D1384210

WITHDRAWN

ETHNICITY IN THE SUNBELT

ITALIAN AMERICAN MIGRANTS IN SCOTTSDALE, ARIZONA

IMMIGRANT COMMUNITIES & ETHNIC MINORITIES IN THE UNITED STATES & CANADA: No. 25

ISSN 0749–5951

Series Editor: Robert J. Theodoratus
Department of Anthropology, Colorado State University

1. James G. Chadney. *The Sikhs of Vancouver.* 1984
2. Paul Driben. *We Are Metis: The Ethnography of a Halfbreed Community in Northern Alberta.* 1985
3. A. Michael Colfer. *Morality, Kindred, and Ethnic Boundary: A Study of the Oregon Old Believers.* 1985
4. Nanciellen Davis. *Ethnicity and Ethnic Group Persistance in an Acadian Village in Maritime Canada.* 1985
5. Juli Ellen Skansie. *Death Is for All: Death and Death-Related Beliefs of Rural Spanish-Americans.* 1985
6. Robert Mark Kamen. *Growing Up Hasidic: Education and Socialization in the Bobover Hasidic Community.* 1985
7. Liucija Baskauskas. *An Urban Enclave: Lithuanian Refugees in Los Angeles.* 1985
8. Manuel Alers-Montalvo. *The Puerto Rican Migrants of New York City.* 1985
9. Wayne Wheeler. *An Analysis of Social Change in a Swedish-Immigrant Community: The Case of Lindsborg, Kansas.* 1986
10. Edwin B. Almirol. *Ethnic Identity and Social Negotiation: A Study of a Filipino Community in California.* 1985
11. Stanford Neil Gerber. *Russkoya Celo: The Ethnography of a Russian-American Community.* 1985
12. Peter Paul Jonitis. *The Acculturation of the Lithuanians of Chester, Pennsylvania.* 1986
14. Dorothy Ann Gilbert. *Recent Portuguese Immigrants to Fall River, Massachusetts: An Analysis of Relative Economic Success.* 1989
15. Jeffrey Lynn Eighney. *Mennonite Architecture: Diachronic Evidence for Rapid Diffusion in Rural Communities.* 1989
16. Elizabeth Kathleen Briody. *Household Labor Patterns among Mexican Americans in South Texas: Buscando Trabajo Seguro.* 1989
17. Karen L. S. Muir. *The Strongest Part of the Family: A Study of Lao Refugee Women in Columbus, Ohio.* 1988
19. Mary G. Harris. *Cholas: Latino Girls and Gangs.* 1988
22. Bruce LaBrack. *The Sikhs of Northern California, 1904–1975: A Socio-Historical Study.* 1988
23. Jenny K. Phillips. *Symbol, Myth, and Rhetoric: The Politics of Culture in an Armenian-American Population.* 1989
24. Stacy G. H. Yap. *Gather Your Strength, Sisters: The Emerging Role of Chinese Women Community Workers.* 1989
25. Phyllis Cancilla Martinelli. *Ethnicity In The Sunbelt: Italian-American Migrants in Scottsdale, Arizona.* 1989
28. Marilyn Preheim Rose. *On The Move: A Study of Migration and Ethnic Persistence among Mennonites from East Freeman, South Dakota.* 1989
30. Bernard Wong. *Patronage, Brokerage, Entrepreneurship and the Chinese Community of New York.* 1988

ETHNICITY IN THE SUNBELT

ITALIAN AMERICAN MIGRANTS IN SCOTTSDALE, ARIZONA

Phyllis Cancilla Martinelli

AMS Press
New York

Library of Congress Cataloging-in-Publication Data

Martinelli, Phyllis Cancilla.
  Ethnicity in the sunbelt.

  (Immigrant communities & ethnic minorities in the United
States & Canada ; 25)
  Bibliography: p.
  Includes index.
  1. Italian Americans – Arizona – Scottsdale – Cultural as-
imilation.   2. Italian Americans – Arizona – Scottsdale –
Ethnic identity.   3. Ethnicity – Arizona – Scottsdale.
4. Scottsdale (Ariz.) – Social conditions.   I. Title.   II. Series.
F819.S37M27 1989   305.8'51'079173   88-45790
ISBN 0-404-19435-4

All AMS books are printed on acid-free paper that meets
the guidelines for performance and durability of the Com-
mittee on Production Guidelines for Book Longevity of the
Council on Library Resources.

AMS PRESS
56 East 13th Street
New York, N.Y. 10003, U.S.A.

MANUFACTURED IN THE UNITED STATES OF AMERICA

TABLE OF CONTENTS

LIST OF TABLES

xi

LIST OF FIGURES

LIST OF MAPS

INTRODUCTION

Whether ethnicity is salient for the descendants of European immigrants or whether these groups are close to total assimilation is a major issue in ethnic studies. To examine if ethnicity was disappearing or persisting in a Sunbelt setting, far removed from a traditional ethnic enclave, Italian American migrants to Scottsdale, Arizona were studied.

The Italian American Family Attitude scale, Identificational Ethnicity scale, (both developed for this research) Cultural Ethnicity scale, National Ethnicity scale, Structural Behavior Ethnicity scale, Religious Ethnicity scale, and Food, Language, and Music scale were the instruments used to test selected variables for evidence of ethnicity. The variables were generation, birth cohort, occupation, education, sex, length of time in Arizona, being married endogamously or exogamously, and being raised in a city with a major Italian American population or raised elsewhere.

The scales were part of an interview schedule administered to 91 full ancestry Italian American men and women. Qualitative comments and participant observation supplemented the instruments that were the basis of the statistical analysis. A shorter interview schedule was administered to 23 respondents of Italian and other ancestry to gain demographic and identificational data. These data were not included in the statistical analysis, however.

While most of the findings showed a lack of significant differences among many of the variables some, for example generation, showed some evidence of declining ethnicity. A fairly cohesive set of attitudes, behavior, and feelings was found among the generally upwardly mobile, middle-class respondents. The majority of the respondents were in the moderate ethnicity category, determined by testing McKay and Lewins' ethnic typology, and were characterized by an emergent ethnicity, termed symbolic ethnicity. It appears that ethnicity still has some salience for the respondents in this study.

Questa dissertazione è dedicata

a mio marito Philip, e
ai nostri figli Vincent, Nicole e Paul;

ai miei genitori Theresa e Frank Cancilla,
e a mia sorella Beverly Cancilla Lamoree;

ai miei suoceri Ann e Nick Martinelli, Sr.,

e ai miei nonni che mi diedero radici in Italia,

Rosa Chirco Cancilla e Vincenzo Cancilla

Maria DiGiovanni Nizza e Francesco Nizza

ACKNOWLEDGEMENTS

I wish to express gratitude to Dr. Bernard Farber, Dr. Melvin Firestone, Dr. Frederick Lindstrom, and Dr. Ronald Hardert for their thorough comments and helpful suggestions. Dr. Albert Mayer offered invaluable assistance in my initial computer analysis of the data.

Dr. Leonard Gordon assisted the study in all phases, and his time and efforts are deeply appreciated.

Assistance was also received from other Arizona State University faculty, they include: Dr. Morris Axelrod, Dr. Mary Benin, Dr. Majel Dominguez, Dr. Richard Nagasawa, and Dr. Joanne Nigg.

Thanks are also due to those expert in Italian American Studies who provided me with assistance. Dr. Richard Juliani, Dr. Vincenza Scarpaci, and Dr. Rose Scherini reviewed and commented on the interview schedule. Dr. Luciano Iorizzo read and commented on an initial draft of the chapter on Italian and Italian American history.

CHAPTER I

INTRODUCTION

Statement of the Problem

In the field of ethnic studies a debate has surfaced in recent years about the continued saliency of ethnicity for the descendants of European immigrants in American society. The focus of this debate has been on those whose ancestors migrated during the last great push of European movement from southern and eastern Europe during the period from the 1880s to the 1920s. Originally this group of immigrants was distinguished from the earlier wave of European immigrants by the label "new" immigrants, with the label "old" immigrants used for groups from Northwestern Europe whose migration peaked prior to 1880 (Lieberson, 1980). More recently the term white ethnics has been used to designate the new immigrants, whose numbers include such groups as Slovak, Greek, Italian, and Polish Americans, as well as many other groups[1] (Ryan, 1973: 2). During the late 1960s and continuing into the 1970s there was an apparent increase in the assertion of ethnicity among white ethnics, including Italian Americans who are the focus of this analysis (e.g., Colburn and Pozzetta, 1979; Krickus, 1976; Wenk, et al., 1972).

The key to the debate was the question of whether the assertion of ethnicity was genuine. Those who did not see an ethnic revival cited a number of reasons for the apparent surge in white ethnic identity. Some

---

[1]Some use a broader definition of white ethnics including Irish Americans (e.g., Krickus, 1976: x) since they are the first of the major Catholic groups, and most white ethnics are Catholic. This study uses the narrower definition stated above.

saw it as a self-serving ploy to hide the fact that white ethnics were really opposing the advancement of minority groups (van den Berghe, 1981). Another view was that the apparent revival was not due to its intensity among most white ethnics, but to the intense ethnic involvement and writings of groups of newly visible white ethnic scholars (Gans, [1962] 1982, 1979). Others have characterized the assertion of a revival as essentially reactionary, at best a temporary halt in the process of assimilation (e.g., Patterson, 1977; Steinberg, 1981).

However, other observers see the recent assertions of an ethnic revival as an expression of a continuing ethnicity that some have ignored because of anticipated assimilation (e.g., Dashefsky, 1976; Glazer and Moynihan, 1971, 1975; Greeley, 1974; Kinton, 1977; Novak, 1973). Basically, this view is one which sees ethnic identity as an important aspect of the core self that is developed during socialization (M. Gordon, 1978). An identity has emerged, according to this view, that is not simply a residue of a European culture, but has been modified into a distinct European American ethnic culture. This ethnic culture is sustained in part by still existing barriers to structural assimilation, and in part by a need for identity in an increasingly depersonalized mass society.

With the revival of interest in this subject some recent researchers involved in the debate over assimilation versus a viable ethnicity for white ethnics look to suburbia to gain insight into the problem. Earlier research on white ethnics has focused on urban, working-class groups in eastern and midwestern locations (e.g., Handlin, 1941; Thomas and Znaniecki, [1918] 1958). Indeed several definitions of white ethnics stress the blue-collar dimension as a characteristic of the group (e.g., Gans, [1962] 1982; Ryan, 1973; Weed, 1973). Many studies have documented the existence of working-class inner-city "Little Italies" (Covello, 1967; Gans, [1962] 1982; Harney and Scarpaci, 1981; Whyte, [1943] 1981). This focus on the working-class has led to predictions that as the younger generation moves into the middle-class and away from the inner-cities there will be an automatic decline in ethnicity (e.g., Hawley, 1971; Rieseman, 1957; Thomlinson, 1969).

This prediction has been denied by other researchers who believe that ethnicity can survive even in a suburban tract (e.g., Etzioni, 1959; Lieberson, 1962; Schnall, 1975; Winch, et al., 1967). Increasingly, Italian American communities in suburban areas are the subject of research (e.g., Fandetti and Gelfand, 1983; O'Brien, 1972; Roche, 1977; Ulin, [1958] 1975).

Purpose of the Study

Given the ongoing nature of this debate, a community in the Southwest is a strategic place to examine the level and nature of ethnicity existing among members of a white ethnic group. It allows ethnicity to be studied in a new, emerging setting, going beyond the boundaries of existing research on the topic. In the decades following World War II there has been a shift in population in the United States. There has been a migration from the Northeast and the North Central Region to the West and the South (U.S. Bureau of the Census, 1980a). One area to receive many new migrants has been Maricopa County, Arizona which increased by 55 percent between 1970 and 1980, from 971,228 to 1,508,030 (U.S. Bureau of the Census, 1981a). Part of this migration has included people of white ethnic ancestry, although current literature is only starting to recognize this trend (L. Gordon, 1973; Martinelli, 1983).

This study was designed to examine the level and nature of ethnicity present among Italian Americans in a Sunbelt community in the Southwest. Table 1 indicates the group is one of the largest of the white ethnic groups in Maricopa County as of 1980. There were then 32,237 single ancestry individuals of Italian heritage in the county, which put the group at 46 percent of the white ethnics in the county. (U.S. Bureau of the Census, 1980b). This is close to the white ethnic percentage of 44 percent in Scottsdale, the community locale of the study.

Research Setting

Scottsdale was chosen as the city to be studied because of its essentially nonethnic background, and its characteristics as a post industrial suburb. The city of Scottsdale is located on the eastern edge of the Salt River Valley popularly known as the Valley of the Sun. The first inhabitants of the area were the Hohokam, a tribe of Native Americans who established a series of canals and villages in the area. They were primarily agriculturalists. The Pimas, whose reservation borders Scottsdale on the east may be the modern descendants of these earliest valley settlers (Wagoner, 1983).

In the 1860s the valley also began to attract white farmers. Despite the desert location, the river valley was fertile and early army expeditions harvested the abundant wild hay. Civilian farmers began to move in, and observing the remains of the Hohokam canals began their own

Table 1. Single Ancestry White Ethnic Groups 1980,[a] for
          Arizona, Maricopa County, Phoenix, and Scottsdale

White Ethnic Groups	Arizona		Maricopa		Phoenix		Scottsdale	
	Number	%*	Number	%	Number	%	Number	%
Greek	4,614	4%	3,075	4%	1,780	4%	354	6%
Hungarian	8,034	8%	5,563	8%	3,020	8%	430	7%
Italian	47,508	46%	32,237	46%	18,915	48%	2,674	44%
Polish	28,066	27%	18,825	27%	9,823	25%	1,497	25%
Portugese	1,807	2%	1,034	1%	710	2%	14	.2%
Russian	11,041	11%	7,422	11%	4,428	11%	989	16%
Ukranian	2,736	3%	1,839	3%	1,037	3%	141	2%
Total White Ethnic	103,806		69,995		39,713		6,099	
Total	2,717,866		1,508,030		764,895		88,364	

[a]The 1980 census expanded the census designation for European
groups. Prior to 1980 only the immigrant generation and their children
were included in the census count. 1980 allowed a self designation of
single or multiple ancestry regardless of how many generations back
ancestry was traced. While the expanded designation allows a more
thorough count of groups, unfortunately the 1980 figures cannot be compared to earlier years to trace the exact growth or decline of a specific group.
  *Percent of white ethnic groups. Percentages may not add to one
hundred due to rounding.

system of irrigation canals. This first area to be farmed grew into the city of Phoenix (G. Johnson, 1982).

The nuclei of what were to become satellite cities of Phoenix also developed as agricultural settlements. An Army chaplain, Winfield Scott, is credited with the foundation of Scottsdale. He homesteaded land nine miles east of Phoenix and developed a ranch. A townsite was established, and by 1895 the town encompassed 40 acres. The town, originally a general store, post office, and some tents, grew slowly. By 1900 only 75 people lived in Scottsdale (Lynch, 1978).

It was not until the 1950s that the small town of Scottsdale began to urbanize, largely as a consequence of the dramatic growth of Phoenix. By 1945 Phoenix had grown rapidly, stimulated by war time industry (G. Johnson, 1982). After the war years the city did not return to an agriculturally dominated economic base. The military bases continued to have an impact as did the electronics industry, and other light industries. Phoenix became part of the growing Sunbelt. Improved transportation, by land and air, competitive utility rates, low-cost housing for new residents, and other inducements became a powerful attraction for businesses and individuals. Phoenix was launched as a major city of the arid Southwest (L. Gordon, 1979; G. Johnson, 1982).

Scottsdale became incorporated in 1951. The official motto, "The West's Most Western Town," was in keeping with the rural ambience of the central city. It had a population slightly over 2,000 people and encompassed an area less than three-quarters of a square mile. The city gradually expanded to the northeast. By 1960 it had grown to 10,000 inhabitants (G. Johnson, 1982; Wilson, 1983).

In 1970 the Scottsdale population had increased to 67,823 (U.S. Bureau of the Census, 1973a). By 1980 Scottsdale's population reached 88,412, and the city encompassed 120 square miles as can be seen in Appendix A, Maps (U.S. Bureau of the Census, 1982a). The city no longer relies on agriculture, although it has become a major center for raising Arabian horses. The economy has shifted to one fairly typical of Sun-belt cities. Tourism, resorts, and the electronics industry are all important to the local economy (Wilson, 1983).

As Scottsdale has grown it has also become more affluent. In 1980 Scottsdale had the second highest median income in the Phoenix area, Paradise Valley had the highest median income, with $10,346 the per capita median income and $22,222 the median household income (U.S. Bureau of the Census, 1982b). The work force was primarily white collar with 33 percent in professional and managerial positions, and 38 percent in clerical, sales and technical occupations (U.S. Bureau of the Census, 1981b). The population was primarily white, with few minorities. The Hispanic population was 3 percent of the population and the black popu-lation was .4 percent of the Scottsdale population (U.S. Bureau of the Census, 1982a).

Because Scottsdale developed so recently it was a useful research setting for several reasons. First, the research was designed to in-vestigate the ethnicity which might be exhibited by people who had migrated to the Sunbelt from other parts of the nation, thus further studying the impact of mobility upon ethnicity. Whereas previous studies of white ethnics in suburban settings studied groups in suburbs which were geographically close to the old ethnic enclaves, this setting allowed the study of people who had moved great distances from any ethnic environment. Phoenix is the main city in Maricopa County, and historically it had a small, diffuse Italian community that had first formed in the 1880s. The community never developed a geographically based "Little Italy," and was generally not visible (Mahoney, 1957a; Martinelli, 1977, 1978).

Scottsdale's Italian community is definitely newer than that of Phoenix. In 1960 the U.S. Census showed only 55 Italians of foreign stock in Scottsdale (U.S. Bureau of the Census, 1962). However, by 1980 Scottsdale had 2,674 single ancestry Italian Americans, who were 3 percent of the total population and 44 percent of the city's white ethnic population. With population growth came an active Italian club, an Italian language program in the local community college, and several Italian owned businesses. All this suggests a rapidly growing number of the group.

Second, Scottsdale has some characteristics that are similar to other suburbs where Italian Americans were studied. Gelfand and Fandetti (1980) studied Italians in Columbia, Maryland, a successful "new town" which contains many upwardly mobile middle-class individuals. Both Roche (1977) and Gabriel (1973), who also studied Irish, studied Italian Americans in Warwick, Rhode Island. Warwick had the second highest median income of the suburbs surrounding Providence. The suburb was mainly white collar, with few minorities, and a low percentage of foreign born residents. Italian Americans represented 5.9 percent of the 1970 population (Gabriel, 1973). Generally, these characteristics resemble Scottsdale in the 1980s.

Third, the community is one which this researcher has been familiar with for several years. Scottsdale was one of the satellite communities examined as part of the historical research done on the Italian community of Phoenix (Martinelli, 1977, 1978). Additionally, secondary materials, such as newspaper articles, have been collected. These materials are part of a research file on Scottsdale's Italian American community that was established in 1975. Since 1975 there has also been participant observation research that has focused on the local Italian club, but has also included any interaction concerning Italian Americans in Scottsdale. The field notes from the participant observation are also part of the research file.

Focus Of This Study

The central focus here is on the strength of ethnicity exhibited in relation to both key variables and exploratory variables. The key variables are ones which have been studied by other researchers in relation to ethnicity (e.g., Gordon and Mayer, 1983; Lazerwitz, 1978). These included generation, birth cohort, occupation, education, and sex. Additionally, exploratory variables which are relevant to the nature of the Scottsdale setting and sample, were studied. These included the length of time in Arizona, being married endogamously or exogamously, and being raised in a major Italian American city or raised elsewhere. These variables are discussed in the following chapters in relation to the assimilation versus the cultural pluralism perspectives. Additionally, the direction in which these variables would be expected to change according to the two perspectives are specified.

The strength of ethnicity exhibited is measured by several scales. The work of Neil Sandberg ([1974] 1977) is the basis for three of the scales. In a study of Polish-Americans in Los Angeles he developed a Likert-type scale to measure cultural, religious, and national ethnicity. This study used part of Sandberg's cultural and national ethnicity scales. However, items that overlapped scales items designed for the Scottsdale study were eliminated. The religious ethnicity scale did not directly apply to Italian Americans, and it was replaced in a more relevant scale. All these changes are discussed fully in Chapter V.

Roche (1977) developed a measure of structural ethnic behavior. His weighting system of measurement of ethnic behavior was used. The modifications are discussed in Chapter VI. Crispino's (1980) scale related to the maintenance of language and cooking skills was modified for the Scottsdale study. An additional scale on religious practices was also developed. All of these are discussed more fully in Chapter VI. The scales were administered as part of an extensive questionnaire which was extensively pretested.

Lengthy interviews were conducted with 91 individuals of full Italian ancestry, and an additional 23 shorter interviews were conducted with those of mixed Italian and other ancestry. The selection of the respondents and their characteristics are discussed in Chapter IV.

Significance Of This Study

The significance of this study can be seen on various levels. First it fills a gap in the literature on white ethnics which Joe R. Feagin pointed out when he called for more regional studies of these groups.

Specifically, he notes that in the Southwest there is a ". . . per-sistence of ethnic consciousness, ethnic identification, and ethnic impact" (1978: 374), and he calls for future research on the topic.

Second, this study carries the current research and broad debate on ethnicity for white ethnics to a middle-class setting in a post in-dustrial suburb. Scottsdale began its development after the technologi-cal advances of the cybernetic revolution in which the development of automation and computers has figured so heavily. Because of developing in this era, it has some characteristics which may not be present in communities which developed earlier. Leonard Gordon (1979: 30-33) noted several characteristics which are different in terms of cities which developed in the post industrial cybernetic era since mid century. Core cities, like Phoenix, often developed according to the multiple nuclei model of Harris and Ullman (1945). As core cities emerged their ad-jacent suburbs, like Scottsdale, developed almost concurrently. Thus little inner city to outer city to suburban movement occurred to set the character of the city and its adjacent suburbs. Further, Gordon notes that the new communities in the Southwest which developed in the cyber-netic era do not have the need for the large numbers of semiskilled workers who swelled the ethnic ghettoes of American cities as the in-dustrial revolution progressed. Rather, cities like Phoenix and Scottsdale have a population relatively dispersed by characteristics like education, income, and ethnicity. If ethnicity remains potent for white ethnics it will have to survive in areas, such as Scottsdale, increasingly alien from the traditional working-class environment of the ethnic enclave. This study was designed to provide insights into how effective the adaptation is.

Third, if ethnicity has some relevance in a new setting it is important to determine if membership in an ethnic group can provide the basis for social contact in a social environment which can be described as amorphous and alienating. Certainly, Italian Americans could easily blend into the general population, because the most distinctive outward aspects of their ethnic identity like language, dress, and folk customs have faded. Evidence from preliminary observation suggests this is not what has happened. Prior to 1940 there was only one formal organization for Italian Americans in the Phoenix area. As of this study the number had grown to twelve active organizations in the larger metropolitan area. While it is true that the overall Italian American population grew, it does not follow that these new migrants would necessarily decide to form organizations unless there was some felt need for contact with others of the same ethnic background. This need could take two forms: one involves the notion of ethnic groups as the basis of vested interests for individuals or groups (e.g., Barth, 1969; Lyman and Douglass, 1973); the other view, which seems more relevant here, is related to self identity and in-group preference. Milton Gordon (1964: 23-7) relates the persistence of ethnicity to the notion that the sense of ethnicity becomes incorporated into the self, and leads to a feeling of peoplehood. Gordon Allport (1958: 29) notes that most individuals accept as basic in-groups their parent's groups, which can include ethnic groups, and these groups often become the basis for reference groups. Thus, ethnic identity in a newly developing setting may prove a significant basis for reference group contact in a social environment characterized by a high divorce and suicide rate (L. Gordon, 1979; Mathews, 1982).

Ethnic enclaves in older cities provided areas that eased the transition to American society for newly arrived immigrants. Ethnic contacts may serve a similar function in developing areas like Scottsdale, serving to combat feelings of anomie and alienation. It will be important to discover if this is the case in the Sunbelt, and this research is designed to provide some answers to this question.

Summary

This study is on the degree of ethnicity revealed by Italian Americans in suburban Scottsdale, Arizona. Using a series of scales designed to measure ethnicity, which were administered as part of an extensive questionnaire, the study attempts to answer some important questions about the specific ethnic group. Additionally, the study addresses some of the issues raised as part of the continuing debate about the relevance of ethnicity for European American groups in general.

CHAPTER II

LITERATURE REVIEW

The central purpose of this study is to address some of the questions raised about ethnicity and assimilation in American society. To
do this it is necessary to examine the various perspectives and models
that have developed regarding ethnicity and assimilation. As noted in
Chapter I, one question that is important in the field of ethnic studies
in America is whether or not there has been a revival of ethnicity among
white ethnics. The origins of this concern are rooted in an earlier
debate that began with the large scale immigration of diverse European
groups to America.

The immigrants became ethnic groups in American society. They were
essentially outsiders, to use the original Greek definition of the
adjective ethnic or ethnos. Ethnos meant a nation or race of non-Greek
peoples, and was applied as a term for outsiders. This use of the term
"ethnic" continued in English (Petersen, 1982: 1-2).

The presence of so many ethnics raised important questions about the
shape that American society would take after the influx of these groups.
Would society become a patchwork of ethnic subsocieties, similar to the
heterogenous nations and subnations of Europe? Or did American society
have the capacity to assimilate the migrants so that the outsiders
adapted to the established society? Or would American society take
another shape that was not anticipated?

Essentially these questions about the status of ethnic groups in
American society still remain unresolved. The following discussion

examines perspectives on assimilation and on ethnicity to clarify these
concepts that are important to the Scottsdale study on the Italian
American ethnic group.

Assimilation

Answers to questions on the possible assimilation of European immigrants first appeared on the American scene in the form of popular
ideologies rather than as theoretical perspectives from the social
sciences (Glazer, 1945; M. Gordon, 1964; Newman, 1973). However, social
scientists were not slow to respond to the urgent societal questions,
and theoretical perspectives began to emerge. Only a few early sociologists, such as Edward A. Ross ([1914] 1965) became caught up in ideology
rather than theory.

Early Models Of Assimilation

Three main models on assimilation, which relates to the processes
involved as a group becomes similar to another group (Feagin, 1978: 27)
emerged, both as ideologies and theoretical perspectives. They have
been called the "Anglo-conformity", "melting pot", and "cultural pluralism" models. These terms for the models are based on the popular
ideologies that were associated with them (M. Gordon, 1964: 184-202).
The following discussion expands upon these models. First the early
models are examined, and then their more contemporary derivations are
explored.

The Anglo-conformity Model

The Anglo-conformity model, the term first being used by Cole and
Cole (1954), grew out of an ideology which stressed the idea that immigrants should conform to the existing Anglo Saxon culture. It left no

room for the culture of the newcomers. Instead this view espoused by Anglo nativists, expected immigrants to assimilate into the American cultural mainstream without leaving a trace of their background (Higham, [1955] 1976). This view was brought to academic circles through the work of Henry Pratt Fairchild (Vander Zanden, 1972: 266).

The Melting Pot Model

The melting pot model is more sympathetic to the immigrant's cultural heritage. The model depicts an American society in which the host society would blend or melt with the immigrant's cultures to form a new, vital culture and society. The notion was first expressed by Ralph Waldo Emerson in 1845, although the popularization of the idea and the term is associated with Israel Zangwill's play "The Melting Pot" introduced in 1908 (M. Gordon, 1964). Historian Fredrick Jackson Turner strongly influenced scholars with his 1893 paper in which he suggested that the western frontier was a potent force in shaping the American people into a nation (M. Gordon, 1964). Turner (1920: 22) presented the frontier as a melting pot, ". . . in the crucible of the frontier the immigrants were Americanized, liberated, and fused into a mixed race, English in neither nationality or characteristics."

However the melting-pot concept was more fully expressed by sociologists, starting with the Chicago school of sociology which established a record for pioneering work on ethnicity in both research and theoretical work. Two important scholars from the Chicago school were Robert E. Park and W. I. Thomas. Thomas was instrumental in bringing Park to Chicago, and initially influenced his thinking on race relations (Edwards, 1968: 34). Emily Green Balch (1911) can be credited with some of the earliest work on Slavic immigrants in Europe and America. However it is Thomas and Znaniecki ([1918] 1958) who are remembered for their massive study of a new immigrant group, the Poles.

Park's (1926) theory of race relations, is clearly the most influential of the early assimilation perspectives in American sociology. His theory, which is also applied to ethnic groups, is part of his human ecological approach to understanding society. Park (1949: xiii) viewed the topic of minority groups relations as related to the more general theme of social processes and social interaction. Large scale migration was breaking down ancient barriers between human groups, thus starting groups through a series of stages of interaction. The first stage of interaction begins with contact after ethnic and racial groups start to move out of their previous niches through exploration and migration. Contact leads to the second stage marked by economic competition and political conflict between the groups. However, in the next stage the conflict and competition become muted through accommodation betweeen the groups. Once a social order is developed the next stage occurs and assimilation takes place. As barriers to intermarriage fell due to assimilation, Park saw amalgamation occurring. The final result of amalgamation would be a global melting pot. People would share a common culture and history (Park, 1949: 149).

While many researchers attempted to apply Park's natural history model of race and ethnic contacts for groups ranging from the Chinese (Lee, 1949) to the Jews (Wirth, 1956), the emphasis was usually on the stages up to the point of assimilation, rather than stressing the final stage of amalgamation and a global melting pot.

Park (1949) held that once the process of contact, competition, conflict, accommodation, and assimilation began it was ". . . apparently progressive and irreversible" (Park, 1949: 150). This emphasis on the inevitability of assimilation led to a wide range of criticism. Additionally, Park's vagueness about why some groups seemed to move through the postulated stages while others, particularly racial minorities, did not seem to be going through the stages also drew criticism. Myrdal ([1944] 1962: 1049) thought too much emphasis was put on the power of natural forces in shaping the stages. This emphasis led Park to take a fatalistic stand. Etzioni (1959: 255-258) also criticized Park. He noted that Park's model, as applied by Wirth, was not specific enough to be scientifically tested. Since Park used the word "eventually" to state when a group would assimilate, Etzioni pointed out that even if a group was not assimilating one could still support the model. It could always be argued that group would assimilate some day. Etzioni also noted that the social conditions under which one might expect the process to work were not specified either, adding to the vagueness of Park's model. Stanford Lyman (1973: 24) pointed to Park's acceptance of Aristotelian logic which led to an emphasis on describing the stages rather than studying the historical reality of ethnic interaction in actual events.

The influence of Park's work led to efforts to refine his natural-history model. E. Franklin Frazier (1953: 298-331) kept Park's original frame of reference, however, Frazier noted that he viewed the stages as logical steps for analytical purposes, not chronological stages in an inevitable process. Talcott Parsons (1966: 709-754) retained the notion of stages as reflecting the process of interaction between racial and ethnic groups. However, he moved away from the stage of assimilation or absorption. Instead Parsons's model places an emphasis on inclusion. In the final stage of inclusion racial and ethnic groups are included in the civic, political, and social organizations of the larger society. However, the groups retain their distinctive subcultures, rather than becoming totally assimilated. As Lyman (1973: 158) notes Parsons's model has flaws similar to Park's model. Both models are teleological, and use the doctrine of obstacles to explain why groups like Black Americans do not follow the progressive stages. The doctrine qualifies the model by noting that some groups encounter obstacles, such as prejudice, that make it difficult to progress through the stages until the obstacle is erased.

Attempts to find stages to explain the interaction between the dominant society and racial and ethnic groups continued (e.g., Greeley, 1969: 53-59), but generally are not influential currently.

The Cultural Pluralism Model

The final model discussed is cultural pluralism. As an ideology it is most closely associated with the work of Horace Kallen ([1915] 1924) who developed the model in reaction to the melting pot model. Kallen's model contained three main points. First, what American society really offered immigrant groups was not conformity or a blending, but a democracy that allowed pluralistic cultures to be maintained within the broader framework of society. Second, American society actually was enhanced by the diversity of many ethnic cultures, and each group offered something valuable to the larger society. Third, keeping an ethnic identity allowed the individual to maintain a tie to their ancestry that assimilation would disrupt (Newman, 1973: 68-69).

Kallen has been criticized because of the lack of precision in his concept of cultural pluralism which left is open to a variety of interpretations. Some areas like the political implications of pluralism were never fully developed. While Kallen foresaw a variety of ethnic groups peacefully coexisting, he never delineated how this cooperative situation would become reality (Gleason, 1982: 96-107).

The cultural pluralist perspective was used, in modified versions, in addressing the problems of immigrant assimilation. Two influential educators Berkson (1920) and Drachsler (1920), supported the idea of cultural pluralism, although both had doubts about the ability of ethnic groups to sustain long-term cultural pluralism (M. Gordon, 1964: 499).

As models were developed in sociology to explain the changes in American society and in the ethnic groups themselves, these perspectives generally moved in the direction of greater flexibility. Some researchers continued to follow Park's model that depicted assimilation as the inevitable outcome of contact between ethnic groups and the dominant society, although definite stages were no longer specified. Other researchers attempted to adapt the somewhat vague cultural pluralist model so that it could be more rigorously studied. The following discussion examines these more contemporary versions of the earlier models.

Contemporary Models Of Assimilation

Generally the Anglo-conformity model does not have salience as a current theoretical perspective. However, there is a continuing migration, both legal and illegal, of distinctive ethnic and racial groups to

American society (Feagin, 1984: 359-364). Therefore, it is possible that factions in American society may endorse the idea that these newest immigrants should conform to American society, and abandon their distinctive cultures. If this occurs, then a revised version of the Anglo-conformity model may appear in the social sciences.

The Straight-Line Assimilation Model

The straight-line model expresses the hypothesis that the immigrant generation represents the high point of ethnicity. As the descendants of the immigrant generation become upwardly mobile it is anticipated that ethnicity will lose its salience (Crispino, 1980). The straight-line model has roots in the early melting pot models (Gans, [1962] 1982) and the natural-history model of Park (Gordon and Mayer, 1983).

Stephen Steinberg (1981) is perhaps the most vigorous neo-Parkist. Steinberg defends Park's model on the grounds that Park was oriented toward long-term historical trends so that Park was ". . . not distracted by the complexities and nuances of the moment." (Steinberg, 1981: 48). Steinberg (1981: 63) asserts that white ethnic groups are in the midst of a crisis due to the loss of the immigrant ethnic culture.

The influence of Park's natural-history orientation can also be seen in the following definition of the straight-line model. "This theory hypothesizes that, once begun, acculturation and assimilation are continuous and permanent processes which end with the absorption of all ethnic groups into the large culture. . ." (Gans, [1962] 1982: 234).

Research to support the straight-line model has focused on ethnicity as related to generation, upward mobility in education and occupation, and intermarriage. Some of the more salient research is presented below.

Several studies support the decline in ethnicity by generation and for the upwardly mobile. Sandberg ([1974] 1977) in his research on Polish Americans concludes that the straight-line theory is supported in the general decline in ethnicity by generation, and among the ranks of the upwardly mobile respondents. Similar conclusions regarding a general decline in ethnicity by generation and among the upwardly mobile are reported for Italian Americans (Crispino, 1980; Roche, 1977). Alba's (1976, 1981) research on intermarriage trends for American Catholic ethnics shows increasing rates of exogamy that accelerate among the younger birth cohorts. Also relevant are the increasing rates of college attendance among the younger cohorts of these Catholic groups. These findings lead Alba to suggest that, "Ethnicity appears to be nearing twilight among the Catholic ethnic groups whose forebears immigrated to the United States in the nineteenth and early twentieth centuries." (Alba, 1981: 97).

Those who advocate the straight-line model have pointed out that despite their emphasis on declining ethnicity, they are not predicting the immediate demise of ethnicity in American society (e.g., Alba, 1976, 1981; Gans, 1979; Steinberg, 1981).

Gans ([1962] 1982: 234-235) has suggested modifications to the straight-line ethnicity model to deal with some of the criticisms that have arisen regarding the basic model. First, he notes that the melting pot image is outdated. America has been transformed from an essentially Anglo Saxon society into a series of multiple subsocieties. Thus, to assimilate one does not necessarily have to become like the Anglo Saxons. Ethnics can assimilate into subcultural groups based, for example, on occupation, religion, or education.

Second, the straight-line model assumes a cohesive ethnic culture was brought to America by the immigrant generation. However, this may often not have been the case. Therefore, the envisioned decline in ethnicity from a cohesive ethnic culture may be overstated.

Third, some researchers have noted that ethnic behavior may be emergent, and be adapting to contemporary situations, rather than reflecting the residue of an immigrant culture (e.g., Yancey et al., 1976).

Fourth, Gans notes that the trends of straight-line assimilation may level off, albeit temporarily. This point is supported by the research of Sandberg ([1974] 1977). He found that the fourth generation still had a measurable level of ethnicity, and further, there was no statistically significant difference between the level of ethnicity exhibited for the third and fourth generations. Sandberg ([1974] 1977: 71) suggests that the decline in ethnicity between generations may have leveled off, or there may be a resurgence in ethnicity.

To explain the presence of ethnicity among the middle-class, younger ethnics, which the straight-line theory does not anticipate, Gans (1979) introduces the notion of symbolic ethnicity. Rather than being ascriptive, as ethnicity was for the immigrant generation, symbolic ethnicity has moved into the realm of a leisure-time pursuit for middle-class

ethnics. Because symbolic ethnicity provides an identity that is easy
to practice, Gans (1979) speculates that symbolic ethnicity may persist
for several generations, or even be replaced by a true ethnic revival,
which he does not see symbolic ethnicity representing. Basically, Gans
sees symbolic ethnicity as part of an assimilation model, and still
anticipates an ultimate assimilation of European ethnics. However, he
is reluctant to predict a demise of ethnicity in the near future.

The straight-line model can be seen as an extension of the melting
pot type of model. Research has supported the anticipated demise of
ethnicity for Europeans in some areas. However, there is also evidence
of continuing ethnicity for white ethnics that belies the straight-line
theory. The idea of symbolic ethnicity has been introduced as an
attempt to explain this variation. In the next section the contemporary
version of the cultural pluralism model is discussed, and compared to
the straight-line model.

The Modified Pluralism Model

In contrast to the straight-line assimilation model the modified
pluralism model retains an emphasis on the continued viability of ethnic
groups. Complete assimilation is not anticipated, rather the continued
salience of ethnicity is stressed. However, unlike the earlier cultural
pluralism, the more modified approaches to pluralism do acknowledge the
reality and even desirability of some degree of assimilation. There is
no one modified pluralism model, therefore it is necessary to discuss
the three main approaches to modified pluralism.

William Newman uses the term modified pluralism (1973: 78) to discuss the ideas of Nathan Glazer and Daniel Moynihan (1963) in Beyond

the Melting Pot. Newman suggests their work represents a synthesis of
the three early models that were discussed, with the main emphasis on
pluralism. Since the work of Milton Gordon and Andrew Greeley also
represent syntheses the term will be used to apply to their work as
well.

Using New York City as a microcosm to explore ethnic groups, Glazer
and Moynihan (1963) look at the history and culture of such diverse
groups as Puerto Ricans, Jews, Italians, Irish, and Black Americans. In
an expanded version of the original book (1971) the authors continue
their main thesis regarding white ethnics while reassessing the status
of minority groups like Black Americans, in light of the social changes
of the late 1960s. They contend that while the white ethnic groups did
lose much of their European culture and identity, they did not move
toward total assimilation. Instead, new ethnic cultures and identities
formed based on the unique historical experiences of each group. The
failure to assimilate came from several dimensions in American society
which sustained ethnicity. Identification with the American core culture was inhibited by varying degrees of prejudice and discrimination,
and by the lack of a simple "American" identity to fix on. As traditional religious practices, working-class status, and ties of national
loyalty to Europe declined in salience for many white ethnics, their
American ethnic identity correspondingly increased in importance.
Glazer and Moynihan (1979) also suggest that ethnic blocks have in some
instances become interest groups. In their capacity as interest groups,

ethnic groups have an impact on the distribution of social and economic
rewards in society, thus providing another element in sustaining
ethnicity.

Milton Gordon in his book <u>Assimilation in American Life</u> (1964) also
wrestles with the problems of assimilation and pluralism; the result is
a model of assimilation that includes several dimensions of assimilation. Assimilation is subdivided into subprocesses. Cultural assimilation, or acculturation, occurs when groups with different cultures come
into contact, and there is a modification of the cultural patterns of
one or both of the groups. This type of assimilation usually occurs
first, and it is possible to have cultural assimilation for an ethnic
group without having the other types of assimilation follow (M. Gordon,
1964: 71). Gordon outlines six other dimensions of assimilation that
could take place in differing degrees depending on the ethnic group.
The dimensions are: attitude reception assimilation or absence of
prejudice, behavior receptional assimilation or absence of discrimination, identificational assimilation or having an identity based on that
of the host society, civic assimilation or a lack of value and power
conflict, marital assimilation or amalgamation, and structural assimilation or admission into the organizations and cliques of the host
society on a primary group level. The key to assimilation is structural
assimilation, once this has occurred all other forms of assimilation
will take place (M. Gordon, 1964: 64).

The various dimensions do not represent stages that ethnic groups
must go through for structural assimilation to occur, so that Gordon's

model is not a variation on the natural-history model. However, because he developed a model of assimilation, Gordon's name is often linked with Park's (e.g., Feagin, 1978; McLemore, 1980), and his name is occasionally associated with the straight-line assimilation model (Crispino, 1980). Consequently, it is useful to note Gordon's observation that structural pluralism is a fact of American ethnic life. Here he differentiates between cultural pluralism, which he sees as hard to maintain because of substantial cultural assimilation, and structural pluralism based on ethnic subsocieties (M. Gordon, 1964: 81). Gordon anticipates that structural pluralism will exist indefinitely in American society (M. Gordon, 1978: 70).

As M. Gordon (1978: 70) notes his assimilation theory was not designed to demonstrate that total assimilation is the inevitable outcome of interaction between ethnic groups. His aim was to create a multidimensional model of assimilation. The subtypes were delineated to allow the study of different rates of assimilation in the different types of assimilation. With his emphasis on structural pluralism, and his lack of expectation in finding a pattern of inevitable assimilation Milton Gordon can be considered one of the synthesizers of the modified pluralism model as specified by Newman.

Greeley further advances the prospect of American pluralism in his outline of the development of ethnic subcultures with his ethnogenesis model (1974: 304-309; 1977: 22-27). This model notes that there were some common points of a broad Western culture shared between the Anglo Saxon host society and white ethnic immigrants, despite the differences which are usually stressed. Gradually, the common culture expands and

the immigrant culture diminishes, but does not vanish in the new
society. Over time an ethnic culture forms that includes some of the
common culture, some of the immigrant culture, and some distinctive
traits of the ethnic group. This perspective was designed to include
elements of the Anglo-conformity, melting pot, cultural pluralism, and
structural pluralism models. Because it suggests the continued
existence of ethnic groups, it is a synthesis that also fits the modified pluralism model.

Research supporting the modified pluralism approach has examined
findings indicating continued ethnicity. The following research includes brief discussions of some of the salient research supporting the
modified pluralism thesis. Goering (1970) did research on Italian and
Irish Americans in Providence, Rhode Island. The findings from this
study indicate that the third generation had a strong ethnic awareness.
However, they were not involved in ethnic behavior such as the formation
of ethnic organizations. Goering suggests that the third generation's
dissatisfaction with the "American Dream" of upward mobility may account
for their subjective type of ethnic consciousness.

Gabriel (1973) also did research on Italians and Irish in the same
area as Goering. Gabriel's findings indicate that ethnic identifications continue to be present even in the upper-middle class members of
the groups he studied (Gabriel, 1973: 145).

Kourvetaris and Dobratz (1976) study was directed at Milton Gordon's
ethclass hypothesis that is part of his emphasis on structural pluralism. Gordon (1964: 51) suggested that ethnic communities are subdivided
into social classes paralleling those in the larger society.

Kourvetaris and Dobratz examined Italian Catholics, Greek Orthodox, and Swedish Lutherans in the Midwest. Their findings on these groups lend support to the ethclass hypothesis. The three ethnic groups tended to marry and form primary relationships within their own pluralistic ethnic groups.

There have been criticisms of the various approaches to modified pluralism. The three approaches represented by Glazer and Moynihan (1962), M. Gordon (1964), and Greeley (1974), have been characterized as basically structural approaches to ethnic behavior (DeVos and Romanucci-Ross, [1975] 1982: x). As Feagin (1982) notes most pluralist analysts accept the loss of much of the immigrant culture. Their emphasis is on the emergence of an ethnic culture (e.g., Glazer and Moynihan, [1963] 1971; Greeley, 1977).

However, critics of the modified pluralism position place an emphasis on the maintenance of the immigrant culture as necessary for viable ethnicity. For example, Steinberg (1981) acknowledges that Glazer and Moynihan's thesis that new ethnic forms have emerged despite the loss of the immigrant culture is essentially correct. However, Steinberg (1981: 59-60) raises the question of whether or not the ethnic culture can be successfully transmitted to a fourth generation that has had no direct contact with the original immigrant culture.

Steinberg further questions the emphasis on structural aspects of ethnicity. He focuses specifically on the structural pluralism thesis of Milton Gordon. Steinberg (1980: 65-68) asserts that Gordon (1964) is merely shifting the focus from the salient issue of the erosion of cultural distinctiveness when he proposes a focus on structural pluralism. Steinberg also questions the ability of structurally distinct communities to maintain themselves without strong roots in an immigrant culture.

Newman (1973: 83-85) takes Gordon to task on several issues. The most salient criticism, for this discussion, is Newman's question regarding the validity of the assumption by Gordon that once structural assimilation has occurred all other forms of assimilation can produce substantial group integration in a pluralist society, and instead turns to social conflict theory for a more relevant approach to group interaction in a pluralist setting (1973: 97-190).

Newman also criticized Glazer and Moynihan for what he sees as a lack of emphasis on interaction between the host society and ethnic groups (1973: 81-82). According to Newman, Glazer and Moynihan focus on the internal dynamics of the communities they studied in New York rather than take a more balanced approach that emphasizes group interaction.

Greeley is also criticized for the apparent difficulties involved in testing the ethnogenesis model. Crispino (1981) notes that while Greeley outlines an agenda to study ethnicity, the model does not present empirically testable propositions. Crispino concludes that the ethnogenesis model is a ". . . one-theme "theory" (the common culture grows larger)" (1981: 12) that does not provide definite relationships between the relevant variables. Hence, in Crispino's view it is impossible to empirically test the ethnogenesis model.

Both the straight-line model and the modified pluralism of assimilation have roots in earlier perspectives on assimilation. Both models recognize that assimilation is a salient feature in the analysis of

ethnicity among white ethnic groups. However, the two models differ in
the assessment of white ethnic groups in contemporary American society.
Adherents of the straight-line assimilation perspective generally hold
that ethnicity is declining for white ethnic groups. Those who take the
modified pluralism perspective hold that ethnicity is still a viable
force for white ethnics in American society.

Ethnicity

A discussion of assimilation would not be complete without a discussion of the issues relevant to ethnicity as related to the preceding
discussion of assimilation. The early definition of ethnic that defined
outsiders (Petersen, 1982) has become complicated by a growing and
sometimes confusing amount of research that often represents differing
perspectives on ethnicity. The global nature of research on ethnicity,
since ethnicity is studied in emerging Third World nations as well as in
more advanced Westernized industrial nations, has added to the variety
of perspectives that need to be taken into account in discussions of the
subject.

Current Discussions On Ethnicity

Fortunately there have been several useful efforts to delineate and
summarize the more salient issues surrounding ethnicity. Some of the
most current discussions are summarized below. Included in the discussions are perspectives from both sociology and anthropology because of
the important contributions being made by both fields, and the overlap-
ping nature of the theoretical perspectives.

Enloe (1981: 4-8) delineates three major debates currently affecting
perspectives on ethnicity. The first debate focuses on whether or not

ethnicity is ascribed or situational. The ascribed approach to ethnicity takes the view that ethnicity is basically fixed in an inherited status (e.g., Shils, 1957). Hence, ethnicity is relatively unchanging, and the major emphasis in research is on the description of existing ethnic patterns. In contrast, the situational perspective views ethnicity as dynamic rather than fixed (e.g., Barth, 1969). This puts the research emphasis on change and interaction rather than on description of a fixed phenomenon.

The second debate, according to Enloe, focuses on the implications of modernization for ethnicity. Those who predict the eradication of ethnicity in the modern age view ethnicity as an archaic kind of affiliation that has no function in a contemporary, rational, rapidly changing environment (e.g., Geertz, 1968; van den Berghe, 1970). However, there are a number of ethnic theorists who see ethnicity as persisting despite modernization (e.g., Isajiw, 1978; Fishman, 1983).

The third debate that Enloe discusses revolves around the question of whether the political sphere influences ethnicity. The accepted view, until recently, is that the political sphere acts in relation to existing ethnic divisions in pluralist societies (e.g., Lipjhart, 1968; Nordlinger, 1972). However, contemporary research (e.g., Cohen, 1969; Roff, 1974) suggests that politics can, in certain settings have a direct impact in, ". . . altering definitions of ethnic belonging" (Enloe, 1981: 8).

In the introduction to their revised book on ethnic identity in a cross-cultural context DeVos and Romanucci-Ross ([1975] 1982) provide a useful discussion of several approaches to the study of ethnicity. They summarize structural and experimental approaches to ethnicity by defining four main approaches. These are (a) the social structural level of ethnicity, (b) ethnicity as a pattern of social interaction (c) ethnicity as a subjective experience of identity, and (d) ethnicity as found in the psychological and emotional structure of individuals.

Burgess' (1978) article on ethnicity provides another useful discussion of major theoretical positions relating to ethnicity. She notes there are rational and nonrational approaches to ethnicity, and both objective and subjective criteria are used in defining ethnicity. Based on the analysis of the major positions Burgess offers a definition of ethnicity which is, ". . . the character, quality, or condition of ethnic group membership, based on an identity with and/or a consciousness of group belonging that is differentiated from others by symbolic `markers'. . . and is rooted in bonds of a shared past and perceived ethnic interests" (1978: 270).

The discussions of ethnicity by Enloe, DeVos and Romanucci-Ross, and Burgess summarize important issues and perspectives relating to ethnicity. These issues and perspectives are incorporated into the final analysis of ethnicity for Italian Americans in Scottsdale.

Typology Of Ethnic Concepts

Further clarification on ethnicity and on the relation between ethnic group and ethnic identity can be gained from the work of McKay and Lewins (1978). Their typology of ethnic concepts offers a way in which individual and group levels of analysis can be distinguished. Since their typology is one that is tested by this researcher, it is discussed at length below.

First, McKay and Lewins discuss the conceptual problems resulting from using the term ethnicity interchangeably with the terms ethnic group and ethnic identification. They note that researchers often classify individuals who have certain similar characteristics, such as race, national origin, or religion, as members of an ethnic group. However, for McKay and Lewins these individuals are aggregates, whom they call "ethnic categories in themselves." Since in these aggregates there is no sense of belonging to a group, the common attributes shared with others is not the basis for meaningful interaction with fellow ethnics.

The term ethnic group is limited by McKay and Lewins to instances when individuals interact meaningfully because of shared ethnic traits. These traits are symbolic elements epitomizing the cultural and social distinctiveness of "peoplehood." Examples of ethnic traits are language, religion, nationality, pheno-typical features, a shared descent, or a combination of these traits.

Second, McKay and Lewins argue that there are two different types of ethnic identity. A person can have either ethnic awareness or ethnic consciousness. Ethnic awareness is the type of ethnic identity a person has who knows he or she possesses a certain ethnic trait(s). However, the trait(s) is only one source of self-identity for the person. Such ethnic awareness can result from interaction in organizations or from perceived membership in a broad social category. This type of ethnic identity fits with the notion of situational ethnicity which originated in the work of Max Gluckman (1940: 1-13) on the situational aspects of interaction between Africans and Europeans. More recently the term situational ethnicity has been used to describe an ethnic identity in a modern society. In this context situational ethnicity rarely encompasses the full range of an individual's social identities (Okamura, 1981; Yancey, Ericksen and Juliani, 1976). This specific type of ethnic identity is likely to be found in the suburbs, among cosmopolitan people (Yancey, Ericksen, and Juliani, 1976: 399). Similarly, Etzioni notes that ethnicity may be operative only in certain social situations for ethnic groups who are residentially dispersed (1959: 258).

For McKay and Lewins ethnic consciousness is much more intense than ethnic awareness. For a person who has ethnic consciousness, an ethnic trait(s) can be the most significant, or one of the most significant, elements of self-identity. Ethnic identity influences the other elements of individual identification. The elementary feeling of solidarity found among ethnically aware people often is translated into a "we" versus "them" orientation. Because of this element, it can be the basis for ethnic group conflict, social tension, and mobilization of ethnic groups along political lines.

Based on these definitions McKay and Lewins develop a conceptual scheme which was tested in this study of the level and nature of Italian American ethnicity in Scottsdale. The following illustrates which people might be found in each cell of the typology. (See Figure 1.)

In the first cell are found people with low ethnic awareness who belong in an ethnic category. These individuals may have few or no ethnic contacts, and be essentially assimilated. McKay and Lewins include Neil Sandberg's Polish Americans in this cell. McKay and Lewins

IDENTIFICATION   STRUCTURAL BEHAVIOR

                          Ethnic Category   Ethnic Group
                              (Low)   (High)

 Ethnic   (Low)   CELL I   CELL II
Awareness

   Ethnic   (High)   CELL III   CELL IV
Consciousness

Figure 1. McKay and Lewins' Typology

would also include an Irish American, for example, who wears a "Kiss Me I'm Irish" button on St. Patrick's Day, but has no other attachment to Irish culture or groups.

In the second cell are people who have ethnic awareness and belong to an ethnic group. McKay and Lewins place those who interact sporadically with members of their ethnic background, or who belong to ethnic groups or organizations, but participate in an intermittent fashion because other groups also attract them in this cell. They also include people who use their ethnic group contacts for instrumental or exploitive reasons, but have no strong feeling of personal attachment to the group. Examples would be people who get political or economic payoffs from their ethnic contacts.

The third cell includes those individuals with a strong ethnic consciousness who are not interacting with members of their group. One example would be people who are physically isolated from members of their group, like Basque sheepherders whose occupation means living alone. Others in this cell are "ethnic orphans," those individuals who are marginal to both their group and to the larger society. Such individuals may have tried to assimilate, but faced rejection at some point. Thus, they are self-conscious of their ethnic identity in a negative way.

The fourth cell contains people who have an "us" versus "them" outlook, and usually includes ethnic group members who are involved in the pursuit of political and economic interests. Many examples of this can be found within American society and cross culturally (e.g., Barth, 1969).

The typology is presented in more detail in Chapter VII when the findings from this study in relation to the typology are presented. The findings examine if McKay and Lewins were correct in their distinctions between types of structural behavior and identification, or if the differences between individuals represent gradations on a continuum as has been suggested by DeVos and Romanucci-Ross ([1975] 1982: xiv). Although mixed, the weight of the evidence from the Scottsdale study supports the views of McKay and Lewins.

Summary

Respecting assimilation, two "camps" currently dominate the thinking on ethnic groups in American society. Despite the appearance of deep divisions in thinking that can be gained from reading the literature supporting the two views, there are some shared points of agreement. Both those who advocate the straight-line assimilationist view and those who advocate the modified pluralism views agree that ethnicity persists in American society today. Additionally, both groups agree that substantial cultural assimilation has taken place, especially in the area of language.

The crux of the debate that remains revolves around the issue of continued ethnic viability. The straight-line assimilationists generally view contemporary ethnicity as a temporary halt in the inevitable process of the erosion of ethnicity for white ethnics. However, there is some disagreement as to how temporary the halt will be. Some see the fourth generation as signaling the end of ethnicity, others concede that ethnicity may persist in a modified form for generations before giving way to assimilation (c.f. Gans, 1979; Steinberg, 1981).

Those in the modified pluralism group predict that ethnic groups will be a viable force in American society indefinitely. No predictions are made regarding the ultimate demise of ethnicity.

The findings from the Scottsdale study on Italian Americans should provide useful information in light of these perspectives on assimilation and pluralism. As has been discussed, the study of a white ethnic group in a new, middle-class, nonethnic setting can offer insights into emergent trends in ethnicity in the Sunbelt, the most rapidly growing area of American society.

The use of the McKay-Lewins' typology along with the statistical tests associated with the various scales used to measure ethnic attitudes, values, behavior, and identity will allow further insight into the straight-line versus modified pluralism debate.

If the straight-line model is basically correct, then most of the tests will show a drop in ethnicity as one moves further away from the immigrant generation and the working class group, although there may be evidence of symbolic ethnicity. This might be represented by an identification with a few clear cultural items, but generally low scores for the most upwardly mobile and youngest of the sample.

If the modified pluralist model is correct then tests will show more complex responses. While some assimilation is not ruled out by this model there should be evidence of an ethnic subculture existing in terms of attitudes, values, and interaction. There might be a decrease in ethnicity in some areas, a trend toward stabilization in other areas, and possibly a resurgence in ethnicity among the third generation.

Regarding ethnicity, the discussion of the salient perspectives of ethnicity are used in the final analysis of these data. The findings from the Scottsdale study add some useful insights into the nature of ethnicity in an emergent Sunbelt setting. Additionally the testing of the McKay and Lewins' typology will help to clarify two important dimensions of ethnicity. These dimensions relate to the distinctions between an ethnic group and and ethnic category, and the distinctions between ethnic awareness and ethnic consciousness.

CHAPTER III

ITALIAN EMIGRATION TO AMERICA, THE REASONS AND

THE RESULTS

To understand Italian Americans today it is first necessary to look
at the historical roots of the group in terms of who emigrated, their
reasons for leaving, the culture brought with them, and their arrival in
America. Then it is useful to examine the reaction of the immigrants
and their offspring to American society and culture. This chapter will
provide a broad overview of those points which need to be explored so
that the remainder of the dissertation can be adequately presented.

Birth of Modern Italy

In the late 1700s the rumblings of vast social changes, later
labeled the Industrial Revolution, began to transform the ancient orders
of the Western world. During the political and intellectual transforma-
tions, which paralled technological innovations, the modern nation of
Italy emerged. The House of Savoy, based in Piedmont in northern Italy,
was the political power which gradually unified the fragmented political
units of the Italian peninsula.

Although Italy emerged as a nation in 1861 it was not until 1870
that the last holdout to unification, the papal states, surrendered.
The goals of the intellectuals and liberals who fought for the
Risorgimento (resurrection), as the movement was called, were modernization, political freedom, and a constitutional government. These goals
were aimed at changing the existing feudal social order (Salomone, 1974:
3-24).

The majority of Italians were peasants, and unification had little direct appeal for them. Denis Mack Smith (1959: 39) contends that unification involved a civil war between the new, upwardly mobile middle-class and the entrenched aristocracy. He notes that the peasants did not actively support a united Italy because they saw no benefit from it for themselves. Their suspicions were correct for they were not brought into the mainstream of national life. The "blessings" of unification came to peasants in the form of increasing taxes, military conscription, loss of what had been traditional privileges under feudalism, and increasing amounts of deforestation, malaria, and land fragmentation (Foerster, [1919] 1968: 47-126). In 1877 a parliamentary inquiry on the condition of rural people was published. The massive report showed that in many areas undernourishment was prevalent, that malaria plagued the South and pellagra the North, and that housing problems, child labor, and illiteracy were prevalent. Important for future emigration and developments, the government was slow to act on the basis of this and other reports on the conditions of the peasantry (Procacci, 1970).

Regionalism and Industrialization

Although the social and economic conditions of the peasant class throughout Italy were basically poor, the northern peasants did not experience the extreme problems of southern peasants (Foerster, [1919] 1968: 106). The economic and social backwardness of the South, compared to the North, which developed after unification became known as the "Southern Question." It referred to the most important regional split in modern Italy, between the industrializing North and the agricultural

South (Smith, 1959: 135). Gramsci (1957: 28) considered the South
to be an exploited colony of the industrialized North. (See Map 1,
Appendix A).

Italy was slow to industralize because it was hampered, in part, by
a lack of natural resources. Since only half the land could be cultivated, food production was limited and no surplus was grown for export.
Italy is poor in mineral deposits such as coal and iron, important in
the early phases of industralization. Transportation was hampered by
the mountains which run like a spine down the length of Italy and by the
lack of navigable rivers. Furthermore, the railroad network was too
limited to unite many remote areas with the rest of the nation
(Tannenbaum and Noether, 1974: xx).

Efforts of the new government to encourage industrialization were
concentrated in the North. The northern area benefitted from early,
major land reclamation projects, the development of a sorely needed
elementary school system, and protective customs tariffs (Iorizzo and
Mondello, 1980: 21; Procacci, 1970: 286). From 1881 to 1887 modest but
steady progress was made in a variety of industries in the North including the cotton, metal, and chemical industries. But, unfortunately,
the industrial boom coincided with the start of an agricultural crisis,
so that as the prices of industrial goods rose, the price of agricultural products declined. As a result, capital was drained from the
South to the North (Procacci, 1970: 286).

In 1887 a new tariff was drawn up which created a tie between the
Northern industrialists and landed gentry of the South. The tariff
favored further industrial development while protecting the interests of

the small class of powerful Southern land owners who wanted tariff protection for cereal products (Dore, 1974: 18). Thus, the interests of the industrialists were encouraged, while the South retained an obsolete agricultural system which primarily benefitted the large land owners. The already substantial social and economic gap between the North and South widened.

One effect of modernization which did reach the South proved, ironically, a mixed blessing. The introduction of modern medicine and sanitation lowered the infant mortality rate and the mortality rate for young children and postpartum women. During the period from 1861 to 1901 the population in the South doubled to 12 million. This rise in population disrupted the balance between the food supply and population (Moss, 1974: 151).

Levi-Bacci (1977: 267-269) sees other factors contributing to the population increase. The South had a much higher illiteracy rate than the North, and the lack of literacy in the South inhibited the circulation of new ideas regarding birth control. Poor transportation hindered the circulation of population that might have also stimulated new ideas and practices. Levi-Bacci (1977: 269-271) also notes that the mass migration from the South did reduce some of the excess population. However, migration also took away the more innovative individuals, and left behind those who were more traditional and less likely to accept the new ideas once they were circulated. Thus, the fertility rate was slow to drop in the South where illiteracy and conservatism flourished.

Migration to America

Many Italian peasants made the decision to emigrate after unification, even as some reform efforts brought improvements after 1900. Once the pattern of leaving had been established, reforms were not enough to convince many individuals that they really had a stake in the future of modern Italy. From 1900 Italian emigration formed the major element in large scale migration overseas from continental Europe (Monticelli, 1970: 4).

While most Italian migration to the United States was from the South of Italy, there were roughly three phases of Italian migration to America; not all were predominately Southern. The first phase was individualistic. In the 1700s emigrants from throughout Italy began to come to the American colonies as explorers, artisans, merchants, and adventurers (Schiavo [1934] 1975: 43-180).

The second phase was a large scale migration (see Table 2) starting in the 1860s as increasing numbers of Italians, mainly from the north, sought their fortunes in America. Emigration was discouraged in some parts of Italy, especially the South where severe laws curbed emigration in the early 1800s. Migrants from the Alpine areas and Ligurian coast, however, were free to move to industralizing European nations, North Africa, and to North and South America. The Northern migration was often of a temporary nature, as agricultural workers left Italy during seasons of slack time (Foerster, 1968: 3-22).

Table 2.   Italian Migration to America from 1860 to 1929*

Period	Numbers
1860-1869	9,853
1871-1879	43,761
1881-1889	255,306
1891-1899	603,761
1900-1910	1,930,475
1911-1919	1,229,916
1920-1929	528,133

*Source: Compiled from data in Iorizzo and Mondello, 1980: 285.

The Northern Italian's experience in the second phase adumbrates the later experience of Southern Italians who formed the bulk of emigrants to America. By the 1860s the New York City colony of Italians at Five Points, originally composed of middle-class merchants and political exiles, became increasingly populated by lower-class peasant immigrants. These immigrants, though few in number compared to those who came later, faced poor working conditions, and were involved in labor disputes with other groups. The myth of lawless Italians emerged during this time, adding to the growing prejudice and discrimination against them (Iorizzo and Mondello, 1971: 24).

The third and largest wave of historical migration began by the 1880s and brought increasing numbers of Southerners to the United States. Poverty was the common lot of rural Italians during the period of mass migration. However, poverty alone did not trigger the decision to leave. As John MacDonald (1963: 491-98) has pointed out in areas with a militant working class, such as Apulia in the South and in Central Italy, the migration rate was low despite the levels of poverty. In the Alpine area and Sicily labor militancy was generally not strong. For those regions, as well as other areas in the South, poverty did lead to a decision to migrate. Briggs (1978: 272-273) in his research on Sicilian emigrants suggests an even further refinement on the broad view of poverty as the push in emigration. He notes that for the town he studied those most likely to leave were from the upper strata of the working class and the middle strata of the rural class. He sees the decision to leave related to a concern on the part of the emigrants that their social positions would deteriorate as the wage-labor system was introduced, which threatened the intricate local status system.

Although the push of conditions in Italy was enough to warrant migration, it was the pull of conditions in an industrializing America which provided a target for the migrants. The rapid expansion of American industry after the Civil War demanded a large pool of cheap labor. Since there were not enough suitable workers in the native population the nation encouraged, at least initially, immigration from Europe. Approximately 23 million individuals responded during the period from the 1880s to the 1920s, until restrictive legislation limited migration for the new European emigrants (Krickus, 1976: 54).

Patterns of Settlement

During the main period of Italian migration the first immigrants were, as was the case with the Northerners before them, men traveling without their families. These immigrants went where the jobs were, and their settlement patterns were fairly clear. They were concentrated on the Atlantic seaboard, in New York, Rhode Island, Connecticut, Massachusetts, and New Jersey and in industrial and commercial centers, like Detroit, St. Paul, St. Louis, Chicago, and Pittsburgh. New York City had the largest number of Italians in the United States, and in the early decades some of the worst living conditions. Dense population, poor housing, poverty, and disease were concentrated in the Italian centers like Mulberry Street. However, similar conditions could be found in other cities like Boston, Chicago, and Philadelphia (Foerster, 1968: 381).

Family oriented migration developed by the 1900s. This meant that more stable Italian communities began to develop in areas of recent settlement. Chain migration based on primary contacts with earlier immigrants allowed tightly knit communities to develop (MacDonald and MacDonald 1964: 82). Barton (1975) showed how the pattern worked for Italians in Cleveland. He reports that early migrants often left in relation to a particular stress, like the drop in the price of cotton in Sicily which caused young spinners and weavers to leave for America. Once established in Cleveland they sent for relatives, in fact some chains extended to include entire villages. Barton found that half the Italians arrived in major village chains of 20 or more members. He also found that those who came in migration chains were more likely to remain than those who came alone (Barton: 1975, 54). Thus, many Italians in Cleveland, as was the case for other communities, found familiar dialects, family, friends, and organizations, which gave indirect parallels to the social structure of the rural communities they left.

Chain migration even functioned in remote areas in the West. However, there was a different settlement pattern in the West. Those who settled in the West were usually Northerners, as opposed to the predominant Southerners. Rolle (1968) attempts to explain this pattern found in the western states by suggesting that Northern Italians seemed ". . . more aggressive about finding place in the sun——particularly the western sun" (1968: 94). An alternative explanation is that Northerners pushed further West because their migration began earlier, allowing more time for "explorers" within their ranks to travel across the vast spaces of America, and send work to their _paesani_ about opportunities in the West (Martinelli, 1981).

Arizona's Italian population was fairly typical. In 1904, for example, 89 percent of the new arrivals were Northern, and in the West 77 percent were Northern. Nationwide for 1904 the overall percentage was 80 percent Southern arrivals to 20 percent Northern (U.S. Commissioner-General of Immigration, 1904). Wherever the arrivals went the goal was to find employment, so patterns of occupation are important to discuss.

Patterns of Occupation

Most immigrants were involved in some type of agriculture in Italy. With a few exceptions, such as truck farmers, most became other kinds of laborers in America. They worked in the textile industry in mills producing silk, wool, twine, and hemp. They also worked at candy making, in canneries, in automobile factories, and followed the Welsh, Irish and Germans into the mines. In the South, Italians worked in lumber and saw mills, and in the tobacco industry. Italians were prominent in the building trades, for this area was one in which Italians were skilled workers. They worked as marble and stone cutters, masons, bricklayers, and at the bottom of the industry as hod carriers and excavators. They also labored on the docks and in gangs on railroad construction and other construction jobs (Foerster, 1968: 333-362).

Southern Italian mores generally did not condone women working outside the home, but in America this began to change. Italian women were heavily involved in the artificial-flower industry and garment industry, although this was often piece work done at home. They also worked in canneries, and the manufacture of tobacco products, candy, and paper, where they frequently worked with other Italian women (Nelli, 1983: 87).

Italians became involved with unions and the labor movement by the early 1900s. This involvement aided them by providing a start in upward mobility. By the 1930s they began to move up in blue collar ranks. Lopreato (1970: 148) notes that although few New York Italians were foremen, electricians, painters, plumbers, and contractors in 1916, by 1931 they were well represented in these areas. Italians also doubled their numbers in other occupations during this period such as clerical, sales, and small business proprietors. Overall, Italians stayed in skilled blue collar occupations into the second generation. Nelli (1983: 185) cites a 1963 study of Italian Americans which found that 52 percent were blue-collar workers and 48 percent white-collar workers. So, well into their first century in the United States most Italian Americans retained their working class origins.

Cultural Patterns

Immigrants brought more with them to America than their desire to advance themselves economically, they brought with them their peasant culture. This culture represents another important area to examine especially in light of the work of the social scientists, discussed in Chapter II, who are interested in establishing whether the immigrant culture has been eroded, continued, or modified into an ethnic culture.

The Family

One theme threading through literature on Italians and Italian Americans is the importance of the family. While the family institution is recognized as a basic social institution, for Italians the family has been described as ". . . the only fundamental institution in the country . . . the real foundation of whichever social order prevails" (Barzini 1964: 198). The centrality of the family stems, in part, from the historical uncertainty of Italian life. Italy, with a desirable geographical position in the Mediterranean, was politically fragmented and often invaded. Peasants, as the most powerless in the social structure, took the brunt of the political struggles. They learned not to rely on outside authority for support or protection.

Family Structure

Despite the focus in literature on the family there is often a lack of agreement on what constitutes the Italian family. Precise definitions of blood relationships are seldom given, especially in American literature, although there is an implicit assumption of kin reckoning through the canon law model (Farber, 1977: 229).

Defining the family system more clearly becomes important in assess
ing the retention of cultural patterns among second and third generation
Italian Americans. Some describe the immigrant Italian family as a
functioning extended system (e.g., Campisi, 1948, Femminella and
Quadagno, 1976; L. Tomasi, 1972). Thus, the nuclear family of the
Italian Americans represents, for some, an example of assimilation
(Vander Zanden, 1972: 357). However, others describe the Italian
peasant family as basically nuclear in focus (Gallo, 1974; Lopreato,
1970; Moss and Thomson, 1959). If the first view is correct and the
Italian family was a functioning extended unit, and today's Italian
American family system is nuclear then there has been a loss of a
cultural pattern. However, if the second view is correct and the
immigrant family system was essentially nuclear, then a nuclear family
system in the 1980s continues to follow the immigrant pattern.

To answer the question about family systems, it must first be recognized that Italy had a wide variety of family types. The Northern
Italians, who were the typical immigrants from the period from 1860 to
1880, were from the regions most likely to have functional extended
families, although specific patterns were found in different provinces.
Two brief examples can highlight the nature of these extended families.
Rina Huber's (1977) study of emigrants from the Veneto region showed the
extended family existed as a working unit until after World War II.
These rural families lived in patrilineal extended households.

In the Alpine culture area which separates northern Italy from the
rest of Europe, Burns (1963) found the patrilocal stem extended family.
The stem structure includes parents with one married offspring living

with them. These studies, then, show the existence of the extended
family system in the North.

Studies of the Southern Italian family indicate a different pattern.
Constance Cronin (1970) summarized references to the Southern family.
She notes that those who describe it as an extended family are primarily
those who studied the family systems of Italian immigrants in America,
and the families of their descendants. Those who studied the family in
Italy stress the importance of the nuclear family as the basic unit,
especially in economic functions.

Based on Cronin's analysis and a review of some later literature two
general types of Southern nuclear families emerge. The first can be
termed the isolated nuclear family. This type of family system became
the source of academic debate because of the work of sociologist Edward
Banfield (1958); a debate which is still being discussed (Gesualdi,
1983). The pejorative undertones of his work, The Moral Basis of a
Backward Society, and the term amoral familism which he used to describe
the isolated nuclear family has served to make Banfield's research a
popular target. While there are some weaknesses in his study the overall description he gives of isolated nuclear units, each seeking to
advance their interests even at the expense of siblings and parents, is
supported by other research. Lopreato (1967), who questions Banfield's
findings actually described a village with characteristics somewhat
similar to the one Banfield studied. Lopreato found evidence of nuclear
households operating for their own interests, with the extended family
nonexistent as any kind of solidarity. Giovanni (1978) also found the
nuclear family dominant. It was a basic economic unit and emotional

unit—love, affection, loyalty belonged within the isolated nuclear family.

In contrast is the family pattern associated with the cannon law model, in which the nuclear family unit is attached to the large kin unit. Cronin's (1970) research describes a kin group which she likens to a series of circles. Furthest out are relatives (i parenti) such as aunts and cousins. Next is the extended family consisting of one's parents, married siblings and their families, and married children. The nuclear family is the innermost circle and commands the individual's loyalty. She points out that Italian law and Sicilian rules of inheritance stressed the primacy of the nuclear family (Cronin, 1970: 45). Chapman (1971) has a similar description of the Southern family. The nuclear family is the most tightly knit kin group and the basic economic unit. The next kin grouping is formed by the male lineage group, the most diffuse group is i parenti (Chapman, 1971: 63, 130). While Miller (1974: 522) found the emphasis on the nuclear family, he did note a sense of obligation to the larger kin unit among the people he studied. He also noted the importance of fictive kin, or godparents (Miller and Miller, 1978).

One could describe differences in Southern regions or even from village to village. As Bell (1979: 75) notes, the Italian family is a process, adapting to ecology, opportunity, economic developments, and even political policy. The basic purpose of the Italian family, as he sees it, is to make the most of existing resources. To do this la famiglia must change with the social and physical context within which it is situated.

Ianni (1977: 104) clarifies why findings on Italian American families and those in Italy differ. The extended family, he notes, was an ideal for Southern immigrants which was not fulfilled for the peasant class because of the hard economic and social realities of the Mezzogiorno (South). The system of chain migration meant that kin were present in America. So in the new environment, initially often as harsh as what immigrants left, kinship ties were reinforced. Ianni doubts that the ideal of the economically independent extended family was ever a reality even in urban American ghettos, but the ideal was kept alive. Where the extended family did serve a purpose was as a "ceremonial network" of relatives who gathered for all important life passages, such as births, marriages, and funerals, and provided some type of aid in times of need. Occasionally the ideal became realized in America when family businesses, an important source of economic upward mobility for Italian Americans, were formed (Ianni, 1977: 104).

In terms of ceremonial functions the ideal of the extended family may have become more important for the second generation, as they became more established in American society, than for immigrants. Palisi (1966a: 49-50) found that, contrary to his predictions, the extended family seemed to play a greater role for the second generation than for the first. The second generation in his study tended to be closer physically and socially to their extended family than the earlier generation did. This suggests that close family ties may be a luxury more easily sustained by more affluent generations.

Based on the above discussion of the family structure it seems likely that the Italian American family of the 1980s will be primarily nuclear in structure, as was the immigrant family. Yet, one would also expect to find evidence of emotional and social ties to a larger, extended family grouping. This issue will be discussed further, when the Scottsdale sample is examined.

Family Values

A unique set of values emerged in the Italian ethos related to the family. Moss and Thompson (1959:39) suggest that family honor is an underlying, basic value. Covello (1967: 152) notes that the concept of family honor (onore) broadly signifies the adherence of family members to the established code of relationships and behavior within an individual family. Family tradition might mean honor is related to meticulous cleanliness, or habitual insubordination to local authorities. Bell (1979: 2) suggests that onore encompasses the notions of honor, respect, and dignity, within the context of the family. The individual earns or loses honor, but it is measured and judged in terms of the whole family. When the individual loses face in a community, (or fails to fare una bella figura), it shames the whole family. Related to the notion of family onore was an emphasis on localism (campanilismo). The family esteem was judged in relation to other families in the local village. Particularly important is the purity of women, with the loss of virginity especially causing shame (Covello, 1967; Cronin, 1970).

Individuals were expected to give family interests priority over their own interests. One turned to the family for physical, emotional, and social needs. There was very little need to rely on outsiders. Often those outside a person's family were viewed with suspicion, for it would be expected that outsiders would be working to advance their own by observing: "in politics, in work, in the economy, in religion, in love, indeed in all of life, perceptions exist and decisions are made primarily in terms of family."

Family Roles

The nuclear family of the Southern Italian immigrants was patri-archal. Men were considered the leaders in family affairs, especially in the public sphere (Femminella and Quadagno 1976: 65). Both legally and socially women were in a dependent relationship to the men in their families, first their father, and then their husband. However, to view the Italian male as an absolute despot and the female as totally sub-servient would miss many of the subtleties of their relationships in the family.

The male was the head of the family, and with that role went many responsibilities. Gambino (1974: 117-145) uses the phrase a man of patience (l'uomo di pazienza) to describe the ideal Mezzogiorno man. It is a description which he sees at odds with many stereotypes of the Italian man as volatile, expressive, and emotional. A real man was expected to protect his family and the order of the family (l'ordine della famiglia). Hard work, self-denial, seriousness, and determination went into being a man of patience. These traits were essential if a man were to advance his family in the hostile circumstances of rural Italy.

The woman's role was that of a unifying force within the privacy of the home. Women often controlled the household finances, and enjoyed the love and respect of the children. Because of their lack of a public role in the family, outsiders often misinterpreted their silence for submission. Gambino (1974: 146-166) describes the ideal Southern woman as a woman of seriousness. Women were related to almost every crucial facet of their society for power usually flowed from the family, and the advancement of the family was dependent equally on the talents and efforts of both the husband and wife. However, the lives of women were more circumscribed than that of men by strict customs, poverty, and illiteracy. A Southern peasant woman, interviewed by Cornelisen (1977: 277) described the authority of women this way, "We decide, but we don't have to talk about it in the Piazza. Call that power if you want to. To us its killing work."

Children were expected to respect and obey their parents. A formal relationship was stressed with a good child measured by good manners (Moss and Thomson, 1959: 40). Children were educated very early for their roles in supporting the family, which was of primary importance. Formal education, when it was available, was a luxury for many. For others it was viewed with suspicion. The nationalist values being taught at the schools established by the Italian government were at odds with the particularistic values of the family (Gambino, 1974: 227). So, children learned by observing the behavior of adults, in an effort to preserve the primacy of the family. Thus, through all this discussion of the family runs the theme of the family as the primary social institution in the lives of those immigrants from Southern Italy who came to America.

Political Attitudes

Most immigrants from the Mezzogiorno brought little direct experience in political participation with them. After unification power in the South was basically left unchanged, for there was not universal suffrage. Even when an electoral reform was passed in 1882, in the South it benefitted those already in power. Southern politics remained controlled by the gentry and small number of the middle-class (Procacci, 1970: 278). Official institutions were weak, the legal system was seen as unreliable, and the government was dominated by the powerful and rich. Barzini (1964: 200) believes that political institutions may have never really succeeded in Italy because they were primarily foreign imports, from France and America, pitting ideas against the entrenched strength of traditional family values.

Lieberson (1980: 77-84) notes that Italians generally had a slow, difficult start in American politics. Initially, as immigrants came to America their earliest encounters with political forces were with urban political machines. This contact reinforced the cynicism of the immigrants who saw political power belonging to forces distant from them, so the desire for naturalization and the vote was not always strong. However, those who did become citizens were encouraged to vote for their own by the Italian intelligensia in their communities, to gain political clout (DeConde, 1971: 18). Gradually Italians began to assert themselves in urban political arenas in cities like New York, Chicago, New Haven, and Philadelphia (Varbero, 1975: 165).

Another factor in slow political advancement was the lack of loyalty to one political party. While many are Democrats, the group has also been found among the ranks of the Republican Party. The unpredictability of their vote seems to stem from a concern with what impinges on their value system. These values are twined around family, home, community, and work. When elections do not revolve around such issues Italian Americans have often shown a poor voting record (Gambino, 1974: 294).

The political advancement of Italians accelerated rapidly after the 1940s. Lubell (1952: 66-75) charting the political climb of John Pastore of Rhode Island, the first Italian American senator, noted several elements present which aided the political advancement of Italian Americans. He sees these elements as operative for other minority groups as well. The Italian Americans of Rhode Island had a growing middle class which provided financial backing and leadership, a growing population base to support aspiring politicians, and prosperous times.

Italian Americans suffered some political losses in the 1960s in cities like Newark and New York, but generally continue to win in heavily Italian areas. They also are winning in some non-Italian areas, like Arizona and Wyoming, according to Acocella (1979: 20-21). However, he notes that they have still not played a role commensurate with their numbers as one of the largest European ethnic groups in America.

Religion

Italians are overwhelmingly Catholic. In the period prior to the unification of Italy the Catholic church was a powerful, autonomous force in most aspects of Italian life. It was an economic force with vast landholdings, an educational force, and political and military force. While opposing Italian unification and the emergence of a modern political state, the Church's conservatism did not halt its own moderni-zation. Lay activities encouraged by the Church gave millions of

Italians experience in organization, propaganda techniques, and coercion
necessary for influence building in modern society (Tannenbaum and
Noether, 1974: xxvii, 258-59). Ventures into Catholic social activities
and the Church leadership primarily focused in the North, however
(Abramson, 1973: 137).

In the South the Church was strongly linked to the upper classes.
Local priests often lived less than exemplary lives, so that understand-
ably many peasants had little respect for the official Catholic Church.
Women went to mass, but peasant men often only appeared in church for
feast days or important rites (Vecoli, 1968: 228).

However, anti-clericalism should not be confused with being anti-
religious for peasants were often religious. Their lives dominated,
according to Vecoli (1969: 228), by a sense of awe, fear, and reverence
for the supernatural. Saints, including some local saints not recognized elsewhere, and the Virgin Mary were venerated. Some Christian
practices, as can be found elsewhere, were merged with some earlier
pagan practices. People also believed in witchcraft and the evil-eye
(Di Stasi, 1981: 59; Mangano [1917] 1972: 76-78).

The Italian Catholics arrived in America to find the Church dominated by the Irish whose version of Catholicism had the stamp of Irish
culture. As immigrants from Italy began to increase in numbers special
services were held in English speaking churches, and eventually Italian
national parishes emerged to serve Italian areas. Traditional feast
days (festa) were held for saints venerated by local clusterings of
immigrants. Thus, those from Cinisi, Sicily might celebrate the feast
of Santa Fara, while those from Ripicandida, Basilicata might celebrate

San'Donato's day. Some saints were more universally recognized. Thousands gather in New York to celebrate the feast of San Gennaro who was first venerated by Neapolitans. S. Tomasi (1970: 191) asserts that since the ethnic parish supported the local *feste* of immigrants it functioned as an intermediary between the immigrants and the larger society. The Italian parishes united people by ritual and social functions.

Protestant attempts to convert Italian immigrants generally failed, and Italian Americans remain basically Catholic. There is some question of whether the group has assimilated into the Irish version of Catholicism. Nicholas Russo (1970: 195-209) in a study of three generations of Italian Americans found that there has been decrease in Italian folk traditions, such as the veneration of local saints by novenas, celebration of feast days, and having masses celebrated. The "cult of the Blessed Virgin Mary" has also declined for the younger generation according to Russo. At the same time there has been an increase in Irish practices among Italian Americans such as attending weekly mass, receiving communion often, donating money to the church, and attending parochial schools. These changes are associated with marriage to non-Italian Catholics, and the assimilation of Italian Americans into the primary groups of other European Catholics (Russo, 1970: 209).

Abramson (1973: 97) sees Italian Catholics retaining their religious distinctiveness. His data suggests that generation has no influence on Italian American religious practices for earlier generations. However, he notes that as the third and later generations become more exogamous, there will be increasing church involvement. Both Russo and Abramson give support to the triple melting-pot thesis advanced by Herberg which predicts that ethnic groups will be exogamous in terms of ethnicity while endogamous within their religion (Herberg, 1955).

Italian Adjustment to America

As discussed in the section on cultural patterns, there has been a scholarly concern on the adjustment of the great wave of Italian migrants to American society. The issue of assimilation has proved salient from the earliest period of the mass migration of Italians. However, as the immigrant generation became settled, and their offspring were raised in an Italian and American culture the concern shifted from looking at immigrants to the results of their settlement, the second, third, and later generations. The remainder of this chapter is devoted to a chronological presentation of the major studies done relating to Italians and their descendants.

Early Period: First and Second Generation

Systematic scholarly studies of Italian American life did not begin during the early years of immigration, although this group of immigrants certainly did receive attention. There was a concern with whether or not the immigrants would benefit America and assimilate into American society (e.g., Dingley, 1890; Foerster, [1919] 1968). Settlement house workers, social workers, journalists, reformers and missionaries observed and described the problems and potentials of Italians in American slums (Cordasco and Bucchioni, 1974: 124-211).

Research of a more academic orientation began to emerge after the turn of the century. Robert Foerster's (1968) The Italian Emigration of Our Times stands as a classic on the world-wide migration of Italians.

Considerable space in this work is devoted to Italians in America. Foerster primarily focused on occupations and settlement patterns, however, he also discussed some of the problems faced by immigrants.

During the 1930s the Federal Writers' Project of the WPA stimulated scholarly efforts on Italian Americans. The work of Leonard Covello, under the auspices of the Federal Writers' Project, was particularly ambitious. He organized the Casa Italiana Educational Bureau in New York City, and proposed a major sociological research project which would cover Italian American communities (Cordasco, 1975: 4). Although he had some early publications, a lack of funds meant the closing of the project and the loss of valuable research data. Covello's 1944 doctoral dissertation The Socio-Cultural Background of the-Italo-American Child was not published until 1967. The three-volume monograph presented a thorough description of the social organization of Italians as well as a study of the assimilation of immigrants in New York.

Paul Radin's ([1935] 1970) work on San Francisco's Italians was also under the auspices of the WPA. Radin, an anthropologist, collected a series of interviews of immigrants. The focus of his study was on the various types immigrants that could be identified through the autobiographies. A brief description of the local Italian community was included in Radin's research, however, like Covello's research, Radin's study was not completed.

Two studies in the late 1930s sponsored by Yale University dealt with Italian Americans. Phyllis Williams ([1938] 1969) studied the folkways of Southern Italians and their modification in America. The work was designed to help social workers deal with their clients. Irvin

Child's doctoral dissertation from Yale was based on his study of second generation Italian males in New Haven, Connecticut. The title of the book Italian or American? The Second General in Conflict ([1943] 1970) delineated the thrust of his research. He saw the second generation facing conflict stemming from the divergence between the American and Italian cultures.

Child observed three kinds of reactions among the second generation in response to being culturally marginal. In the Rebel reaction the individual prefers acceptance by Americans, trying to minimize his Italianess while becoming American in behavior and association. This reaction could be stressful. Initially, the individual had to reject, at least in part, his immigrant parents in order to identify with Americans. However, once the individual had rejected his Italianess he could face rejection from American society, since Italians were still the targets of prejudice and discrimination. The In-group reaction as when the individual identified with the Italian community to the exclusion of the larger American community. Child saw strain arising from this reaction because the individual would be aware of the rewards of the larger society which were not being attained. The third response he called the Apathetic reaction which was a compromise strategy. The person avoids strong attachment to the Italian community, but does not go as far as rejecting it.

Since Child's reaction patterns are frequently cited, one criticism of his work should be mentioned. Cronin (1970) notes that while Child interviewed 53 boys, only 31 fit into one of the three reactions. The remaining 22 respondents were not included in his analysis because they did not fit any reaction pattern. Thus, one needs to be cautious about applying Child's reaction patterns to discussions of other Italian Americans.

In the same period a Harvard graduate student was involved in a study of the Italian community of North Boston which became a sociological classic. William F. Whyte's Street Corner Society ([1943] 1981) gave a view of an ethnic slum's social networks. Whyte assumed the second generation was different from the first, but detailing these differences was not the main purpose of his research. Like Child he focused on second generation males. He called those oriented to the community the "corner boys", and those who were upwardly mobile the "college boys".

Two decades later another Boston community, on the west side, came under sociological scrutiny, this time by Herbert Gans in his well known study The Urban Villagers ([1962] 1982). Gans was astute in capturing the powerlessness of a community of lower-class individuals faced with the razing of their area for urban renewal projects. Gans was also astute in describing the West End's close social ties thriving in an urban neighborhood. His term "urban villagers" passed into general usage within urban sociology to describe people who live in a city area characterized by intimate, face-to-face relationships.

The third area Gans dealt with was describing Italian American life. He contended that the Italian culture had largely disappeared among the second generation West Enders, as Gans called them. However, he observed very little change between generations in regard to their social structure. This led him to conclude that while the Italian culture had been eroded, assimilation had still not taken place (Gans, 1982: 35).

The Later Period: The Third Generation

By the 1950s studies began to include the third generation. Ulin ([1958] 1975) studied second and third-generation Italian American boys in a suburb of Boston. Ulin was interested in differences in high school performance between Yankee and Italian American boys. Italian American boys appeared similar to their Yankee peers, were elected to class offices, and enjoyed high school social life. However, the Italian American boys had a distinctive pattern in the curricula they chose, the courses they took, their close friends, after school socialization patterns, and extra-curricular activities. Perhaps most importantly they scored differently than Yankee boys on standardized achievement tests, got lower grades, and showed lower intelligence scores on IQ tests (Ulin, [1958] 1975: 164-165).

Ulin studied the values of the two groups of boys and concluded that in several areas there were no reliable differences in values to be found. However, among those values which were different two seemed to account for the scholastic difference between the Italian Americans and the Yankees. The Italian American boys scored higher on Family Allegiance and lower on Urge for Upward Mobility, and these values combined with the overall lower SES level of the Italian American boys contributed to the scholastic differences (Ulin, [1958] 1975: 166-167). Like Gans, Ulin concluded that assimilation, in terms of attitudes, had not occurred.

Ianni (1957: 65-77) studied the Italian community of Norristown, Pennsylvania during the 1950s. Using historical records he traced the gradual occupational and residential mobility of the group from 1930 to 1950. The overall mobility trends indicates, for Ianni, the gradual trend toward the acculturation of the ethnic group. Mobility also served as a measure of the changing status of the Italian Americans in that city. Ianni's (1961: 70-78) later article on third generation Italian American teens parallels Ulin's findings. Ianni's teens also came from marginal families. They kept ties to their Italian families and culture while Americanizing. Even the younger generation retained elements of ethnic identification, although Ianni saw the Irish-Catholic Church as an important factor in shaping Italian American teen-agers' attitudes in the future.

Angelo Danesino's (1960) doctoral dissertation looks at personality patterns formed by an ethnic cultural environment. Danesino focused his research on low and high achievers among male college students of Irish and Italian descent. Using a battery of tests he was able to conclude that even for second and third-generation college students who were similar in age, intelligence, and SES, consistent ethnic differences could be found (Danesino, 1960: 104).

Patrick Gallo's research (1974) examined the political attitudes of Italian Americans. Using Milton Gordon's paradigm as the basis for his analysis, Gallo concluded that cultural assimilation was extensive. Other forms of assimilation were not as extensive, with identificational and structural assimilation only minimally present (Gallo, 1974: 195).

His small sample was almost all lower SES, residentially stable, and urban. As such, it was typical of the traditional working-class white ethnic.

Clement Valletta ([1968] 1975) did a study of three generations in an Italian American town in Pennsylvania. As he traces the changes in the world view of the three generations in "Carneta" he notes the gradual intrusion of the larger society in terms of the value structure. He holds that even for the upwardly mobile third-generation who leave, an Italian identity is important. Valetta concludes that the ethnic framework of Carneta will be worn away by outside influences, but that through the three generations he studied Italian traditions were evident in the way American society was perceived and approached.

Thaddeus O'Brien's (1972) study of Italian Americans in the Chicago area focused on the retention of core values from Southern Italy. His dissertation was based on in-depth interviews of 50 individuals from an ethnically homogeneous suburb and additional seven with "emigrants" who had moved. Many key values, such as the importance of the family, close ties with the extended family, concern with family honor, and the role of the father as head of the household, were retained. The major change he saw was that women had greater freedom. The suspicion of outsiders, distrust of officials, and inability of the community to work together was seen by O'Brien as evidence of "amoral familism." Changes in the Catholic Church related to the Second Vatican Council were interpreted as undermining core values, and were disliked. While he did interview second and third generation Italian Americans the focus was not on differences between these groups. O'Brien did note that the small sample of people who had left the ethnic community exhibited attitudes which were not as clearly Southern Italian (O'Brien, 1972: 217-326).

The last three studies to be discussed have some similarity because all rely, in part, on Sandberg's scale of ethnic attitudes. Roche (1977), whose dissertation was mentioned in the discussion of straight-line assimilationism in Chapter II, used Sandberg's attitude scales and added a behavioral scale. He studied an Italian American suburb and an ethnically mixed suburb near Providence, Rhode Island. Roche found that generally generation was the main independent variable that showed differences in ethnicity. The most important decline in ethnicity was between the first generation and second generation. The decline between the second generation and the third was slight, and often not statistically significant. The other two key variables he explored, class and suburb type, failed to show declining ethnicity. Based on his findings Roche predicts that ethnicity will gradually decline, and that ours will not be an ethnically pluralistic society (Roche, 1977: 219-226). The questionnaire was administered directly, with an overall completion rate of 80 percent, resulting in 260 interviews.

James Crispino (1980), whose study was also mentioned in the straight-line assimilationism discussion in Chapter II, added items to Sandberg's scale. His research focused on the Italian Americans in Bridgeport, Connecticut, and the suburbs surrounding the city. While Crispino found an indication of increased ethnic self identification among younger generation Italian Americans, he concluded that overall his results support the straight-line assimilation thesis. He ties the symbolic ethnicity argument of Gans into the findings in Bridgeport on self-identity since the identification does not correlate with high

levels of ethnic activities (1980: xxiii, 99). He also found evidence

of increasing structural assimilation with the exception of highly

educated first and second generation individuals. Crispino speculates

that these individuals are presumably those who serve the Italian

community, and thus are likely to express support for the continuation

of the Italian culture (1980: 89). Crispino's study was based on a

mailed questionnaire with a 60 percent response rate which resulted in

469 respondents. Part of the sample was selected from city directories.

Italian Americans who could not be identified by name were included in

the study by soliciting the aid of such respondents.

Fandetti and Gelfand (1983) did a similar study of Italian Americans

in Columbia, Maryland in an attempt to look at middle-class suburban

individuals. In addition to Sandberg's scale they utilized the highest

loading items, based on factor analysis, from Kohn's (1977) index of

parental values, social orientation, and self-conception. Their mailed

questionnaires had a 56 percent response rate which yielded 113 usable

responses (Fandetti and Gelfand, 1983: 115).

Fandetti and Gelfand found that for their sample there was a gener-

ally neutral response to Sandberg's scale, similar to Child's "apathetic

reaction." Respondents did not favor ethnic church organizations, poli-

tical candidates, or neighborhoods. But there was a positive response

to cultural heritage and history. Respondent's scores on Kohn's indexes

gave results similar to the upper-class individuals in Kohn's sample,

indicating the men valued self-direction, exhibited self-confidence, and

were able to take responsibility for their lives. They conclude that the Columbia sample shows an overall convergence between middle-class Italian American values and the values of the core society. These individuals are selective in the values they transmit. While retaining pride in their heritage they will not transmit values which would limit success (Fandetti and Gelfand, 1983: 122-125).

Conclusion

The history of the third phase of mass Italian migration to America is the movement of a peasant people into a rapidly developing industrial nation. Italians left behind their struggle for survival in a harsh rural environment to take up the struggle in an urban environment that was also harsh in many ways. While little of their rural material culture was of use to them in the new setting, they did bring attitudes and values that persisted. Some of these values, such as loyalty to the family, aided them in a new and sometimes hostile country. Other attitudes, such as a distrust of formal education and the political system, proved dysfunctional for rapid social advancement. In the Scottsdale study attitudes and values that correlate with those from the peasant experience are examined to see if they are relevant for Italian Americans in a Sunbelt setting.

The preceding also examined some of the salient research done on Italian Americans in regard to their ethnicity and assimilation. Overall there is little doubt that increasing acculturation is evident from the very beginning of the Italian experience in America. The data on assimilation is less clear. Studies which were based on in-depth research and participant observation show assimilation, but seem to find many Southern Italian values still evident even in the third generation.

Those studies based on survey research techniques have larger samples, and found some evidence to support the straight line assimilation thesis. All of the studies were of local communities, and most researchers cautioned about generalizing from their studies. This could explain some differences in findings. Finally the studies were in different time periods, with most of the quantitative studies being done most recently, and most of the qualitative done earlier. Some differences could arise from the studies being done in different periods.

As important as many of these studies are, none of them deal with emerging Italian American settlements in upwardly mobile suburban communities. This gap in the literature on Italian Americans and their continuing adjustment to a changing American society is addressed by this study located in the most rapidly growing Sunbelt region in American society. In Chapter IV the demographic trends represented by the Scottsdale sample are presented, and compared to some of the studies presented in this chapter. In Chapters V through VIII the findings from the study are presented, and again compared to some of the research that has been presented. Thus the Scottsdale study can be evaluated as a study of an emergent community, and as another example of upwardly mobile, suburban Italian Americans.

CHAPTER IV

DESCRIPTION OF METHODS AND SAMPLE

The purpose of this chapter is to explain the methods used in the study of Italian Americans in Scottsdale. It also includes a description of the sample which was generated by this study. Together these serve as a preface to the following chapters which will contain the analysis of the research.

Methodology

The research is primarily based on quantitative data collected through an interview schedule. In an effort to delve more fully into ethnicity in an emergent setting qualitative data were also included as a supplement. The combination of these two techniques, along with the historical perspective utilized in Chapter III, constitutes the methodological techniques employed in this study.

Research Setting

A brief look at the Italian community of the Valley of the Sun is useful to explain the ethnic research setting. The type of community which formed was a consideration in the sample selection.

In the 1880s the first Italian settlers began to arrive in Phoenix. They formed a loosely knit community based on business and social ties (Mahoney, 1957a; Martinelli, 1977). The community was small, scattered, and lacked a gathering place. There was no Italian Catholic church, store, or mutual aid society to serve the community. Additionally, there was no evidence of chain migration which would have unified the group with at least a common dialect (Martinelli, 1977).

Many of the Italians of Phoenix did enter into businesses together, with saloon keeping the most typical occupation. Saloon keeping compared to the general trend of Italian employment in Arizona represents a specialization. In 1900 74 percent of the Italians in Arizona were in manufacturing, with most of these men working in the mines (U.S. Bureau of the Census, 1904). In contrast, close to 40 percent of Phoenix's Italians were in some area of the saloon business. Many were saloon proprietors. Others worked as bartenders, porters, musicians, or in other jobs related to the saloon business.

Casual socializing characterized the other important local network for Italian families. Networks extended throughout the Valley and the state. The Scottsdale community, described in Chapter I (pgs. 4 - 8), had few Italians historically. However, the few Italian families were part of the Phoenix socializing network.

Thus, in many ways the Italian community of the Valley of the Sun was not typical of Italian communities in the East or Midwest, where heavy concentrations of immigrants led to long lasting, cohesive ethnic enclaves. Nor was it necessarily typical of Italians in the West or even Arizona. Several western cities, like San Francisco and Denver, had large Italian communities. In Arizona some towns had small but distinct Italian communities. Globe's Italians, for example, were geographically concentrated. There were ties of kinship and region which were usually based on chain migration from northern Italy. In addition, most men worked in the local mines which forged another tie. The Globe community had several social organizations, grocery stores, and saloons which catered to the Italians. Overall, the experience of living in

Globe might not be different than living in another small Italian community (Mahoney, 1957b; Martinelli, 1981). However, Phoenix did present a different experience which, as noted became a factor in the selection of the sample.

Selection of the Sample

The selection of a sample of respondents who must be members of a particular ethnic group is one with several methodological difficulties. There is, in fact, no one research strategy to give the researcher total confidence in finding an unbiased sample. However, by being aware of the methodological pitfalls a researcher can hope to avoid or at least minimize the problems inherent in a particular strategy.

The classic sociological studies of Italian Americans were based, as previously mentioned, on participant observation (Gans, [1961] 1982; Whyte, [1943] 1981). The participant observation technique was well suited for the research topics in which the researchers were interested. The geographical concentration of the groups under study facilitated the research. Such a technique could have been used in Scottsdale, but would have been unsuitable for two reasons. First, the lack of a geographical base for the group means that one can not simply enter an Italian neighborhood to start research. Second, while this researcher has lived in the Scottsdale community for several years and has contacts within the community, many of these tend to be with Italian Americans who have at some time belonged to an Italian American organization. Since a person who would join such an organization might be expected to be less assimilated than a nonjoiner, starting to sample from such a group could tend to bias the sample in favor of individuals with stronger ethnic identities.

In the interests of locating a sample from which some generalizations could be made about the Italian American population of Scottsdale, a sample was drawn from the 1982 Scottsdale telephone book. Respondents were selected by their Italian surnames. Both surnames and the use of the telephone book represent sampling problems for which this study tried to compensate.

The use of surnames to identify European ethnic groups for research purposes is an established technique (Bugelski, 1961; Crispino, 1980; Fandetti and Gelfand, 1983; Roche, 1977). Gabriel (1973: 30) tested the use of surnames for his study and concluded that using surnames was valid. His pre-test did not show any misidentification, and the final study only had a 5 percent misidentification rate.

However, even if the researcher, on the basis of his or her assumed familiarity with the surnames of the ethnic group under study, can identify those names which are typical with up to 95 percent accuracy not all the problems of using surnames are solved. Another problem is that in many instances the surnames have been changed from typical European surnames to either Americanized surnames or a mixture of European and American surnames. Fucilla (1949: 236) has pointed out several major categories of name change patterns for Italian names in America. These include translating names directly into English, dropping the final vowel, Gallicizing the name to a French surname, shortening a compounded surname, or phonetically respelling a name. While some names become unrecognizable as Italian, by knowing these patterns it is possible to identify some changed Italian names.

Besides those who would be lost due to an unidentifiable surname, the technique of using surnames excludes women who are exogamous. Some researchers have solved this problem by limiting their research to males (e.g., Fandetti and Gelfand, 1983). Others have decided to allow the loss of such individuals by assuming that exogamous females are already assimilated to some degree (Bugelski, 1961: 149). Neither solution was acceptable for this study. The first solution excludes all women, who were important since sex-role identification is so generally important and since it cannot be assumed that ethnicity is the same for men and women. The second solution to be consistent would also need to exclude all exogamous men and would place a major limitation on who could be included in the sample. Further, it would not allow an exploration of the assumption that exogamous individuals are more assimilated than their endogamous peers, an assumption that this study does explore.

It was decided to compile a list of exogamous women and individuals with changed names by asking the respondents for such names. At the end of the interview, people were asked if they knew of anyone who would fit either criterion. From these responses a list was compiled which would be used for drawing a random sample.

This method was useful in locating exogamous women. A list of 27 exogamous women was compiled and 8 women were chosen from the list on a random basis. The number of women to include was determined by ascertaining the percentage of exogamous women among the respondent's siblings according to the data collected. The proportion among the siblings gave some guide as to how many exogamous women to include, since there was no reliable, current guide in the literature on the proportion of endogamous versus exogamous females which one could expect to find.

The method of asking respondents for names did not prove useful for locating individuals with changed names. Only a few names were collected, so it was not possible to sample randomly from the list. Therefore, the changed names were excluded.

Another problem with using surnames in the Southwest, although not necessarily everywhere else, is the number of Spanish surnames, some of which can be similar to Italian surnames. This problem is particularly relevant in some parts of the Phoenix metropolitan area. In Scottsdale only 3 percent of the population is Spanish origin so the problem is not as salient as it would be in Phoenix, but it was still a concern since the Italian origin population is about the same percentage of the population (U.S. Bureau of the Census, 1982a).

In the interest of accuracy about 180 names which were possibly Spanish or changed from Italian were checked by a professor of Italian language at the university. If a name was even possibly Italian, although not clearly so, it was included. It was considered more desirable to misidentify an individual, and have to drop them from the sample, than to exclude someone who might be Italian American.

The final problem with the use of surnames is that a person may have an Italian surname but be of mixed ancestry rather than full ancestry. Several researchers have simply included these respondents in their sample with those of full ancestry (e.g., Bugelski, 1961; Crispino, 1980; Roche, 1977). The logic for this is that a person would likely identify with his or her surname and the group associated with that surname (Abramson, 1973: 67). However, Alba (1976) argues that one cannot assume that people will identify with their surnames, or even have an ethnic identity.

This study reached a compromise between these two positions. The initial screening interview determined a person's ancestry. Those of mixed ancestry were included in the sample. However, they were not treated in the same manner as respondents of full ancestry. Those of mixed ancestry were given a shorter interview schedule since research suggests that to adequately study people of mixed ancestry an interview schedule designed for this purpose would need to be developed (C. Johnson, 1978). The shorter schedule obtained information about the respondent's background, demographic characteristics, and self-identity.

Consequently, the responses of the mixed group are not part of the statistical analysis. The information collected about this group will serve in related research as the basis for a full scale study of mixed ethnic identity.

Sampling Frame

There was no one list available for use as a sampling frame for Scottsdale's Italian Americans. The City of Scottsdale has lists of utility users, but these exclude apartment dwellers. This could bias the sample against older and younger people who are more likely to be renters. There are no census tracts with heavy concentrations of Italian Americans from which to sample (U.S. Bureau of the Census, 1983b). Consequently, although there are limitations, the telephone book seemed a practical primary source for obtaining a sample. In a

middle–class suburb one can assume most residents can afford a telephone, an assumption which cannot be made for lower-income areas. One
will, of course, miss unlisted phone numbers. An effort was made to
correct for this problem by asking respondents to supply names of
Italian American acquaintances with unlisted phone numbers. However,
this did not result in enough names to select from randomly so these
numbers were not included in the sample.

The Scottsdale telephone book yielded 1,064 Italian surnames with
Scottsdale addresses. A systematic sampling method with a random start
was used to select the sample. This is a technique which Babbie (1973:
92-93) describes as sampling every kth element, in this case Italian
surname, in the total list for inclusion in the sample. Further, this
sampling began by selecting a random number, to avoid bias.

A further guard against bias was used in the actual selection of the
individual within a household to be interviewed. Kish (1949) pointed
out that if more than one member of a household fits the criteria
designated for inclusion in a sample, it becomes necessary to make an
objective selection of whom to interview. He designed what is now
called the Kish table for this purpose. During the screening interview
for the Scottsdale study the interviewer would initially determine the
number of eligible respondents in the household. Then the individual to
select for the interview was determined by consulting the Kish table.
Each interview had a unique table, generated by a computer program. The
tables were supplied by the Survey Research Laboratory in the Department
of Sociology at Arizona State University.

To be eligible for the study the individual had to be eighteen or older, of Italian ancestry, and have been raised in a state other than Arizona. The last criterion was chosen for several reasons. Since the study is interested in exploring migration patterns and the retention of ethnic identity in an emergent setting, someone born and raised in Arizona would not have migrated. Further, their ethnic identity would have been formed in a community, Phoenix, which was non-typical of many Italian communities. However, this turned out not to be the problem anticipated, since only one household contacted was an old Arizona Italian family.

Overall, the sample selection was made with an effort to follow the principles of objective, random sampling. However, the researcher has attempted to point out some of the limitations in locating members of an ethnic group in the general population.

Interview Schedule

The interview schedule was based on both original questions and those developed by others (e.g., Crispino, 1980; Gallo, 1974; Parenti, 1975; Roche, 1977; Sandberg, 1977). Questions were asked on family, migration, friendships, and ethnicity. The schedule was first pre-tested on five Italian American respondents personally known to the researcher. They all were migrants, and lived in the larger Phoenix area, not in Scottsdale. These individuals were encouraged to give suggestions and criticisms of the interview schedule, and did so.

This early version of the interview schedule for Scottsdale was also sent out for review by research faculty familiar with Italian Americans. The schedule was reformulated based on the comments and criticism from

both the initial respondents and the research faculty. The new schedule
was then tested on 15 Italian Americans who were also migrants, and
lived in the Phoenix metropolitan area. None of those pre-tested lived
in Scottsdale.

During the second phase of pre-testing the respondents were not
asked for comments. However, it became apparent that the interview
schedule frequently stimulated spontaneous replies. It was decided to
record these comments, since they were given in an effort by the respondent to more fully explain to the researcher how the person was
reacting to the question. The spontaneous comments given by respondents
in the final sampling were to become the basis for the qualitative
interpretive data included in this study. Originally, when the idea of
including qualitative data was noted in developing the proposal for this
study, it was thought that a small group of respondents could be given
in-depth, unstructured interviews. However, because the projected size
of the sample made it feasible to record comments from all respondents,
and because the pre-test respondents offered such informative replies to
the questions all spontaneous comments were recorded and indexed. This
provided the study with data that served to enhance the statistical
analysis which is the principal basis of the analysis.

The final basic interview schedule contained 120 questions, and 24
scale items. A shorter schedule for mixed ancestry had 31 questions.
(See Appendix B for both schedules.) The administration of the full
ancestry schedule averaged between 45 to 90 minutes. Some interviews
were longer. Respondents were asked to schedule the interview at a time
which would allow them to complete the interview without feeling

pressured. All interviews, including the pre-tests, were conducted over the telephone. In some instances the use of a telephone hindered building a rapport, but in many more cases it proved an asset. Several respondents seemed to project a favorable role on the interviewer, who was for all cases the principal investigator. For some individuals the anonymity of the telephone allowed expressions of attitudes which might have been suppressed in an initial face-to-face interview. As one older man interrupted the interview to say, "I'm an unusual person . . . I'm controlled as far as food and drink and talking to people, and I'm proud of it. I'm talking more to you than to my wife."

To gain the initial acceptance of potential respondents, the household was first contacted by a letter. The letter gave a brief description of the search project, introduced the researcher, and gave the phone number of the Sociology Department to contact for any questions. (See Appendix B for the letter.) To further legitimate the research, the university sponsored radio program mentioned the launching of the research project.

The interviewing lasted from October 11th, 1982 to March 28, 1983. There were 169 households contacted. Thirty-eight of the households were not eligible. Nine were ethnically misidentified, although four of this group had Italian surnames but were of other ancestry, such as Swiss or Yugoslavian ancestry. Four were non-Italian women formerly married to Italian men, 24 had moved or changed to unlisted numbers, and one was born in Arizona. Of the 131 eligible households contacted 17 refused (13%) and interviews were conducted with 114 respondents.

Although the Scottsdale sample size was moderate, it is believed that the extent of the questionnaire, random selection, and addition of qualitative data help to compensate for this. In a larger funded project this study would have followed the procedures outlined above, but would have employed a number of interviewers. No one technique can adequately capture the essence of ethnic identity for a given individual. The participant observation method allows for a good deal of qualitative material to be gathered, but lacks the scope of a broader survey. And, since most participant observation studies have focused on Italian Americans in slums they are not generalizable to this study's concern with the more upwardly mobile segment of the ethnic group. Survey data allows a broader segment of the group under study to be explored, and permits the use of statistical analysis. One weakness of such a technique is that the more "human" side of ethnicity is not brought out. However, with adequate preparation research can combine both quantitative and qualitative approaches to ethnicity as was done on a limited basis in this study.

Techniques for Data Analysis

Information in the study is frequently presented in a tabular form. For the primary task in data presentation and analysis, this study employed basic descriptive statistics including the mean, median, and frequency distribution.

For inferential statistics the Student's t was used to determine whether a statistically significant difference could be found between the sample means of any two groups being examined. The t-test statistics used to test the central tendencies of the various ethnicity scales were computed through the use of the subprogram T-TEST (Nie et al., 1975: 167-275). The significance levels considered necessary to reject the null hypothesis for this study are the .05 or .01 level. Both are reported in this analysis.

All t-tests presented are one-tailed tests. The one-tailed tests can be used when it is possible to hypothesize the direction a mean should take. One-tailed tests are preferable since one can concentrate the entire critical region at the correct end of the sampling distribution (Blalock, 1979).

Based on the literature the following one-tailed tests were specified for the independent variables.

Hypothesis One: It is anticipated, based on the literature (e.g., Alba and Chamlin, 1983; Eisenstadt, 1956; Park, 1949; Sandberg, 1977) that ethnicity, as exhibited by the various scales, will decline with younger birth cohorts, and with each generation removed from the immigrant generation.

Hypothesis Two: It is anticipated that higher occupation and educational groups will have lower mean scores on the ethnic scales. This assumption is based on literature which indicates that ethnicity declines with upward social mobility (e.g., Borhek, 1970; Gans, 1982; Warner and Srole, 1945).

Hypothesis Three: It is anticipated that the exogamous group will have lower mean scores on the ethnicity scales than the endogamous groups. This is because exogamy represents a close tie with members of other ethnic groups (e.g., Alba, 1976, 1981; M. Gordon, 1964).

Hypothesis Four: It is anticipated that the group that resided in Arizona the longest will have lower mean scores on the ethnicity scales than the group which had migrated recently. This assumption is not based on the literature. This is because little research has been done on this variable (Roche, 1977), and none of the research done involves a community like Scottsdale. Scottsdale, as has been noted, had no Italian community and is geographically removed from any such community. Therefore, if a sense of ethnicity is supported by contact with an ethnic community, even a suburban ethnic community, it was expected that it would diminish in a nonethnic environment like Scottsdale.

Hypothesis Five: It is anticipated that men will have lower mean scores on the ethnicity scales than women. This assumption is not based however, on clear differences between the sexes in the literature on ethnicity. Research on the differences between men and women in terms of ethnicity is not abundant, and it is often conflicting. For example, Roche (1977: 220) reported that Italian American men had stronger ethnic attitudes than the women exhibited, but that there was no difference in regard to the behavior of the men and women. Krase's (1978) study of Italian American women at Brooklyn College shows that the female students had slightly higher career aspirations than their male counterparts, and had better grade averages than the males. He concludes that Italian American women are not handicapped by their immigrant heritage. In contrast are findings, based on case studies, that point out the mixed messages young Italian American females receive regarding education (Scelsa, 1983). Young women may be encouraged to get an education, but it should be one that will benefit the family and not interfere with family obligations. Scelsa (1983: 251) concludes that Italian American women are experiencing difficulties in educational aspirations that can be linked to their immigrant cultural heritage.

Since this literature does not offer a clear direction to anticipate for mean scores it was decided, based on the more traditional roles for Italian women that are still influential (C. Johnson, 1978), to predict that Italian American men will have lower mean scores on the ethnicity scales. This is because women, as discussed in Chapter III pages 56 - 58, were traditionally oriented to home, family, and religion. Therefore, it is anticipated that overall Italian American women will be more involved with the traditional ethnic culture than men who would be more exposed to the American social milieu.

Other Statistical Techniques

There were a number of statistical techniques employed to test the scales employed for this research. The testing of the scales is appropriate especially since several researchers (e.g., Crispino, 1980; Fandetti and Gelfand, 1983; Roche, 1977) have used Neil Sandberg's ([1974] 1977) scale of ethnicity. If a uniform measure of ethnicity is going to be available it must be thoroughly tested to assure that the measurement is actually tapping into the variables under study.

In Appendix C the interested person will find a brief description of the statistical techniques used to test the scales.

To assess the relationship between the scales a Pearson correlation matrix was prepared. This produced a matrix which showed the strength of the association between the scales.

The matrix and a discussion of its significance is in Appendix D. Additionally, the overall findings regarding the utility of the scales for future research are discussed. Furthermore, each scale is tested for internal reliability. These findings are also presented in Appendix D. Finally, discriminant analysis was used to determine which items contributed the most to each scale (Klecka, 1981; Nie et al., 1975).

Presentation of the Sample

The following is a description of the sample of Scottsdale Italian Americans. This description details the social characteristics of the respondents. Whenever possible, comparative data from other studies of similar samples will be introduced. The significance of the trends among the Scottsdale sample will be discussed in relation to these other studies. The discussion will focus on the 91 single ancestry respondents. The characteristics of the 23 mixed ancestry individuals are given in Appendix D.

Age, Generation, Birth Cohort, Gender

The 91 respondents ranged in age from 22 to 75 years old. Forty-nine was the median age. This is close to the median age for second generation Italian Americans, which was 46.6 in the most recently available national data (U.S. Bureau of the Census, 1973b). It is a higher median age than is found for the city of Scottsdale where 35 was the median age in 1980. It is also higher than the median age for the state of Arizona which was 29 in 1980 (U.S. Bureau of the Census, 1982a). (See Table 3 for a summary of the characteristics of age, and generation, birth cohort, and gender for the Italian Americans of Scottsdale.)

Table 3. General Characteristics of the Scottsdale Italian American
         Sample

Scottsdale Sample	Number (N=91)	Percentage
AGE		
20-29	7	8%
30-39	14	15%
40-49	26	29%
50-59	25	27%
60-69	13	14%
70-79	6	7%
GENERATION		
First (Immigrant)	16	18%
Full Second	32	35%
Half Second	17	19%
Third	24	26%
Fourth	2	2%
BIRTH COHORT		
Pre-1914	6	7%
1914-1929	34	37%
1930-1945	32	35%
1946-1960	19	21%
SEX		
Female	35	38%
Male	56	62%

Generation is an important variable indicating distance from the immigrant generation. The sample contained 16 people (18%) in the first, or immigrant, generation. Most of the first generation migrated after World War II, so they were not part of the earlier wave of Italian immigration. The second generation contained 49 people, 54 percent of the sample. This group was subdivided for analytical purposes into two groups because some second generation individuals have two immigrant parents and some have only one immigrant parent. Those who have two immigrant parents are called full second generation; there were 32 such individuals in the sample. Those with only one foreign born parent are called half second generation; there were 17 such individuals in the sample. The third generation had 24 respondents, 26 percent of the sample. The fourth generation is underrepresented since only two people were in the sample from this generation. Consequently the fourth generation is not included in the statistical analysis.

In addition to age and generation some researchers use birth cohort to look at changes in ethnicity which are not related to generation but to being part of a particular historical cohort. Using the four birth cohorts designated by Alba and Chamlin (1983: 242) the sample yielded six respondents in the cohort born before World War I. This cohort was not included in the analysis due to its size. The second cohort includes those born between 1914 and 1929; 35 people (37%) in the sample were in this cohort. The third cohort encompasses those born between 1930 and 1945; 32 individuals (35%) were in this cohort. The fourth cohort includes those born after 1945; 19 individuals (21%) in the sample were in this cohort.

The sample included 56 men and 35 women. The higher male representation reflects the number of exogamous men contacted during the sampling. In terms of generation the first generation had 7 men and 9
women. The full second generation had 22 men and 10 women, and the half
second generation had 12 men and 5 women. The third generation had 14
men and 10 women. The fourth generation had one man and one woman. The
distribution by birth cohort showed 2 men and 4 women in the pre-World
War I cohort. There were 26 men and 8 women in the cohort for 1914 to
1929. The cohort from 1930 to 1945 had 22 men and 10 women. The
youngest cohort had 6 men and 13 women.

Regional Origin

Since the sample was composed of in-migrants, it was of interest to
ascertain the origins of the respondents. (See Table 4 for a summary of
the regional origins of the Scottsdale Italian American sample.) Nine
of the first or immigrant generation were from the southern Italian
regions of Calabria, Campania, Puglia, Abruzze, and Lazio. Seven were
from the northern Italian regions of Tuscany, Liguria, Lombardy, and
Friuli.

The majority of the American born respondents were of Southern
origin (77%) and came primarily from the regions of Campania and Sicily.
No one Northern region had any strong representation.

Those born in America came mainly from the East coast states and the
Midwest. Most respondents came from two states. New York contributed
30 respondents, which is 40 percent of the American born respondents.
Illinois contributed another 15 respondents, or 20 percent of the American born group. Seven people came from New Jersey, 5 from Massa-

Table 4. Regional Origins of the Scottsdale Italian American Sample

Scottsdale Sample	Number (N=91)	Percentage
ITALY (Immigrants N=16)		
Abruzze	2	2%
Calabria	1	1%
Campania	3	3%
Friuli	1	1%
Lazio	3	3%
Liguria	1	1%
Lombardia	2	2%
Puglia	1	1%
Toscana	2	2%
STATE BORN IN (N=75)		
California	2	2%
Colorado	2	2%
Connecticut	1	1%
Illinois	15	20%
Indiana	1	1%
Massachusetts	5	5%
Michigan	3	3%
Missouri	1	1%
Nebraska	1	1%
New Jersey	7	8%
New York	30	40%
Ohio	2	2%
Pennsylvania	4	4%
West Virginia	2	2%
RAISED IN AN ITALIAN AMERICAN METROPOLIS (N=37)		
Albany	4	4%
Boston	1	1%
Chicago	11	12%
Cleveland	1	1%
Detroit	2	2%
New York	15	16%
Phildelphia	1	1%
Rochester	2	3%

chusetts, 4 from Pennsylvania, and 3 from Michigan. Two people apiece came from California, Colorado, West Virginia, and Ohio. One person each came from Connecticut, Indiana, Missouri, and Nebraska.

When the percentage of Italian Americans for each state as of 1980 is computed, the Scottsdale sample shows a higher representation than the national percentage for some states (U.S. Bureau of Census, 1983a). New York still had the highest percentage of single ancestry Italian Americans. However, its national percentage is 28 percent, yet in the Scottsdale sample New Yorkers represent 40 percent of the group. Illinois shows an even bigger contrast. While Illinois represents only 5 percent of the national Italian American population, 20 percent of the Scottsdale sample comes from this state. Other states are underrepresented in Scottsdale. For example, New Jersey has 12 percent of the nation's Italian Americans but only 9 percent of the Scottsdale sample is from this state. California has 8 percent of the national Italian American population, but is only represented by 2 individuals (2%) in the Scottsdale sample.

A survey study of all newcomers to Scottsdale for 1979 to 1980 does not show a pattern of general migration which might account for the migration pattern of the Scottsdale Italian Americans. California is the state that contributed the highest percentage to the general Scottsdale population, 15 percent, followed by Illinois, 12 percent, and Michigan, 11 percent. New York only contributed 4 percent, and Connecticut and Pennsylvania 2 percent (Gardner, 1980). Of course such a limited survey does not cover enough years for an adequate explanation of general migration patterns.

There is some evidence of chain migration for the Italian American Scottsdale sample, to be discussed in the section on kinship. However, it is not compelling enough to suggest the patterns of migration from states is primarily related to kinship ties. Nor was there any evidence of chain migration of friends. A clearer explanation of the actual migration pattern of Italian Americans to Scottsdale must await further research.

City of Origin

In addition to ascertaining the state in which people were raised, data was collected on the city of origin. This was to see if being raised in a city with a major Italian American population had an effect on ethnic identity. This idea is an extension of the argument that living in an area with large, diverse ethnic communities would enhance ethnic identity and permit ethnic subcultures to survive (Alba and Chamlin, 1983; Fischer, 1982).

The argument seems particularly salient for Italian Americans who have traditionally been a heavily urbanized group. Velikonja (1970: 23-39) pointed out that in 1960 Italian Americans were concentrated in 23 Standard Metropolitan Statistical Areas. Each contained at least 25,000 Italian stock people. Velikonja notes this constitutes a sufficient number to allow the formation of Italian cultural and social networks. Even in metropolitan areas like Los Angeles, St. Louis, or Chicago where the relative number of Italians is small, less than 2 percent of the population, the concentration of Italian Americans has been dense enough to permit the continuation of the Italian culture (Velikonja, 1970).

In the sample 37 people were raised in the Italian American metropolises identified by Velikonja. These cities included New York, with 15 people, Chicago with 11, Albany, with 4, Rochester and Detroit, with 2 each, and Boston, Cleveland, and Philadelphia with 1 person each. The salience of ethnicity for this group will be compared with the rest of the sample.

Migration Trends

The 1980 census cannot show the actual increase of Italian Americans in Scottsdale from 1970 due to the changes in census designation previously noted in Chapter I. The sample does show, however, recent arrivals. (See Table 5 for a summary of the migration trends of Scottsdale Italian Americans.) The length of time in Arizona ranges from 3 months to 37 years, with 6 years the median number of years for the sample, and 9 the mean number of years. Sixty respondents (69%) had lived in Arizona for 10 years or less. Thirty-four respondents (39%) had lived in Arizona for 5 years or less.

Four respondents were part-time residents of Scottsdale. They had wintered in the state from 6 to 20 years. Two of them planned to make the move permanent in the near future.

The sample was divided almost evenly in terms of prior mobility. Forty-six respondents (51%) had moved from their home state before moving to Arizona. Forty-five (49%) had remained within their home state. Of these, 24 respondents still lived in the city they were raised in until moving to Arizona, and 21 had moved to other cities in their home state.

Table 5. Migration Trends for the Scottsdale Italian American Sample

Scottsdale Sample	Number (N=91)	Percentage
YEARS LIVED IN ARIZONA		
0 to 6	46	51%
7 to 10	18	20%
11 to 15	11	12%
16 to 20	6	7%
21 to 37	10	11%
MOVED PRIOR TO ARIZONA		
Yes	46	51%
No	45	49%
CITY SIZE LIVED IN PRIOR TO SCOTTSDALE		
Under 4,999	10	11%
5,000 to 19,999	12	13%
20,000 to 49,999	13	14%
50,000 to 99,999	8	9%
100,000 to 499,999	20	22%
500,000 to 1,000,000+	28	31%
ETHNIC COMPOSITION OF AREA MOVED FROM		
All or Mostly Italian	11	12%
Italian and Other Ethnic	29	32%
Few Italian	28	31%
No Italians	20	22%
Unsure of Ethnic Composition	3	3%
REASON FOR MOVE		
Job or Business Reasons	19	20%
Climate/Life Style	22	23%
Health	21	22%
Family Moved Here	7	8%
Relatives Already Here	15	16%
Other	10	11%

Respondents were asked about the community they had lived in just before moving to Scottsdale. Twenty-eight respondents (31%) moved from cities with populations of 500,000 to a 1,000,000 of more. Another 20 (22%) had moved from cities with a population from 100,000 to 499,999. Only 8 (9%) had moved from cities of 50,000 to 99,999; an additional 13 (15%) had moved from cities of 20,000 to 49,999 in size. Of the remainder 12 (13%) moved from communities of 5,000 to 19,999, and 10 (11%) moved from communities which were under 4,999.

Respondents were asked about the ethnic composition of the area they had moved from right before moving to Scottsdale, to determine how many had moved from traditional Italian American neighborhoods. Eleven (12%) had moved from a heavily Italian American area. Another 29 (32%) moved from an area with Italian Americans and other ethnic groups. In contrast 28 (31%) moved from an area with few Italian Americans. An additional 20 (22%) moved from an area with almost no Italian Americans. Three respondents were not sure of the ethnic composition of the area they moved from prior to moving to Scottsdale.

Generally the sample is not as rooted as studies show residents of traditional Italian American neighborhoods to be (Gallo, 1974; C. Johnson, 1978, 1982; Juliani, 1981; Scarpaci, 1981). However, when compared to the middle-class respondents of Columbia, Maryland the Scottsdale group is less mobile. Fandetti and Gelfand (1983: 116) report that only 4 percent of their sample had moved directly from an ethnic neighborhood which is lower than 12 percent for the Scottsdale sample.

Most respondents were pleased with their decision to move to Arizona. Sixty-seven (73%) would not return to their home state, even if financial considerations were not a factor. Eleven (12%) indicated they would move back, while 13 (14%) were unsure about staying.

When asked their reason for moving to Arizona 20 (22%) indicated they moved for health reasons, related to either their own poor health or that of a family member. Eighteen people (20%) moved for job or business opportunities for themselves or a family member. Twenty-one people (23%) moved because of the climate or life style, although these are somewhat general reasons for specifically choosing Arizona. Fifteen people (16%) moved at the encouragement of a relative who was already in Arizona. Another 7 people (8%) moved because their parents moved them. The remainder of the respondents moved for a variety of reasons, including attending college in Arizona, or because of having been stationed in Arizona during military service.

Marital Status

Most of the respondents, 69 (76%), were married although not always for the first time. The rest of the sample contained 10 divorced people, 7 single people and 5 widowed people.

Seventy-nine of the respondents had children. The average number of children was 2.8 per family. This is slightly higher than the average of 2.3 children reported by Greeley (1977) for Italian Americans. Half of the 223 children were living at home, that is 112 children (50%). Another 50 children (22%) lived independently in Arizona. The remaining 60 children (17%) lived outside of Arizona.

Ethnic Endogamy and Exogamy

The significance of whether or not an ethnic group remains endogamous or marries outside the group is one which has received considerable
attention in the debate on the assimilation of European ethnics. For
most groups the immigrant generation maintained a high degree of endogamy. So, many researchers see increasing rates of exogamy as an indication of increasing assimilation (Alba, 1976, 1981; Gans, 1982; M.
Gordon, 1964; Steinberg, 1981). Other researchers are not as willing to
see marital assimilation as a clear indicator of increasing assimilation
(Farber et al., 1979; Greeley, 1971; Isajiw, 1975; Newman, 1973).

The majority of the sample was exogamous in terms of ethnicity, with
54 (64%) of those ever married exogamous, and 30 (36%) endogamous. The
exogamous marriages tended to be to individuals of European ancestry
such as Slavics, 8 or 15 percent, Irish, 9 or 17 percent, German, 10 or
19 percent, or those of other or mixed European ancestry, 9 or 17
percent. Another 9 married Anglo Saxons. Four married individuals of
Hispanic origins and the remainder were not ascertained.

This lack of a distinct pattern of outmarriage to primarily only one
ethnic group, such as Irish Americans, may be typical of Catholic Americans. Alba and Kessler (1979) report, based on national data, that they
failed to find a pattern of selective intermarriage among Catholic
ethnics.

Data was collected on the marriage patterns of the respondents'
siblings to compare to the Scottsdale sample's rate of intermarriage.
Of the 193 married siblings 108, or 56 percent, were endogamous and 85,

or 44 percent, were exogamous. This is a higher rate of endogamy than for the sample, and more in keeping with other studies. (See Table 6.)

Other studies of endogamy among Italian Americans will be discussed in the following. This will help to assess the importance of such patterns, and to compare the Scottsdale sample to other studies of Italian American marital patterns.

As an ethnic group Italians have exhibited a high rate of endogamy. Although the rate has declined across the generations it has remained high, in some instances the highest rate for studies of ethnic endogamy. Kennedy (1944; 1952) found that 97 percent of the Italians of New Haven were endogamous in 1900. By 1940 81 percent were endogamous, and by 1950 there was a further decline to 77 percent. One exception to the generally slow trend toward exogamy for Italians was found in Buffalo, New York where the rate of endogamy dropped from 71 percent in 1930 to 27 percent in 1960 (Bugelski, 1961). However, national data from 1966 found 59 percent of the Italians endogamous (Alba, 1976; 1036-1039). In a study of "Forest City", in the Midwest, done in the 1970s Italian Americans had an endogamy rate of 67 percent (Korvetaris and Dobratz, 1976: 46). Crispino's (1980: 104-105) study of Bridgeport showed that 44 percent of his respondents married endogamously, while another 12 percent married someone with one parent who was of Italian ancestry. Coleen Johnson's (1982) sample from Syracuse, New York was similar. Forty-three percent of the sample was endogamous and 57 percent was exogamous. Fandetti and Gelfand (1983) reported that three-fourths of their sample was exogamous, which would given an endogamy rate of about 25 percent for Columbia.

Table 6. Ethnic Endogamy for Italian Americans, by Percentage

Location	Year of Study	Percent Endogamous	Sample Size
New Haven, Conn.	(1900)	97%	*
	(1940)	81%	*
	(1950)	77%	*
Buffalo, New York	(1930)	71%	368
	(1960)	27%	417
United States	(1966)	59%	606
"Forest City"	(1972)	67%	103
Bridgeport, Conn.	(1975)	44%	448
Syracuse, New York	(1975)	43%	172
Columbia, Md.	(1979)	25%	113
Scottsdale, Ariz.	(1982)	36%	84
Scottsdale Siblings	(1982)	56%	192

*Findings reported in percentages only.

The Scottsdale sample in relation to the above findings shows an endogamy rate which is rather low, although not as low as Buffalo or Columbia. The sibling's rate of ethnic endogamy is certainly closer to what other studies report. This indicates that those Italian Americans who migrate to Arizona may be less traditional regarding endogamy than other Italian Americans. Whether exogamy affects the ethnic identity of those who have married out of their group is a question that is explored in later chapters.

Religion

In terms of religion the group was primarily Catholic. Overall 69 (76%) respondents were Roman Catholics. Four people were Protestants, 3 preferred the designation Christian, while 10 respondents had no affiliation, and the remaining 5 had other responses, such as humanist. (See Table 7.)

Most of the respondents were endogamous in terms of religion. For those ever married respondents 52 (62%) had Catholic spouses. The remaining 32 (38%) had nonCatholic spouses.

Forty-five (65%) of those currently married had Catholic spouses. Eight respondents (12%) had Protestant spouses, 2 (3%) Jewish spouses, 8 (12%) spouses with no religious preference, and additional 6 (9%) spouses with a general Christian designation.

The religious activities of the respondents will be discussed in more detail in Chapter VI. The chapter contains an analysis of a scale, with a limited number of items, on religious ethnicity for Italian Americans.

Table 7. Religious Profile for Scottsdale Italian American Sample

Scottsdale Sample	Number (N=91)	Percentage
RESPONDENT		
Catholic	69	76%
Protestant	4	4%
(Specific Denomination)		
Christian	3	3%
(No Denomination)		
None	10	11%
Other	5	5%
RESPONDENT'S SPOUSE FOR CURRENTLY MARRIED*		
Catholic	45	65%
Protestant	8	12%
(Specific Denomination)		
Christian	6	9%
(No Denomination)		
Jewish	2	3%
None	8	12%

*Respondent's spouse for currently married based on N=69.

Kinship Ties

This study looked at the migration pattern of the Scottsdale sample to see if kinship ties could be found in Arizona. This was important to assess for several reasons. First is the emphasis on family which stems from the Southern Italian culture. Second is the literature which reports that Italian American families are strong in their ties to kin (e.g., Greeley, 1977; C. Johnson, 1982; Palisi, 1966a). Finally, it was of interest to see if evidence of chain migration, which characterized the migration of Italians to America, could be found in the migration to Scottsdale, Arizona.

The sample showed evidence of kinship ties in Scottsdale. (See Table 8.) As was mentioned, 17 percent of the Scottsdale respondents gave relatives as their main reason for moving here. Another 6 percent indicated that having relatives in Arizona was an influence in moving, if not the main motivation. Another 7 percent noted that they had moved as a dependent child, with their family. Overall more than half the sample, 47 people, or 52 percent, had relatives other than adult children living in the Phoenix area. When adult children living on their own are included 58 respondents, 64 percent of the sample, had some family locally. This indicates that the Scottsdale sample is not composed of isolated families.

When asked if the respondent had relatives planning to move to Arizona 22 (24%) replied yes, 63 (69%) said no, and the remainder were unsure of their relative's plans. Those who indicated that relatives were not interested in moving often mentioned that their families were rooted in the home area. A few indicated that their relatives preferred

Table 8. Family Characteristics of the Scottsdale Italian American
Sample

Scottsdale Sample	Number (N=91)	Percentage
FAMILY LOCALLY		
Yes	58	64%
No	33	36%
WHICH RELATIVES LOCALLY		
Parent(s)	14	33%*
Older Sibling	5	11%
Younger Sibling	20	33%
Grandparent(s)	5	11%
CONTACT WITH LOCAL RELATIVES		
Daily	17	29%*
Weekly	24	41%
Semi-Weekly/Monthly	23	22%
RELATIVE IN CONTACT WITH MOST IN ANOTHER STATE		
Parents	33	37%
Older Sibling	14	15%
Younger Sibling	7	8%
Maternal Aunt	7	8%
KIND OF CONTACT WITH RELATIVES IN OTHER STATES		
Reciprocal Visits	38	42%
Relatives Visit Arizona	28	32%
Respondent Returns Home	14	15%
Do Not Visit	11	12%
IMPORTANCE OF CLOSENESS		
Very Important	43	47%
Important	32	35%
Mixed Feelings	10	11%
Not Close	6	6%

*Percentage based on number of respondents, 58, with local relatives.

Florida to Arizona. Although Florida has some Italian immigration historically (Pozzetta, 1974), it is another area in the Sunbelt with many Italian American migrants. As of the 1980 census 274,202 single ancestry Italian Americans lived in Florida, 4 percent of the Italian American population (U.S. Bureau of the Census, 1983a).

Parents and younger siblings were most typically the relatives respondents had locally. Fourteen respondents, (33%) had one or both parents in the area. Twenty (33%) had younger siblings locally. Five of the respondents (11%) had an older sibling present, and five had grandparents present. The remainder had an assortment of relatives who included aunts, uncles, nieces, nephews, cousins and in-laws.

Most of the families gathered for a variety of occasions such as birthday celebrations and for major holidays, such as Christmas and Easter. They also socialized for weekly dinners, chats, or just to be together.

It has been demonstrated that Italian Americans have higher rates of contact with their families than do nonItalian groups (Greeley, 1969; C. Johnson, 1982). Scottsdale respondents with local relatives were asked how often they saw those relatives to whom they felt the closest. Seventeen respondents (29%) saw their closest relatives on a daily basis. Twenty-four respondents (41%) saw their closest relatives weekly. When combined, this means that 70 percent of the Scottsdale respondents with local relatives saw those relatives at least weekly.

It has been ascertained that kinship networks can operate over distances, aided by rapid transportation and long distance communication (Adams, 1971). So, it was decided to see if the Scottsdale Italian

Americans kept in contact with relatives living elsewhere. When asked to identify which relatives not living in Arizona the respondents kept in close contact with only 9 had no contact with relatives. Twenty-one (23%) reported their mother as the person they communicated with the most, with 7 (8%) mentioning both parents, and 5 (6%) their father. The high percentage of contact with mothers is related, at least in part, to surviving widows rather than to a lack of closeness to fathers.

Siblings were the next group of relatives mentioned frequently. Since respondents were most likely to have younger siblings locally, it is not surprising that fourteen (15%) mentioned older siblings as first choice for contact. Younger siblings were indicated by 7 respondents (8%) and both younger and older siblings by 8 (9%) people. This may reflect the importance of siblings to each other in the Italian American family, which has been reported recently (C. Johnson, 1982). The only other relatives who received as much contact were maternal aunts, who were first choice for 7 of the respondents (8%).

Eleven of the respondents, 12 percent, indicated they did not visit with their relatives. Twenty-eight, 32 percent, had relatives who visited them in Arizona, while 14, 15 percent, visited their relatives back home. Thirty-eight, 42 percent, said they had reciprocal visiting patterns.

Telephone calls were frequently used by respondents to keep in contact with relatives back home. Seventeen, (18%) called relatives weekly. Twenty-five (64%) called monthly and 33 (36%) called their relatives only occasionally. No one corresponded weekly with relatives, 7 (8%) wrote to relatives monthly, and 33 (36%) wrote occasionally. The remaining 48 (53%) did not write.

Respondents were asked how important a feeling of closeness between family members, not living together, was to them. Forty-three respondents, 47 percent, felt it was very important to them. Another 32 respondents, 35 percent, felt it was important. Ten respondents, 11 percent, had mixed feelings about being close. Six respondents, 7 percent, indicated closeness was not important to them.

The analysis of the scale on family attitudes in the next chapter will give added insight to the family patterns and attitudes toward the family for the Scottsdale Italian Americans.

Occupation

The Scottsdale sample reflects the general trend of upward mobility in occupations for Italian Americans. The majority fall into the broad white collar designation. A much smaller number belong to the blue collar category which has, until recently, held the majority of the Italian American ethnic group, as noted in Chapter III.

Of the 79 respondents who had worked full-time 25 (32%) were in management, with twelve (15%) of this group self-employed. Fourteen respondents (18%) were professionals, and 4 (5%) had technical occupations. Twelve respondents (15%) were in sales, and five (6%) in clerical occupations. Only 2 respondents (3%) were in the service category. There were 7 (8%) in the craftsman category and 10 (11%) were operatives. The rest had not worked full-time including 9 housewives (10%) and 3 college students (4%).

The occupational patterns of the Scottsdale sample are compared to
Crispino's recent study of the Bridgeport community, and to a national
sample compiled by Crispino from NORC studies between 1962 and 1973
(1980: 40-41). (See Table 9.) Although it would have been preferable
to compare the sample to the 1980 census figures for Italian Americans,
these figures have not yet been released.

The differences between Scottsdale and the national sample indicates
the gap between Italian Americans who live in the more traditional urban
areas and the suburbs. As Feagin (1984: 127) notes the clearest upward
mobility in occupations is in the latter areas. In two metropolitan
areas with concentrations of Italians, New York City and San Francisco,
the percentage of Italian Americans in professional and managerial
positions was about 25 percent (Aiello, 1979: 227; Scherini, 1976:
12). This is in contrast to the Scottsdale study and the Bridgeport
study, which as mentioned in Chapter I, included the seven suburbs
surrounding the core city. In Scottsdale 55 percent were in professional and managerial occupations, and in Bridgeport 46 percent were in the
same categories.

When compared to the Scottsdale work force the Italian American
sample was somewhat higher than average in the professional and managerial category, but lower in the clerical, service, and production
category. The categories used for Scottsdale are those compiled by the
census (U.S. Bureau of the Census, 1981b). Thirty-three percent of the
work force in Scottsdale was employed in the professional and managerial
category, with 43 percent of the Italian Americans in the same category.
Thirty-eight percent of Scottsdale workers were in the clerical, sales

Table 9. Occupations* for Italian Americans in Scottsdale, Bridgeport,
          and the United States, by Percentages

Occupation	Scottsdale (N=79) (1982-1983)	Bridgeport (N=399) (1975)	United States (N=346) (1962-1973)
Professional, Technical	23%	25%	15%
Managers, Proprietors	32%	21%	12%
Sales, Clerical	21%	21%	12%
Craftsmen, Operatives	22%	23%	44%
Laborers	0%	2%	3%
Farm	0%	0%	1%
Service	3%	8%	13%

*1980 census data on occupation for European ancestry not available
as of time of this analysis.

and technical category as were 22 percent of the Italian Americans. Finally 27 percent of Scottsdale workers were in the service, production or operative category compared to 21 percent of the Italian American sample.

The Scottsdale sample represents what would be expected in terms of occupational patterns for contemporary suburban Italian Americans. Occupation will be one of the variables to be examined in later chapters to see if upward mobility in this area does correlate with a loss of ethnicity.

Education

As with occupation one might expect a higher educational level among suburban Italian Americans, since movement to the suburbs, as has been indicated, seems to correlate with upward mobility. The Scottsdale sample conforms to this expectation. Of the 81 respondents educated, at least partly, in America 11 respondents (13%) did not finish high school. Twenty-three (28%) respondents finished high school. Twenty respondents (25%) attended at least one year of college, but did not receive a four year degree. Twenty (25%) finished four years of college, and 7 (9%) respondents completed graduate school. Most of the respondents attended public rather than parochial schools. Sixty-five (80%) went to a public grammar school. Fifty-six (80%) of those who finished high school went to a public high school.

The numbers of respondents who attended college is part of a new trend in educational mobility for Italian Americans as an ethnic group. Educational mobility for Italian Americans has been slow (Lopreato, 1970: 161). It may be even slower than mobility in occupation since some of the occupational mobility into the managerial category represents a high proportion of self-employed proprietors. Advanced education is not necessarily a prerequisite for being self-employed.

Several factors worked against the early Italian immigrants taking full advantage of educational opportunities in America. As mentioned in Chapter III, some peasants had a negative attitude toward education, and other peasants simply had little experience with it. In America, families often took their children out of school as soon as they could work.

Those who remained in school were often encouraged to pursue a vocational education rather than to set their sights on professions. Finally, educators often took the early, low scores of Italian Americans on IQ tests as an indication that these children were not as capable of learning as those from other backgrounds. So many children did not receive encouragement from home or school to continue their education (Rolle, 1972: 117).

Greeley's (1976) analysis of white ethnic educational trends shows that Italian Americans were one of the last of the Catholic groups to reach the national average in terms of college attendance. The Irish reached the national average by the 1920's cohort. The German Catholics were even by the World War II cohort. Polish and Slavic Catholic were at the national average by the Cold War cohort, but the Italian American Catholics did not approach the national average until the Vietnam War cohort. Only the French and Spanish-speaking Catholics were behind Italian Americans in terms of college attendance (Greeley, 1976: 60-63).

Although as a group the Italian Americans were entering college at percentage close to the national average, this mobility reflected the youngest cohorts. As late as 1970 the overall ethnic group still showed signs of slow educational mobility. The average number of years of school completed for immigrant men was 7 years. Native born men over twenty-five completed an average of 11.9 years. Women were slightly behind men in both categories (U.S. Bureau of the Census, 1973b).

Studies on patterns in particular states reveal variations within the younger cohort. Korbin and Goldscheider (1978) showed for Rhode Island the percentage of younger Italian American males going to college more than doubled to 21 percent. However, over 50 percent of the same group had not finished high school. Aiello (1979: 224) noted a similar pattern in New York City. The numbers going on for a college education increased but overall Italian Americans were still below the achievement level of other white groups in the city. He further stressed the high dropout rate among young Italian Americans. Thus, as a group younger Italian Americans are not yet showing a clear pattern of high educational attainment, particularly in metropolitan areas.

Again it is useful to compare the Scottsdale, Bridgeport, and the national sample compiled by Crispino (1980: 41). (See Table 10.) The Scottsdale sample shows almost twice the percentage of those attending college with the exception of graduate school. Overall, the Scottsdale sample indicates a definite trend toward educational upward mobility for the ethnic group. In terms of the Scottsdale community, Italian Americans are about the norm for all levels of education (U.S. Bureau of the Census, 1981b).

Table 10. Educational Attainment of Italian Americans in Scottsdale, Bridgeport, and National Sample, by Percentage

Education	Scottsdale (N=81) (1982–1983)	Bridgeport (N=461) (1975)	United States (N=346) (1962–1973)
Less Than High School	13%	20%	46%
High School Graduate	28%	39%	36%
Some College	25%	15%	11%
Four Years of College	25%	13%	6%
Graduate School	9%	13%	1%

Summary of the Sample Characteristics

The Scottsdale sample shows social characteristics which might be expected in a suburban sample. While the age of the group is fairly high, Scottsdale in general has a population with an age which is higher than the surrounding communities. Young adults, who would fall into the fourth generation and youngest birth cohort, are likely to live in less affluent communities than Scottsdale.

The Italian Americans of Scottsdale are about equally divided into migration patterns, with about half having moved to another state prior to moving to Arizona. About half of those who lived in the same state had moved from where they were raised. This characteristic contradicts the traditional image of Italian Americans as being strongly rooted in an ethnic neighborhood.

The group exhibits a unique migration pattern which does not seem to fit either the proportion of the Italian Americans in the states they came from, nor the general population pattern to Scottsdale. More research needs to be done in this area.

The group exhibited high ethnic exogamy but a lower rate of religious exogamy.

Since Italian Americans exhibit a strong family orientation, it was of interest to find that the Scottsdale sample, despite its being migrant, tended to have some relatives in the area. Additionally, ties to the family not in the area were maintained, and an emotional attachment to absent kin remained strong.

In terms of occupational and educational mobility the group exhibited upward trends. This was expected, since mobility for the

Italian Americans as a group has been faster for those in the suburbs rather than in central cities.

Salient aspects of these variables presented are explored to see what level of ethnicity is exhibited by this suburban sample of Italian Americans. The results are presented in the following chapters.

CHAPTER V

FINDINGS: ETHNIC ATTITUDES

This chapter presents findings on Italian American ethnicity among
the sampled respondents. The findings are based primarily upon three
scales on ethnic attitudes. As discussed in Chapter I on the statement
of the problem, the scales are on attitudes related to the Italian
American family, ethnic culture, and ethnic nationality. The first
scale on the Italian American family was developed for the Scottsdale
study. The other two scales are taken from the instrument developed by
Sandberg ([1974] 1977).

The first scale on the Italian American family attitudes is presented in the following order. A lengthy discussion of the development
of the scale is presented, since the instrument was developed for the
Scottsdale study. An analysis of the scale items is presented, and then
an analysis of the t-tests, with one-tailed probability scores, is
presented.

For each of the other scales, on attitudes toward ethnic culture and
ethnic nationality, the rationale behind the instrument is presented
briefly. An analysis of the scale items is presented, and then an
analysis of the t-tests, with one-tailed probability scores, is given.

Finally, the Scottsdale study findings which are based on all three
scales are presented and discussed. The overall responses to the scale
items are presented, as are the results of a statistical analysis of
each of the scales.

Italian American Family Attitude

Scale: Development

The Italian American Family Attitude scale, (IAFA scale), was
developed to supplement the scales designed by Sandberg (1977). The
final form of the IAFA scale is related to needed modifications on the
"Group Cohesiveness" scale developed to measure ethnicity by Sandberg
for his study of Polish Americans in California. The scale is subdivided into the three dimensions of culture, nationality, and religion.
Despite the name given to the scale it primarily measures attitudes.
For as Sandberg (1977: 26) notes, "the ethnic scale tended to produce a
series of conscious attitudinal responses." Sandberg assumed these
attitudinal responses stemmed from the psychological symbols in the
instrument that evoked unconscious attitudes.

Sandberg's scale was designed to focus on the dimensions he believed
represented a "broad-gauged measure of ethnicity" (1977: 25). The
Polish American culture and experience in the United States were the
baseline for the scale items. Sandberg also hoped that the scale would
prove a useful instrument for research efforts of those interested in a
variety of ethnic groups. He thought it would be most useful to those
who studied European groups who might share broad cultural and historical experiences with Polish Americans. Sandberg does note that some
minor adjustments would be necessary to use the instrument for specific
groups, in order to focus in on the unique dimensions of the group under
study.

Researchers using Sandberg's scale to study Italian Americans have
not modified the instrument, although other measures of ethnicity were

added to the Group Cohesiveness scale (e.g., Crispino, 1980; Fandetti and Gelfand, 1983; Roche, 1977). However, Italian Americans differ sufficiently from Polish Americans so that Sandberg's instrument calls for modification as a valid measure of ethnicity for Italian Americans.

The Religious Ethnicity scale is particularly problematical for studying Italian Americans. The Catholic church in Poland was histori- cally an important social institution. In America it was important in linking Polish immigrants to the ethnic community (Sandberg, 1977; Thomas and Znaniecki, 1918-20; Wytrwal, 1961). The role of the Polish Catholic church apparently continues to be important to this ethnic group, according to contemporary research (Lopata, 1976; Wrobel, 1979). This can be seen as different from the experience of Italian immigrants who, as discussed in Chapter III, were often anticlerical, or interested in local saints rather than the larger church. Nor did Italians see their church as representative of Italy when it became a nation. Thus, Polish immigrants had different attitudes toward their church when they migrated than did Italian immigrants and some of these differences apparently persist, and influence the basis of ethnic identity for each group.

In an effort to develop a subscale which would reflect the culture of Italian Americans more clearly than using Sandberg's instrument without modification, this study employed the use of ethnic ideological themes. Francis. X. Femminella (1983) suggests that deep in the person- ality structure of ethnic individuals are ethnic ideological themes, even though these themes may be overlayed with themes from the dominant culture. It is these themes as well as the more overt aspects of ethnicity, such as social and political organizations, that allow ethnic groups to survive in the United States. Drawing upon the work of psychologist Erik Erikson (1959) Femminella defines ethnic themes as "the generalized leit-motifs and underlying principle features (of which an individual may or may not have awareness) of one's ideals, aspirations, and interests, and the specific pattern of variation . . . of value orientations of individuals" (1983: 113).

Applied to the individual, these ethnic themes become part of the personality and are not easily erased, at least without deep social and personal costs. Femminella holds that ethnic themes will survive over time because they are internalized ideologies often retained at the subconscious level, but evident in the expression of certain values. The ethnic ideological themes which identify a group become, therefore, instrumental in maintaining the group's identity. Sandberg's comments about his scale relating to psychologically based group symbols seems to reflect Femminella's view. So it was reasonable to turn to the notion of ethnic ideological themes to modify Sandberg's scale for Italian Americans.

Italian American Ethnic Themes for the

IAFA Scale

An effort was made to find a theme as relevant to Italian Americans as religious ethnicity was in the study of Polish Americans. The themes Femminella identifies for Italian Americans provided the initial focus for modifying the instrument. While Femminella recognizes that Italian themes did not pass unchanged into Italian American themes, he did identify some basic themes which could still be found.

In an effort to confirm Femminella's insights, while at the same time search for other Italian themes, other studies on Italians and Italian Americans were examined. Several themes emerged which were salient for the immigrant generation. The major themes were (1) family, (2) honor, (3) localism, and (4) fatalism. The family attachment theme has been observed by many analyses (e.g., Bell, 1979; Femminella, 1983; Ulin, 1975; Vecoli, 1978). The concept of honor is closely related to the family (e.g., Bell, 1979; O'Brien, 1972). Localism as another theme was represented in Italy by an attachment to home and village. In America this theme became translated into an attachment to home and neighborhood (Bell, 1979; Femminella, 1983, Vecoli, 1978). A fatalistic attitude, related to one's destiny, is also a theme which is often stressed for Italian Americans (e.g., Bell, 1979; Femminella, 1983, Ulin, 1975).

In the initial interview schedule several of these themes were included in an effort to bring to the scale items which would reflect the ethnic ideological themes of Italian Americans. The themes which were incorporated related to the primacy of the family, honor, localism, and fatalism.

However, pretesting revealed difficulties in using so many complex themes in an instrument such as a Likert scale. A brief example points out some of the difficulties involved, particularly for a study in an upwardly mobile suburban setting. Crispino (1980) prepared a two item fatalism scale, which he based on items from NORC studies. Like the view of fatalism or destiny repesented by other researchers on Italian Americans (e.g., Ulin, 1975), Crispino's scale reflects the passive side of fatalism. However, Bell (1979) has pointed out that the peasant's seemingly passive acceptance of fate or destiny was a realistic assessment of a harsh life in a hostile environment. Fatalism did not always lead to resignation, but to a defiance of fate and a treasuring and celebration of life. Comments from respondents during the pretesting revealed considerable ambivalence about the notion of life being controlled by fate. As one woman commented, she planned for the future even while accepting the possibility that her plans, for a new business, might not work out. She felt her plans for the future were clouded by this concern over fate or destiny having an influence in her plans, but she continued to make plans.

Rather than attempt to refine and correct the problem of studying complex and sometimes contradictory themes it was decided to take one main theme and explore it more thoroughly. The theme which clearly emerged as a central theme was the family. Based on the literature on the family already discussed in Chapter III twelve items were prepared which formed a scale on attitudes relating to Italian American family values.

Analysis of the Italian American
Family Scale Items

In Table 11 the items which were included in the scale are listed, as well as the responses to those items. Generally, the responses to these items seem to indicate the importance of the family value system to the Scottsdale respondents. Overall, 75 percent of the responses were in the general agree categories. An average of 21 percent of all responses were in the strongly agree category, 37 percent were in the

Table 11. Scottsdale Sample, Responses to Italian American Family
Items, by Percent (N=91)

Strongly Agree	Agree	Mildly Agree	Mildly Disagree	Disagree	Strongly Disagree	Unsure

1. Children show respect for their parents by being obedient and not
talking back.

| 27.5 | 36.3 | 17.6 | 3.3 | 12.1 | 2.2 | 1.1 |

2. The family is all you really have because friends can come and go.

| 16.5 | 35.2 | 16.5 | 13.2 | 16.5 | 2.2 | 0 |

3. Your job should not come before your family.*

| 40.7 | 34.1 | 12.1 | 6.6 | 3.3 | 1.1 | 2.2 |

4. Girls should be supervised more closely than boys, even when they
are teenagers.

| 15.4 | 26.4 | 12.1 | 7.7 | 27.5 | 9.9 | 1.1 |

5. One way a parent shows love for a child is by setting strict
standards for the child.

| 9.9 | 40.7 | 30.8 | 5.5 | 8.8 | 2.2 | 2.2 |

6. If a women works outside the home she should find a job that will
interfere with her family as little as possible.

| 18.7 | 50.5 | 15.4 | 2.2 | 2.2 | 5.5 | 5.5 |

7. A person who puts their trust in their family is better off than
someone who puts their trust in outsiders.

| 33.0 | 35.2 | 11.0 | 11.0 | 9.9 | 0 | 0 |

8. When a person does something wrong, it reflects on the whole
family.

| 9.9 | 23.1 | 16.5 | 17.6 | 20.9 | 8.8 | 3.3 |

9. The father is the head of the family, and the mother is the heart
of the family.

| 31.9 | 37.4 | 13.2 | 5.5 | 7.7 | 3.3 | 1.1 |

10. A well kept home is the symbol of a sound family.

| 26.4 | 36.3 | 13.2 | 5.5 | 11.0 | 6.6 | 1.1 |

11. A person should be willing to put the needs of their family ahead
of their own needs.

| 17.6 | 41.8 | 25.3 | 4.4 | 7.7 | 0 | 2.2 |

12. A person has a duty to help their relatives.

| 9.9 | 48.4 | 18.7 | 11.0 | 12.1 | 0 | 0 |

*Reverse wording on the interview schedule, see Appendix B.

agree category and the remaining 18 percent were in the mildly agree
category. The items associated with the Culture and Nationality scales
had a lower percentage agreeing.

Additional insights about responses to the Italian Family items came
from the spontaneous comments of the respondents. These comments were
of utility in explaining some of the attitudes which the items were
related to. On item 2, pertaining to putting one's job before one's
family, people favored family in the highest overall agree responses (87)
percent. Comments indicate this might have been higher except that some
saw the job as instrumental in preserving the family. As one person
noted, "Your job might have to come first to feed the family." The job
was seen not as a goal to be pursued instead of the family relationship,
but as a means to aid the family. This is a different emphasis than one
would expect from a primarily career oriented individual.

Items which related to differences within the family between males
and females showed interesting responses. Item 4, which stated that
girls needed to be supervised more closely than boys showed 38.5 percent
of the responses in the disagree categories. This item pertains to the
traditional role of the purity of the unmarried female representing the
family's honor. Some comments of those who agreed did reflect traditional attitudes, as one would expect. One woman said, "I know it's a
biased view, it's a double standard, but it's true, girls need more
protection [to preserve their purity]."

Those who disagreed were also often very clear about why they had
rejected the item. Only a few, however, expressed views which indicated
a "raised consciousness" associated with the general liberation of

women. One man noted, "Emotionally I agree [that girls should be more supervised], but objectively I must disagree."

The response which came out most strongly, in 11 comments, was that boys needed protection, too. As one woman said, "You need to supervise boys too, they can get in trouble too, like get herpes or something." So answers in the disagree category indicated, for some, that instead of reflecting the idea that girls should be given more freedom and treated equally with boys, people were now concerned with extending the same protection to boys which had been given to girls.

Item 6 on not letting an outside job interfere with a woman's family looked changes relating to working women (e.g., Ericksen et al., 1979). Eighty-five percent of the respondents generally agreed that an outside job should not interfere with the family. There were mixed feelings about the statement, however.

Some of the men in the older birth cohorts said that they objected to the idea of women working at all, while other men recognized the changing times and indicated that their attitudes had also changed. Surprisingly, no women expressed disagreement in their comments on this item.

Item 9 reflects a traditional role division within the Italian family which was discussed in Chapter III (pgs. 57 - 58), that the father is the head of the family, and the mother is the emotional center of the family.

Overall people agreed with item 9, 82.4 percent, however comments from both men and women indicated that there was not an unthinking acceptance of this item. Comments from two men in their forties were similar, "Both need some degree of equality," and "It's cooperative." One man indicated that he saw the woman as the central figure in the family when he said, "The mother is the big wheel in the family, she runs the whole show." Interestingly two immigrant women in their sixties provided the strongest statements regarding the equality of sexes within the family. The first woman said "I don't believe the father should be a total boss like the old days." The second woman stated, "They should be equal, he isn't the head just because he is a man."

The item which had the lowest agreement for the family scale was number 8 which was associated with the idea of family honor. It reflects the view that the individual is basically an extension of the family, and the behavior of the individual reflects in a positive or negative way on the family. The respondents only gave a 50 percent overall agreement to this item. Many of those who expressed disagreement indicated that their view was related to the situation, as several people noted, "It depends on the crime or wrong;" "It depends on the wrong done;" or "It depends on the act." Others indicated they saw the item as typical of attitudes their parents would have taken. One second generation woman who disagreed with the item expressed this point clearly when she noted, "My mother used to say "Il pesche puzza dalla testa [The fish stinks from the head.] It used to be true, that's how we used to think, the whole family would be tainted." This comment and similar ones suggest a movement away from the immigrant familistic values toward more individualistic acculturated values and views for this item.

Analysis of the Italian American

Family Attitude Scale

The analysis of the independent variables shown in Tables 12 and 13 showed some significant changes in the mean scores on the IAFA Scale. The maximum number of points was 72.[1] There was a range in scores from 25 to 69, with a mean of 51.8 and a standard deviation of 8.8 for the scale.

The scores for the generations and birth cohorts are shown in Table 12. The differences between the generations show some decline in family values across the generations. However, there is no statistically significant difference between the first and full second generation. There is the expected decline in mean scores between the first generation and half second and third generations. There is also the expected decline between the full second and the half second and third generations that is statistically significant. There was, however, not a significant decline between the half second and third generation.

When birth cohorts are examined the expected significant decline between the 1914 and the 1930 cohorts is not present. However, there is

---

[1]The data were collected for the scale, and the other scales in this chapter, using the same scoring system that other researchers used (e.g, Crispino, 1980; Sandberg, 1977). Respondents were asked to rate their responses to the attitude statements according to a scoring system which meant that the strongest agree response was scored 1, an agree score was 2, up to a strongly disagree which was equated with a 6 score.

However, intuitively it made sense to have the strongest ethnic statement a strongly agree, except in the case of a reverse worded question, worth the most points. Therefore, when the scale scores were computed the points were reverse coded.

Thus, the higher the mean score, the higher the ethnicity. This facilitates the discussion of ethnicity, and the inclusion of the Likert scale data with other measures of ethnicity if a total combined ethnicity scale were constructed.

Table 12. Scottsdale Sample's Scores, Italian American Family
Attitude Scale by Generation and Birth Cohort: One-tail
Probability (P), T-values (T)*

		Probability and T-Values			
Generation	$\bar{X}$**	First	Full Second	Half Second	Third
First (N=16)	54.0	————	P=.31 T=-.48	P=.05[a] T=1.6	P=.002[b] T=2.1
Full Second (N=32)	55.2		————	P=.01[b] T=2.3	P=.002[b] T=3.0
Half Second (N=17)	49.5			————	P=.34 T=.39
Third (N=24)	48.5				————

		Probability and T-Values		
Birth Cohort	$\bar{X}$	1914–1929	1930–1945	1946–1960
1914–1929 (N=34)	52.1	————	P=.34 T=-.37	P=.03[a] T=1.8
1930–1945 (N=32)	52.9		————	P=.01[b] T=2.1
1946–1960 (N=19)	47.3			————

*72 points maximum score.
**The standard deviations and degrees of freedom for these variables
are in Appendix E.
[a]Significant at the.05 level or less.
[b]Significant at the .01 level or less.

Table 13. Scottsdale Sample's Scores, Italian American Family Attitude
Scale*

Scottsdale Sample		X	s	T Value	Degree Freedom	1-Tail Probability
OCCUPATION						
Blue Collar	(N=19)	55.7	6.3	2.27	77	.01[b]
White Collar	(N=60)	50.5	9.3			
EDUCATION						
High School	(N=34)	54.2	7.3	2.37	79	.01[b]
College	(N=48)	49.5	9.5			
TIME IN ARIZONA						
0 to 6 Years	(N=42)	52.3	8.8	.46	85	.32
7 or More Years	(N=45)	51.4	9.0			
RAISED IN ITALIAN AMERICAN METROPOLIS						
Yes	(N=37)	53.1	8.3	1.69	73	.04[a]
No	(N=38)	49.6	9.3			
MALES/FEMALES						
Males	(N=56)	52.7	7.7	-1.26	89	.10
Females	(N=35)	50.3	10.3			
ENDOGAMOUS						
Yes	(N=30)	54.0	8.6	1.37	81	.08
No	(N=54)	51.3	8.6			

[a]Significant at the .05 level.
[b]Significant at the .01 level.
*72 points maximum score.

a significant decline between the 1914 cohort and the youngest cohort, and between the 1930 cohort and the youngest cohort.

The educational and occupational groups show statistically significant differences in the direction anticipated. (See Table 13.) The blue collar group has a mean score on the IAFA scale which is higher than for the white collar group, and the difference in scores for the one-tail t-test is significant at the .01 level. Similarly, the lower educational group with a high school education or less shows a higher mean score on the IAFA scale than does the college educated group. The difference in scores is significant at the .01 level for these groups.

Only one other variable shows a statistical difference. As anticipated, those who were raised in an Italian American metropolis had a higher mean score on the IAFA scale. The difference was significant at the .04 level.

Those who lived in Arizona the least amount of time were expected to have a higher mean score on the IAFA scale, but no statistically significant difference was found. The score for the endogamous group was higher than the exogamous, which was in the direction anticipated. The difference was not significant, but was close to the .05 level of significance.

Finally, no statistically significant difference was found between the mean scores of the men and women in the sample, although it was anticipated that women would score significantly higher than men on the scale.

Taking one of the key variables and looking more closely at where the decline in values had taken place, gives insight into the question of whether there was a decline across all the values, or if there was a decline in certain specific items. It was decided to examine the third generation more closely to trace changes between this group and the full second generation which is closer to the immigrant generation. The findings are shown in Table 14. An examination showed that the changes were not across all items, but instead related to certain ones.

The items to be discussed are those with significant changes. In all there are six items where a statistically significant difference was found between the full second and third generation. However, on one item a statistically significant increase in the direction of the third generation was found. On the remainder of the items, no statistically significant differences were found.

On IAFA items 2, "The family is all you have because friends can come and go," and 4, "Girls should be supervised more than boys," the third generation showed a change from a mildly agree category of the full second generation to the mildly disagree category. For item 8 "When a person does something wrong, it reflects on the whole family," there was a change from the mildly disagree to the disagree category for the third generation. On item 9, "The father is the head of the family, and the mother is the heart of the family," the change was from the agree category to the mildly agree category. On item 10 "A well kept home is the symbol of a sound family," there was a change from agree to mildly disagree. Finally, for item 11 which was "A person should be willing to put the needs of their family ahead of their own needs," there was a change from a high agree to a low agree.

Table 14. Scottsdale Sample Full Second and Third Generation Scores,
Italian American Family Attitude Scale

Scottsdale Sample	X	s	T Value	Degree Freedom	1-Tail Probability
1. Respectful Children			1.27	54	.10
Full Second (N=32)	4.8	1.3			
Third (N=24)	4.3	1.2			
2. Family All You Have			2.03	54	.02[a]
Full Second (N=32)	4.5	1.1			
Third (N=24)	3.7	1.4			
3. Family Before Job			- .76	54	.04[a]
Full Second (N=32)	4.6	1.4			
Third (N=24)	5.2	.7			
4. Girls Supervised			2.20	54	.01[b]
Full Second (N=32)	4.2	1.6			
Third (N=24)	3.2	1.5			
5. Strict Shows Love			- .38	54	.35
Full Second (N=32)	4.0	1.5			
Third (N=24)	4.1	.8			
6. Woman/Family			.71	54	.23
Full Second (N=32)	4.6	1.3			
Third (N=24)	4.4	1.4			
7. Put Trust Family			1.4	54	.07
Full Second (N=32)	4.9	1.2			
Third (N=24)	4.4	1.2			
8. Wrong Reflects			2.5	54	.003[b]
Full Second (N=32)	3.8	1.7			
Third (N=24)	2.7	1.1			
9. Father Head Family			2.2	54	.01[b]
Full Second (N=32)	5.0	1.2			
Third (N=24)	4.1	1.5			
10. Home Symbol Family			3.7	54	.0001[c]
Full Second (N=32)	5.1	1.0			
Third (N=24)	3.8	1.5			
11. Put Family First			2.1	54	.01[b]
Full Second (N=32)	4.8	1.1			
Third (N=24)	4.0	1.4			
12. Duty to Relatives			1.27	54	.10
Full Second (N=32)	4.5	1.2			
Third (N=24)	4.0	1.1			

[a]Significant at the .05 level.
[b]Significant at the .01 level.
[c]Significant beoynd the .0001 level.

On item 3 which put one's family before one's job, the third generation answered in the agree category, while the full second generation answered in the mildly agree category. This is contrary to the anticipated decline, and is a statistically significant difference in mean scores between the two generations.

These findings on the IAFA scale for the third generation suggest that the youngest generation in the Scottsdale study still holds to many traditional Italian family values. Apparently the younger Italian Americans of this sample are not clearly moving toward attitudes that are related to the "standard" American family model, characteristics of middle—class, white Protestants, where "intimacy at a distance" in terms of kin and egalitarianism are favored (Farber, 1981).

This finding on the retention of many of the traditional Italian values is in keeping with other research specifically on Italian Americans, and white Catholic groups in general. Both Greeley (1977) and Colleen Johnson (1982) demonstrate that Italian Americans families possess distinct traits compared to non-Italian families. Additionally, white Catholics still exhibit distinctive family traits when compared to non—Catholic families, in areas such as sex role structures, age at marriage, and contraception (e.g., Korbin and Goldscheider, 1978; Scanzoni, 1975).

As American family patterns, in terms of values and structure, change (e.g., Glick and North, 1979; Masnick and Bane, 1980; Pleck, 1979; Ross and Sawhill) continuing comparative research on ethnic American families, including Italian Americans, and non—ethnic American families will be needed. Such research will help to determine if changes in traditional ethnic families are related to assimilation or linked to a general decline in traditional family patterns.

The following section contains a discussion of the findings that are based on the cultural and national ethnicity scales developed by Sandberg. The final section contains a comparison of the findings based on the three scales utilized in this analysis.

Cultural Ethnicity

The purpose of the scale on Cultural Ethnicity is to assess the willingness of respondents to support and preserve the traditions of the group. The scale, as developed by Sandberg, contained items about a variety of Polish institutions including formal cultural organizations, schools, and the ethnic newspaper. Items were also included on attitudes relevant to the attachment to language, art forms, and the history of the Poles (Sandberg, 1977: 29). Six of the ten items which were used by Sandberg were included in the Scottsdale scale for Italians. (See Table 15.) Some of Sandberg's items were not included because they lacked relevance in the Scottsdale setting. For example, Sandberg's item about the need for a local ethnic newspaper does not apply to the Phoenix area because it does not have an Italian American newspaper. Another question in the structural behavioral ethnicity scale, presented in Chapter VI, covered respondents who might receive an ethnic newspaper from another community.

Analysis of the Cultural Ethnicity Items

Generally, the cultural ethnicity items did not elicit many spontaneous comments. This may be related, as mentioned, to the

Table 15. Scottsdale Sample's Scores, Cultural Ethnicity Items by
         Percent (N=91)

Strongly Agree	Agree	Mildly Agree	Mildly Disagree	Disagree	Strongly Disagree	Unsure

1. Public schools should teach more about the contributions of Italian
   people to America.

| 9.9 | 19.8 | 33.0 | 17.6 | 14.3 | 5.5 | 0 |

2. We need to know the history of the Italian people.*

| 30.8 | 40.7 | 15.4 | 8.8 | 2.2 | 1.1 | 1.1 |

3. I would be willing to give money to preserve the Italian tradition.

| 8.8 | 29.7 | 38.5 | 7.7 | 7.7 | 3.3 | 4.4 |

4. Our children should learn Italian dance and music.

| 5.5 | 22.0 | 34.1 | 17.6 | 15.4 | 1.1 | 4.4 |

5. It is too bad that the Italian tradition is not being carried on by
   many of our young people.

| 19.8 | 37.4 | 22.0 | 7.7 | 7.7 | 0 | 5.5 |

6. Our children should learn to speak Italian.

| 19.8 | 29.7 | 30.8 | 6.6 | 9.9 | 2.2 | 1.1 |

*Reverse wording used in interview schedule, see Appendix B.

somewhat lower percentage of agree comments compared to the IAFA scale. However, two items did generate several comments.

Item 5, "It is too bad that the Italian tradition is not being carried on . . . by young people," elicited the most comments. Four respondents disagreed with the statement because they felt the statement was not correct. As one younger person noted, "I see it [the Italian tradition] being carried on. I have many Italian American students and they talk to me about their families, and the traditions, for example food, being carried on."

Item 6, "Our children should learn to speak Italian," brought several qualifications to those who answered in the agree categories. Seven respondents stressed that children should learn Italian or another foreign language. As one man stated, "They should learn any other language besides English." The agree categories may represent a generalized support of learning foreign languages for some of the respondents, rather than a support of the Italian language exclusively.

Analysis of the Cultural Ethnicity Scale

There were 36 possible points for the scale. The range of scores was from 13 to 36 for the scale. The mean score was 24.7 and the standard deviation was 5.6 for the scale.

Few of the independent variables showed statistically significant differences between groups (See Tables 16 and 17). In several cases there were almost no differences between groups.

Table 16.   Scottsdale Sample's Scores, Cultural Ethnicity Scale for Generation and Birth Cohort: One-Tail Probability (P), T-Values (T)*

			Probability and T-Values		
Generation	$\bar{X}$**	First	Full Second	Half Second	Third
First (N=16)	25.4	------	P=.31 T=-.50	P=.16 T=.98	P=.21 T=.80
Full Second (N=32)	26.2		------	P=.03[a] T=1.8	P=.04[a] T=1.7
Half Second (N=17)	23.2			------	P=.34 T=-.04
Third (N=24)	23.9				------

		Probability and T-Values		
Birth Cohort	X	1914-1929	1930-1945	1946-1960
1914-1929 (N=34)	24.6	------	P=.48 T=.03	P=.42 T=.19
1930-1945 (N=32)	24.6		------	P=.41 T=.21
1946-1960 (N=19)	24.3			------

*36 points maximum score.
**The standard deviations and degrees of freedom for these variables are in Appendix E.
[a]Significant at the .05 level or less.

Table 17. Scottsdale Sample's Scores for Cultural Ethnicity Scale, One-tail T-Tests*

Scottsdale Sample		$\overline{X}$	s	T Value	Degree Freedom	1-Tail Probability
OCCUPATION						
Blue Collar	(N=19)	25.5	5.9	1.02	77	.15
White Collar	(N=60)	24.0	5.4			
EDUCATION						
High School	(N=34)	25.5	4.9	.76	79	.22
College	(N=48)	24.5	6.0			
TIME IN ARIZONA						
0 to 6 Years	(N=42)	25.0	5.4	.41	85	.34
7 or More	(N=45)	24.6	5.7			
RAISED IN ITALIAN AMERICAN METROPOLIS						
Yes	(N=37)	25.0	5.3	.70	73	.24
No	(N=38)	24.1	5.6			
MALES/FEMALES						
Males	(N=56)	24.6	5.3	.27	89	.39
Females	(N=35)	24.9	6.1			
ENDOGAMOUS						
Yes	(N=30)	26.7	5.7	2.51	81	.005[a]
No	(N=54)	23.5	5.3			

[a]Significant beyond the .01 level.
*36 points maximum score.

Table 16 represents the findings for generation and birth cohort. Only some of the changes expected between generations were found. There was no statistically significant difference in scores between the first generation and the other three generations.

The expected significant declines were found between the full second generation and the half second and the third generation. There was no significant difference between the half second generation and the third generation. Crispino (1980: 57) found a similar increase from the half second to the third generation, followed by a decline for the fourth generation.

Interestingly, none of the expected statistically significant changes were found between the birth cohorts.

The other statistically significant difference in mean scores was between the endogamous and exogamous group. (See Table 17.) Endogamous respondents did have a significantly higher mean score which was in the direction anticipated.

The expected differences betwen the mean scores for occupational and educational groups were not present at statistically significant levels. The findings were similar for other variables. Those who lived in Arizona longest had a slightly higher mean score than did those who lived in Arizona 6 years or less, but the difference was not significant. The same pattern was found for those who were raised in an Italian American metropolis. They had a slightly higher, but not significantly higher, score than respondents raised in another kind of setting. Finally, women and men did not exhibit a significant difference in their mean scores.

Generally both Sandberg (1977: 46-66) and Crispino (1980: 50) found that the Cultural Ethnicity scale items had basic agreement. Sandberg noted that clearer patterns of generational decreases in ethnicity were found for the religious and national ethnicity scores. Crispino found that overall the Bridgeport respondents supported maintaining the Italian cultural traditions. However, most responses were in the mildly agree to agree category. The Scottsdale respondents also seem to generally support the items in this scale at a similar mildly agree to agree level.

National Ethnicity

The scale on National Ethnicity was designed by Sandberg to study attitudes about ties to the ethnic group (1977: 32). Five of the items on the National Ethnicity scale used for the Scottsdale instrument are taken directly from Sandberg's ten items on national ethnicity. These items are listed in Table 18. Another item was added, number 5, which related specifically to a belief that Italian American families were different than other groups' families. This item was included in consideration of the importance of the family as a central symbol for the Italian American ethnic group.

As was the case for the Cultural Ethnicity scale, some of Sandberg's items were not included because his items were too close to items included in another scale, on Identificational Ethnicity, designed for the Scottsdale study.

Analysis of the National Ethnicity Items

The National Ethnicity items showed more variation in responses than did the scale on Cultural Ethnicity. (See Table 15.) The six National

Table 18. Scottsdale Sample's Scores, National Ethnicity Scale, by
           Percent (N=91)

Strongly Agree	Agree	Mildly Agree	Mildly Disagree	Disagree	Strongly Disagree	Unsure

1. We need stronger organizations to express the views of Italian
   Americans.*

| 5.5 | 16.5 | 18.7 | 18.7 | 24.2 | 4.4 | 12.1 |

2. An Italian neighborhood is a friendlier place to live.

| 7.7 | 18.7 | 26.4 | 12.1 | 12.1 | 4.4 | 18.7 |

3. I feel more comfortable with Italian American people.

| 5.5 | 16.5 | 27.5 | 22.0 | 23.1 | 3.3 | 2.2 |

4. You can be for your own people first and still be a good American.

| 23.1 | 38.5 | 11.0 | 11.0 | 5.5 | 3.3 | 7.7 |

5. Italian American families are warmer and express more feelings than
   other families.

| 14.3 | 31.9 | 16.5 | 19.8 | 8.8 | 2.2 | 6.6 |

6. You can count on Italian people to help you if you're in trouble.*

| 18.7 | 34.1 | 19.8 | 14.3 | 4.4 | 2.2 | 6.6 |

*Reverse worded on interview schedule, see Appenix B.

Ethnicity items showed a generally lower percentage in the agree categories than the items in the other two attitude scales. The overall agree responses averaged 58 percent in the agree categories. An average of 12 percent of the replies were in the strongly agree category, 26 percent were in the agree category, and 18 percent were in the mildly agree category. The items on National Ethnicity did, however stimulate more comments than did the Cultural Ethnicity scale.

Item 2, on living in an Italian neighborhood brought some interesting comments. Several people commented that they had never lived in an Italian American neighborhood so they could not evaluate if such a neighborhood were really a friendlier place to live. This lack of experience in living in such an area was reflected in the highest percentage, for all three scales, of responses in the undecided category. As white ethnics continue their move out of their traditional urban enclaves, this type of question may become increasingly less salient to assess ethnicity.

Interestingly item 4, "You can be for your own people first and still be a good American," did not elicit the responses which were anticipated for Italian Americans. It was expected that there would be a generally negative response to this item because of the sense of conflict over divided loyalties experienced by many Italian Americans about the role of Italy during World War II (e.g., Gambino, 1974: 284-293). However, only one respondent mentioned the issue of divided loyalties stemming from World War II. Overall, the item received the highest percentage, 73 percent, in the agree categories given to items that were on the National Ethnicity scale.

Item 5, on Italian families being warmer and expressing more emotions, rated the next highest agree score. This generally positive response was anticipated because of the importance of the family to the Italian American ethnic group. However, agreement was sometimes modified by comments which indicated that the respondents also found other ethnic families warm and emotional. Specific groups mentioned included Greek, Polish, Irish, and Jewish families. It seems that for those respondents who made the comments, the Italian family was considered warmer when it was looked at in relation to the larger society. One respondent said specifically, "Italians are especially warmer than Americans, but other groups, like the Greeks, are warm too."

Item 6, on being able to count on fellow Italians for help rated an overall response in the agree categores of 73 percent. This item is considered a meaningful indicator of ethnicity by both Crispino (1980: 63), who found 82 percent of his respondents in the general agree category, and Sandberg (1977: 66), whose respondents generally rejected the statement that you cannot count on Polish people for help. Fandetti and Gelfand (1983: 118) also found this item to be an important discriminating variable for National Ethnicity because of the strong response in their study.

Similar to Crispino's (1980: 60) respondents, the Scottsdale respondents gave a relatively low level of agreement to item 1, "We need stronger organizations to express the views of Italian Americans." His suggestion that this generally negative response is related to a continuation of the suspicion with which Italians viewed formal organizations seems reasonable (Crispino, 1980: 59).

In the next section the mean scores on the National Ethnicity scale
will be discussed.

Analysis of the National Ethnicity Scale

The maximum points for the National Ethnicity scale were 36 points.
The range of scores was from 3 to 33 points. The mean score was 21.7
and the 6.3 was the standard deviation.

The mean scores for the various independent variables under analysis
are presented in Tables 19 and 20. As Table 19 shows there was no
decline in the mean scores between any of the generations. Nor did the
birth cohorts show any statistically significant differences between
their mean scores. Apparently for these two variables there is a
general agreement on the scale items. These findings are in contrast to
the findings in both the study of Polish Americans in Los Angeles and
the study of Italian Americans in Bridgeport (Sandberg, 1977; Crispino,
1980). Both studies reported declining ethnicity by generation on the
National Ethnicity scale. Furthermore, the Bridgeport sample showed the
expected decline by age groups on the National Ethnicity scale
(Crispino, 1980: 64).

For Table 20 only two variables showed any differences in mean
scores which were considered statistically significant. Respondents who
were raised in an Italian American metropolis had a significantly higher
mean score than those who were not. It is possible that being raised in
an Italian American neighborhood does influence a person's feeling of
ties toward their group, and their views toward other groups as well.
Also, men had a significantly higher mean score than women did, and this
difference was not in the direction anticipated.

Table 19. Scottsdale Sample's Scores, National Ethnicity Scale for Generation and Birth Cohort: One-Tail Probability (P), T-values (T)*

Probability and T-Values

Generation	X**	First	Full Second	Half Second	Third
First (N=16)	20.3	———	P=.12 T=-1.2	P=.43 T=-.02	P=.16 T=-.09
Full Second (N=32)	22.8		———	P=.13 T=1.1	P=.38 T=.28
Half Second (N=17)	20.7			———	P=.17 T=-.93
Third (N=24)	22.4				———

Probability and T-Values

Birth Cohort	X	1914-1929	1930-1945	1946-1960
1914-1929 (N=34)	20.8	———	P=.12 T=1.2	P=.40 T=-.26
1930-1945 (N=32)	22.7		———	P=.19 T=.87
1946-1960 (N=19)	21.3			———

*36 points maximum score.
**The standard deviations and degrees of freedom for these variables are in Appendix E.

Table 20. Scottsdale Sample's Scores, National Ethnicity Scale:
T-tests, One-Tail Probability*

Scottsdale Sample		X̄	s	T Value	Degree Freedom	1-Tail Probability
OCCUPATION						
Blue Collar	(N=19)	20.7	7.4	- .80	77	.21
White Collar	(N=60)	22.1	6.0			
EDUCATION						
High School	(N=34)	22.2	6.1	- .33	79	.37
College	(N=48)	22.6	5.6			
TIME IN ARIZONA						
0 to 6 Years	(N=42)	21.5	6.4	- .20	85	.42
7 or More	(N=45)	21.8	6.3			
RAISED IN ITALIAN AMERICAN METROPOLIS						
Yes	(N=37)	23.3	5.5	1.90	73	.03[a]
No	(N=38)	20.8	5.9			
MALES/FEMALES						
Males	(N=56)	22.7	5.6	-1.81	89	.03[a]
Females	(N=35)	20.2	7.1			
ENDOGAMOUS						
Yes	(N=30)	22.4	7.3	.81	81	.21
No	(N=54)	21.2	6.0			

[a]Significant at the .05 level.
*36 points maximum score.

The remainder of the variables did not show statistically significant differences in mean scores, so the following discussion of differences should be considered with caution.

The endogamous group had a mean score that was higher than for exogamous respondents, which was expected. However, the difference was not significant. The remaining variables showed differences in means which were not statistically significant.

Both education and occupation showed the higher status groups having slightly higher mean scores than the lower status groups. The Bridgeport respondents showed a significant increase on the National Ethnicity scale for the highest occupational and educational levels (Crispino, 1980: 65). No difference was found between recent arrivals in Arizona and those respondents who had lived in the state for seven or more years.

Comparative Analysis of the Scales

This section contains a discussion of the three scales presented in this chapter and focuses on the independent variables. Each of the variables is examined to show the pattern the mean scores exhibited for the scales. An analysis of all seven scales, with four more presented in Chapter VI, is presented in Chapter VIII.

As has been discussed, generation is considered a key indicator of declining ethnicity. Each generation from the immigrant generation was expected to have a lower mean score than the preceeding generation. However, the expected decline is not clearly evident. Scores of the three scales do not show a significant difference between the first and the full second generation. While the first generation does show a significant difference between the half second and third generations for the IAFA scale, it is not significantly different from these two generations on the other two scales. This lack of significant differences may be because most of the immigrants in the Scottsdale sample came to America after World War II, so that these respondents are not as traditional as earlier immigrants.

The second generation shows the expected decrease in ethnicity scores between the full and half second generation. While the decrease is not significant for the National Ethnicity scale, it is significant for the IAFA scale at the .01 level and for the Cultural Ethnicity scale at the .03 level. Additionally the full second generation has a mean score that is significantly different from the third generation for both the IAFA scale and the Cultural Ethnicity scale. It is only on the National Ethnicity scale that there is no significant difference.

The next comparison is between the half second and the third generation. The expected decline between generations did not occur at a statistically significant level. There is apparently a leveling off of ethnic decline between these two groups.

Birth cohort is a variable for which a decline is expected between each of the cohorts. However, the differences in mean scores between the cohorts was not always statistically significant. There was no statistically significant decline between the 1914 to 1929 and the 1930 to 1945 birth cohorts for any of the scales. When the 1930 to 1945 and the 1946 to 1960 cohorts are examined, the expected decline is found for the IAFA scale. The difference in mean scores is statistically significant at the .01 level. However, for the other two scales the decline is not significant. The same pattern holds for the differences between the 1914 to 1929 cohort and the 1946 to 1960 cohorts. The statistically significant decline is present for the IAFA scale, but not the Cultural or National Ethnicity scales. There seem to be a fairly consistent level of ethnicity as represented by these two scales for the three age groups.

This examination of birth cohort suggests that for these three scales birth cohort may not be a good indicator of declining ethnicity, except on the IAFA scale for the middle and youngest cohort.

Being raised in an Italian American metropolis seems to be a fairly good indicator of a higher level of ethnicity for these three scales. For all three scales those raised in an Italian American metropolis had higher mean scores than did those who were raised in another type of area. The difference was significant at the .04 level for the IAFA scale, and the .03 level for National Ethnicity. However, the difference was not significant for the Cultural Ethnicity scale.

The two variables which indicate upward mobility, higher education and higher occupational status did not always show the expected decline in ethnicity with mobility. For those with a higher education and those with a higher occupational status there was a decline in scores on the IAFA scale that was statistically significant. However, for the other two scales neither of these variables showed the expected changes in mean scores at a significant level.

The pattern of differences between male and female respondents was significant for only one scale, the National Ethnicity scale and it was not in the direction anticipated. The women had a lower mean score on that scale, and the difference was significant at the .03 level. The anticipation that women would score higher on the Ethnicity scales was based, as discussed in Chapter IV on literature which showed women oriented to home and the family, which are bastions of the Italian American culture. Perhaps women did not exhibit the expected significantly higher scores on these scales because of the relatively high percentage of younger women in the sample. Thirty-seven percent (N=13) of the women in the 1946 to 1960 birth cohort, and 29 percent (N=10) are in the 1930 to 1945 cohort. This means that 66 percent of all the women in the sample are from the youngest and middle cohorts. It is possible that these women, especially those in the 1946 to 1960 cohort, have been exposed to the changes in American society that led toward more egalitarian expectations about the roles of women (Thornton et al., 1983). These egalitarian trends could mean that younger Italian American women may not accept as fully the traditional role expectations for Italian American women.

It is also possible that expecting women to have generally higher ethnic scores is an oversimplification of the various dimensions of ethnicity represented by these scales. Perhaps men are more likely to be nationalistic in ethnic attitudes than are women. Other research, based at least in part, on ethnic attitudes scales does not clarify the issue. Roche (1977: 220) found that the Italian American men in his sample were stronger in their ethnic attitudes than were the Italian American women. In contrast, Crispino (1980: 179) found little difference between Italian American men and women in terms of the sub-processes explored by his study. Apparently more research needs to be done to clarify the relationship between ethnicity and gender.

The endogamous respondents exhibited the anticipated higher mean scores at a significant level for the Cultural Ethnicity scale. Additionally, their score was close to being significantly higher for the IAFA scale.

The final variable to be discussed, the length of time in Arizona, did not show any statistically significant differences between groups. Apparently for the attitudes represented by these three scales there was not a significant erosion of ethnicity even after living in Arizona for seven or more years.

Of the three scales the IAFA scale showed the most overall significant declines in ethnicity. This appears to reflect some changing attitudes about the family, which has been a central social institution in the Italian and Italian American culture. However, it is necessary that caution be used in interpreting such changes rather than to assume there is now a lack of attachment to family values.

First, an examination of the overall percent agreeing to the IAFA scale items showed a generally high level of overall agreement with 75 percent of the respondents answering in the general agree category to all the items. The Cultural Ethnicity scale also had 75 percent in the general agree category, but the National Ethnicity scale had a lower percent, 58 percent, in the general agree category. However, the IAFA scale had the highest percentages in the strongly agree and agree columns in comparison to the other two scales. Twenty-one percent of all the responses to the IAFA scale were in the strongly agree column compared to 16 percent for the Cultural Ethnicity scale and 12 percent for the National Ethnicity scale. For the agree column 37 percent of the IAFA responses were in this category compared to 30 percent of the Cultural Ethnicity scale and 26 percent of the National Ethnicity scale. The Cultural Ethnicity scale had the highest percentage in the weaker mildly agree category, with 29 percent of the responses to this scale in this category. The National Ethnicity scale had 20 percent of the responses to this scale in the mildly agree column while the IAFA had 17 percent of the responses to the scale in this column.

Second, an examination of the scores of the third generation on the IAFA items indicated that although this generation's mean scores dropped on some items, there was not a drop in scores on all items. This seems to indicate a selective decline in values. Additionally, a significant increase on item 3 on one's job not coming before one's family could indicate a return to a traditional attitude.

Finally, respondent's comments on the item which received one of the lowest overall percentages in the agree categories, item 4 on stricter supervision for girls, indicated that a new value might be emerging which favored closer supervision of both boys and girls, not a rejection of supervision.

In Chapter VIII all the data collected on the family will be reviewed to assess the overall importance of the Italian American family to the Scottsdale respondents. The IAFA scale will be looked at in relation to the other indicators of the importance of family.

The Cultural and National Ethnicity scales will also be reexamined in Chapter VIII, as was mentioned, to look at the total ethnicity exhibited when all seven scales are reviewed.

CHAPTER VI

FINDINGS: ETHNIC BEHAVIOR, IDENTITY, AND TRAITS

The preceding chapter contained an analysis of the findings from three scales used to test for ethnicity. However, other researchers have attempted to explore different dimensions of ethnicity than those which are related to attitudes. These other dimensions are studied through the findings from the four scales presented in this chapter. The first of these scales deals with behavior relating to ethnicity. The second scale deals with identity relating to ethnicity. The third and fourth scales deal with the retention of cultural traits relating to language, food, music, and religion.

Each of the scales are examined in the following order. The rationale for the development of the scale is discussed. The modifications to the scale, when they were needed, are specified. The actual scale used is delineated. The responses to the items in the scales are presented, and the findings relating to the scales themselves are presented and discussed.

Finally, a summary of the results of the findings from the four scales is presented. An overview is given to see what trends are represented by an examination of the scales.

Behavioral Ethnicity

For his study of Italian Americans in Rhode Island John Roche (1977) developed an instrument to measure ethnic behavior. As Roche (1977: 66) noted most studies of ethnicity seek to measure attitudes (e.g., Borhek, 1970; Masuda et al., 1970; Sandberg, [1974] 1977).

As Roche (1977: 113-114) observes attitude and behavior do not always coincide. Attitude is an internalized belief system which may or may not directly guide behavior. Behavior is external and usually occurs in interaction with others. The few studies which focused on ethnic behavior developed research instruments which were primarily applicable to the group under study, and hence cannot be readily generalized to other ethnic groups (e.g., Uyeki, 1960).

Development of the Structural Behavior

Ethnicity Scale

Because of the lack of a suitable instrument to measure ethnic behavior Roche devised a scale of ethnic behavior. The scale is based primarily on a typology of ethnic behavior. Structural behavior ethnicity or SBES is used to label the scale (Roche 1977: 67, 75).

The typology of ethnic behavior which was developed focuses on structural ties to the ethnic subsociety (Roche, 1977: 66). Milton Gordon's (1964: 32) definition of structure was used to describe social relations which link individuals to groups. The groups may be formal or informal, big or small, and short term or long term. The groups serve to link their members to the major social institutions and their activities.

Because of this focus any behavior related to family, including the preparation or eating of ethnic foods, was excluded from the scale by Roche. He holds that family behavior does not necessarily link the individual to the larger ethnic subsociety. Behavior which was considered principally cultural, such as language usage, was not included either (Roche, 1977: 67).

Roche (1977: 68) delineated certain structural behaviors which he sees as relevant to behavioral ethnicity. These include belonging to an ethnic organization or to a church that is designated as an ethnic or national church, by the Catholic church in the case of Italian Americans, or belonging to an ethnic organization or church that was not designated an ethnic or national church, but had a high (51 percent or more) ethnic membership. Other ethnic behaviors include the following: shopping at a store specializing in ethnic foods, listening to ethnic radio programs or watching ethnic television programs, reading a local ethnic newspaper, subscribing to an ethnic publication, wearing or using an ethnic insignia, and using the services of a professional person of one's ethnic background.

Roche divided the above activities into four basic types of behavior. For measurement purposes the types were weighted differently, and in some cases the frequency of the behavior was also weighted (Roche, 1977: 69-75). Behavior that is overtly ethnic and involves ten or more people is Type A behavior. An example of this would be belonging to an ethnic club or church. This type of behavior is given four points for membership and four points for frequent participation, which would be at least once a month.

Type B behavior is behavior which involves many others of one's ethnic group, but is not specifically ethnic in purpose. Examples of this would be belonging to a club or church that was not designated ethnic but had a high proportion of the membership from the same ethnic group. Since this behavior is not overtly ethnic it received fewer points. Two points are given for membership and two points for frequent

participation in the type of club or church specified, with 51 percent
or more of the membership from the particular ethnic group.

Type C behavior is behavior which, like Type A, is overtly ethnic
but does not require interaction with many other ethnic individuals.
Examples of this type of behavior include shopping at an ethnic store,
viewing or listening to ethnic programs, reading local ethnic papers,
subscribing to ethnic publications, or using an ethnic insignia on one's
clothing or car. This behavior was given three points for the activity
and three points for frequent activity.

Type D behavior is not overtly ethnic and it only involves a few
individuals of the same ethnic background. This behavior would be
represented by having a person of one's ethnic background render professional services, such as a doctor, lawyer, or insurance agent. This
behavior was given one point for the activity and no points for
frequency, since frequency was not viewed as important to the relationship.

Finally, friendship with a fellow ethnic was included in the scale
but not in the typology, since Roche does not consider friendship
essentially ethnic. However, Roche holds that primary group contacts
with ethnic friends is a form of structural ethnic behavior. Therefore,
it is weighted as if it were Type B behavior receiving two points for
each ethnic friend, for up to six friends (Roche, 1977: 73-75).

Modifications to the Structural Behavior
Ethnicity Scale

While the examination of behavior is a useful approach to studying
another dimension of ethnicity, it is not easy to apply Roche's measure-

ment to Scottsdale. Many of the types of structural behavior ethnicity did not exist in Scottsdale, in the surrounding communities, or even in the state of Arizona.

There are no Italian Catholic churches in the Valley of the Sun. A check of the local parishes failed to find evidence of a Catholic church which might have 51 percent or more of the parish of Italian descent. Therefore, Type A and Type B behaviors related to ethnic parishes were not measurable for the Scottsdale study.

There are Italian American clubs locally. There is one in Scottsdale, and one each in the neighboring communities of Paradise Valley and Fountain Hills. These three clubs tend to have low profiles. None have club houses or permanent meeting places. The only Italian American clubs in the Valley that have established meeting places are both in central Phoenix. Neither the Scottsdale club nor the two clubs in nearby communities had listings in the Scottsdale or Phoenix telephone books at the time of the study.

While an effort would need to be made to find an Italian club, it is possible to participate in this activity. Belonging to an ethnic club was given four points for each club a person belonged to, and four additional points for each club a person attended frequently, as specified by Roche.

Since there are so few possibilites for ethnic behavior in Scottsdale, it was decided to include a measure for nonmembers who indicated they attended functions of an ethnic club with a friend or relative who was a member. Since this is not as overtly an ethnic behavior as actually belonging to a club, it was decided to assign the behavior three points, since it is similar to Type C behavior. No points were given for frequency, since there was a lack of close involvement with the club.

Respondents were asked if they belonged to any club or organization which was not ethnic but had Italian Americans as a majority, 51 percent or more, of the membership. No one reported belonging to such a club. Nor did anyone report belonging to a group which might have a smaller percentage of visible, active Italian Americans. So this type behavior was not included in the scale.

One of the principal behaviors which one can readily participate in locally is shopping in an ethnic food store. Within recent years the number of Italian delicatessens in Scottsdale had increased considerably. Shopping at an ethnic food store was given three points and frequent shopping an additional three points.

There were no Italian American radio or television programs at the time of the study, so this type of behavior was not included. Nor was wearing an insignia or emblem included in the measurement since such items were not sold at any local stores at the time of the study.

There was no local Italian American newspaper, so this type of activity was not used in the measurement. However, subscribing to an ethnic publication was included, with three points given for each publication.

Since there are Italian American professionals locally this type of behavior was included, with one point for each professional who served the respondent.

Finally, friendship with a fellow ethnic was included, with two points given for each friend. The pre-testing showed that respondents had a difficult time ascertaining the ethnic background of six friends, so the number was dropped to five friends for the Scottsdale study.

Analysis of the Structural Behavior

Ethnicity Items

One of the primary activities that was available for the SBES in Scottsdale was membership in an ethnic club. However, very few respondents actually belonged to an ethnic club. Only 11 of the respondents (12 percent) belonged to Italian American clubs. Eight belonged to clubs in Scottsdale and three belonged to clubs in nearby communities. Nor did many respondents seem to have been members of Italian American clubs where they lived previously. When asked if they had belonged to an ethnic club before moving to Arizona, only 13 (14 percent) replied they had been members before their move to Arizona.

Actually, the respondents were generally not active in many clubs of any type. Forty-three respondents, 47 percent, indicated that they did not belong to any club or organization, while 53 percent of the sample did belong to a club or organization. The 53 percent of the Scottsdale sample who were joiners is somewhat higher than was observed for a national sample of Italian Americans where 62 percent did not belong to any organization (Greeley, 1969).

Twenty-one percent of the sample (N=19) did attend the social activities of the local Italian clubs although the respondent was not a member. An additional 22 percent of the sample (N=20) indicated that they had considered joining one of the local clubs. So while actual members in the sample were few in number, an additional 43 percent had been in some kind of contact with the clubs, or considered joining.

One of the structural behaviors that involved many respondents was shopping in an ethnic food store. At the time of the study there were 13 delicatessens located in the Scottsdale area. The majority of the respondents, 64 or 70 percent, shopped at such a store. Respondent's comments indicated strong preferences as to the best store, although some were loyal to stores "back home."

The respondents generally did not subscribe to ethnic publications. Twenty-one percent (N=19) of the respondents received an Italian American publication of some kind. Nine received OSIA, the publication of a national ethnic organization, the Sons of Italy. Four received "Attenzione," a national Italian American magazine. The remaining six received various publications from their home states.

Overall the respondents did not use the services of Italian American professionals. Only 21 percent (N=19) of the respondents could name professionals whose services they used. Some of these respondents did use the services of more than one professional. Over half of this group, 59 percent or 12 respondents, used the services of an Italian American physician. The only other service used fairly consistently was that of dentist, used by 26 percent (N=5) of the respondents serviced by Italian Americans.

A total of 304 friends were identified by ethnic background for this portion of the scale. Out of this number 132, or 43 percent, were identified as Italian or Italian American. No strong preference was shown for friends from any other specific ethnic group. Instead friends were from various groups. Fifty-four, 18 percent, were of white ethnic background. Forty-four friends, 14 percent, were from earlier European groups, and 58, 19 percent, were of Anglo Saxon stock.

Twenty-seven respondents, 30 percent, reported having no close friends who were of Italian ancestry. Thirty-one percent (N=5) of the first generation was in this group, as was 22 percent (N=7) of the full second generation, 47 percent of the half second generation (N=8), and 29 percent (N=7) of the third generation. The remainder of the respondents reported from one to five close Italian ancestry friends.

Twenty-two individuals, 24 percent, in the sample reported that they had more Italian American friends where they had lived previously. The majority, 50 respondents or 55 percent, found no change in their friend-ship patterns. This suggests that friendship patterns are a somewhat reliable indicator of behavior patterns for most of the respondents.

The use of behavioral ethnicity as a measurement of ethnicity must be viewed with some caution because of the lack of potential for activity in a setting such as Scottsdale. One could argue, of course, that ethnic behavior probably did not matter to the respondents or they would not have moved to such a setting in the first place. However, if one reviews the immigrant experience from Italy, it becomes apparent that the earliest immigrants often settled in communities which were decidedly nonItalian (e.g., Rolle, 1968). The salient issue in choosing a community involved concerns like employment possibilities, since the survival of the family was of primary importance. So, the respondents from Scottsdale should not be automatically viewed as less ethnic be-cause they moved to a community which offered few opportunities for ethnic behavior. Their basic reasons for moving, as noted in Chapter IV, were most often for employment and health concerns. Thus, it would not be surprising if issues such as finding an ethnic church or newspaper were not paramount in deciding to move to Arizona.

Analysis of the Structural Behavior

Ethnicity Scale

This section presents the results of the statistical analysis of the SBES scores. The scores ranged from 0 to 26. The mean was 8.7, and 6.0 was the standard deviation. The first variable to be examined is generation. (See Tables 21 and 22). The mean scores between the generations do not fully show the anticipated statistically significant decline by generation. There is not a significant decline between the first and full second generations. However, there is a significant decline between the first generation and the half second and the third generation. The difference between the full second and the half second generations is significant at the .01 level. The difference between the full second generation and the third generation is not as pronounced, however it is close to the .05 level of significance. No significant difference exists between the half second and the third generation.

Roche (1977: 223) found that ethnic behavior generally declined by generation. There was a statistically significant decline between the first and second generation, which he did not subdivide, in the Italian American suburb of Johnston. There was also a statistically significant decline between the second and third generation in Johnston (Roche, 1977: 104). Warwick, which had a mixed ethnic population, had a slightly different pattern. The difference in means between the first

Table 21. Scottsdale Sample's Scores, Structural Behavior Ethnicity
Scale for Generation and Birth Cohort: One-tail Probability
(T), T-Value (T)*

Probability and T-Values

Generation	X**	First	Full Second	Half Second	Third
First (N=16)	11.4	——	P=.18 T=.89	P=.004[a] T=2.81	P=.02[a] T=2.0
Full Second (N=32)	9.8		——	P=.01[a] T=2.2	P=.07 T=1.44
Half Second (N=17)	6.2			——	P=.25 T=-.66
Third (N=24)	6.4				——

Probability and T-Values

Birth Cohort	X	1914-1929	1930-1945	1946-1960
1914-1929 (N=34)	8.7	——	P=.27 T=.60	P=.45 T=-.11
1930-1945 (N=32)	7.9		——	P=.28 T=-.57
1946-1960 (N=19)	9.0			——

*26 points maximum score.
**The standard deviations and degrees of freedom for these variables
are in Appendix E.
[a]Significant at the .01 level or less.

Table 22. Scottsdale Sample's Scores, Structural Behavioral Ethnicity
           Scale: T-tests, One-Tail Probability*

Scottsdale Sample		$\bar{X}$	s	T Value	Degree Freedom	1-Tail Probability
OCCUPATION						
Blue Collar	(N=19)	8.6	6.3	.19	77	.42
White Collar	(N=60)	8.4	5.4			
EDUCATION						
High School	(N=34)	8.9	6.2	.92	80	.18
College	(N=48)	7.7	5.8			
TIME IN ARIZONA						
0 to 6 Years	(N=42)	8.0	6.3	-1.08	89	.14
7 or More	(N=45)	9.4	5.6			
RAISED IN ITALIAN AMERICAN METROPOLIS						
Yes	(N=37)	8.2	5.8	.23	73	.40
No	(N=38)	7.9	6.1			
MALES/FEMALES						
Males	(N=56)	7.6	5.0	2.28	89	.01[a]
Females	(N=35)	10.4	6.9			
ENDOGAMOUS						
Yes	(N=30)	11.5	5.8	3.6	81	.0001[b]
No	(N=54)	6.9	5.2			

*26 points maximum score.
[a]Significant at the .01 level
[b]Significant beyond the .0001 level

and second generation was not statistically significant. However, the difference between the second and third generation was significant (Roche, 1977: 140).

No significant differences were found between the three birth cohorts. This was not anticipated.

In Table 22 two other variables show significant differences on the SBES scores, and both are in the direction anticipated for one-tailed tests. Those who married endogamously had a mean score that was significantly higher than the scores of exogamous respondents. Apparently marrying within one's ethnic group means that one is also likely to interact with other members of the group.

Women in the Scottsdale sample had a mean score that was higher than men's score, at the .01 level of significance. In contrast, Roche found no significant difference between men and women on the SBES (1977: 221).

The difference between blue-collar and white-collar workers in Scottsdale was not statistically significant. In Johnston the blue-collar workers had a mean score for the SBES that was significantly higher than the score for white-collar workers (Roche, 1977: 101). However, for Warwick no significant difference in scores was found between the two occupational categories (Roche, 1977: 136).

No significant difference was found between the mean scores of the high school and college respondents in Scottsdale. Similarly, Roche's regression analysis of education and ethnic behavior did not show a statistically significant correlation for either Johnston or Warwick (Roche, 1977: 107, 143).

The findings for the remainder of the variables studied for the Scottsdale sample, length of time spent in Arizona, and being raised in an Italian American metropolis, did not show any statistically significant differences.

The type of behavior used by Roche in his scale may not, in the final analysis, be the most relevant type of behavior to measure in an emergent ethnic setting such as Scottsdale. Herbert Gans (1979) in his discussion of symbolic ethnicity suggests several types of behavior which could be measured, even in a setting with few opportunities for the behaviors Roche mentions. For example, one can send money to an ethnic cause, observe ethnic ceremonial occasions, such as saint's days for Catholic ethnics or Chanukah for Jewish ethnics, attend an ethnic festival, or vote for a fellow ethnic (Gans, 1979: 9-10). The kind of community and the opportunities for activities need to be carefully studied before attempting to measure structural behavior ethnicity.

Identificational Ethnicity

Identificational ethnicity refers to a sense of identification with an ethnic group. As Milton Gordon (1964: 76-77) noted American ethnics think of themselves as Americans, but they also have an additional level of identity that is based on a sense of peoplehood related to their ethnic group. He used the label identificational assimilation to denote the loss of a sense of identificational ethnicity for members of an ethnic group.

The importance of identificational ethnicity, or ethnic identity as it is sometimes referred to, as a dimension of ethnicity has been noted by many researchers (e.g., Gans, 1979; Greeley, 1970; Isajiw, 1975;

Royce, 1982). None of the scales presented so far focus on this dimension of ethnicity. Attitudes and behavior are two important elements in studying ethnicity. However, in examining identificational ethnicity the basic focus is on an emotional attachment to the ethnic group.

Development of the Identificational
Ethnicity Scale

It was necessary to develop a scale for the measurement of identificational ethnicity since there was not a satisfactory measurement available. Crispino (1980) studied identificational assimilation in the Bridgeport sample, but he used only one question for the assessment of identity. The question that was used in his study was, "How do you think of yourself: Italian, Italian American, or American" (Crispino, 1980: 96). This question was used in the Scottsdale study, in a modified form, but it was not considered adequate to measure the dimensions of identity which were considered relevant.

Feelings of ethnic identity can extend beyond one's own identity to identification with other members of the ethnic group. If can also involve feelings of the individual in relation to the larger society. The following will examine how these various feelings of identification were operationalized for the instrument which was developed. Several of the items used in the Scottsdale instrument were used as individual items in other interview schedules (Crispino, 1980; Gallo, 1974; Parenti, 1975; Sandberg, 1977). However, none of them had been incorporated into a scale of identificational ethnicity.

The first dimension measured was self-identity. Crispino's question was used. One other choice was included which the respondent could identify with, that choice was American Italian. This choice was included after the initial pretesting. One respondent noted her lack of identification with the three self identities offered, saying that she viewed herself as an American Italian. This designation was included for the rest of the pretest interviews. The number of respondents choosing the category made it apparent that an American Italian identity was salient for the respondents.

The item on self-identity was one of the few items on the scale that was weighted. The categories Italian and Italian American represented the strongest responses and received two points. American Italian was considered to be a more moderate response, and was given one point. The category American and Other were not considered to represent an ethnic identity, and were not given any points.

Another question was asked relating to self identity and surname. Since surname remains the one easily identifiable ethnic label for many of the respondents, it was considered important to self-definition. The question was, "If you thought it would help you socially or professionally would you change your Italian name?" A negative answer received one point, and a positive answer did not receive a point.

The second dimension measured was identification with members of the ethnic group. Self-identity, while important, is a personal reaction. Feelings of identification with other members of one's ethnic group goes beyond an individual, psychological identification. Several questions were included to explore this dimension.

The first question asked was, "Do you feel any special sense of closeness to Italian Americans." If the response was yes, the

respondent was then asked the second question relating to closeness,
"How close would you say you feel to Italian Americans?" The options
were do you feel, "A slight sense of closeness, a moderate sense of
closeness, a strong sense of closeness, or a very strong sense of closeness."

This question was also weighted. Two points were given for answering very strong or strong sense of closeness. One point was given for
answering moderate or slight sense of closeness.

The third question asked in this series was, "When you meet an
Italian American for the first time, how do you feel?" The options were
"I assume we have something in common." "It is just like meeting anyone
else." "I try to avoid talking about my Italian background." "I have
another feeling." One point was given for the first option, "I assume
we have something in common." The other responses did not receive a
point.

The fourth question related to identification with successful
Italian Americans. The respondents were asked, "Do you ever feel proud
when you see someone with an Italian name do well or succeed, for
example in sports, business, or entertainment?" The options for the
respondents were, "Yes," "No," or "I never notice Italian names." One
point was given for a yes, the other responses did not receive a point.

The fourth question related to identification with successful
Italian Americans. The respondents were asked, "Do you ever feel proud
when you see someone with an Italian name do well or succeed, for
example in sports, business, or entertainment?" The options for the

respondents were, "Yes," "No," or "I never notice Italian names." One point was given for a yes, the other responses did not receive a point.

The fifth question related to negative identification with public Italian American figures. The question asked was, "Does it bother you when Italian names appear in connection with criminal activities or other negative events." The options were the same as for the fourth question. One point was given for a yes, the other responses did not receive a point.

The sixth question related to political identification. Gans (1979) notes that as ethnic politicians transcend representing only their ethnic group, they become identity symbols for their ethnic group. To assess if the respondents would respond to an ethnic politician they were asked, "If during an election you had to choose between two people you thought had equal ability, with no real political differences, and one was Italian American and the other was not, would you vote for the Italian American?" A yes response was given one point, and a negative response was not given a point.

The final dimension explored was the respondent's perception of barriers to identification in the larger society. This dimension is important to explore since identification with a group can be based on ties to the group, but it can also be based on barriers to participation in the larger society. One question which was included on the scale dealt with this dimension. The question was, "Some people think that Italian Americans face prejudice and discrimination. Would you agree with them?" A yes response was worth one point, a no did not receive a point.

The total number of points which could be obtained was 11 points.
The following section will present the scale items in terms of individual items and comments from the respondents regarding these items.
Then the mean scores of the independent variables on the scale will be
presented and analyzed.

Analysis of the Identificational
Ethnicity Items

As noted, this section deals with the individual items and the
spontaneous comments relating to the items. In general these items
produced numerous comments. Perhaps this was because identificational
ethnicity is something the respondents felt strongly about, or had at
least thought about.

The first question asked about self-identity. Sixteen of the
respondents, 17.6 percent, identified themselves as Italian. This
response was mostly from the immigrant generation. However, some of the
immigrants had other responses, and some of the American born
respondents identified as Italians. As one American born full second
generation woman who identified as Italian said, "The way I used to wear
my hair and dress I looked Italian . . . I used to live near a bunch of
comari [friends] in Chicago, so funny as it sounds I feel Italian even
though I was born here."

Thirty-one respondents, 34 percent, identified as Italian American.
Ten individuals expressed pride in their identity, but did not make
longer statements. One younger woman of the half second generation
noted that her Italian American identity was, ". . . a way to define
myself among masses of people."

Twenty-six respondents, 29 percent of the sample, chose the identity American Italian. Responses typical of this category included a second generation man who said, "I was born here, but from an Italian family."

Ten respondents out of the 73 in the above three categories expressed how their identity had changed. For some the identity had declined. One full second generation man said, "I thought of myself as Italian, because of the area I grew up in, there were so many Italians. As I get older I'm thinking of myself more as an American of Italian heritage, because of location [living in Arizona]." A third generation man expressed a similar transition. He said, "I was brought up saying I was Italian, ... But now I've changed. After I went in the service [in Vietnam] I see myself more as an American of Italian ancestry."

However, for some ethnic identity increased. One full second generation man who expressed increased identity said. "When I was younger I saw myself as American, but now I realize the Italian side of me that I was raised with."

Sixteen individuals, 17.6 percent, identified as American. This group did not state many attitudes about their identity. As one half second generation man noted, "I was not brought up in an Italian type household." Another third generation man said, "I have ties toward my background, but I'm an American."

Two individuals chose other identifications. One said, "I'm just a person." The other said, "I'm a humanitarian, I love all people and animals."

In Crispino's (1980: 96) sample 7 percent chose the category
Italian, 61 percent chose Italian American, and 32 percent chose American. Since the Scottsdale respondents had another choice, American
Italian, it is difficult to compare the two groups directly. However,
if Italian American and American Italian are combined then 62.6 percent
of the Scottdale sample could be placed in the Italian American
category, which would be close to the response of the Bridgeport sample.

In terms of generation, the half second generation was the group
most likely to identify with American or other. Thirty-five percent of
this generation identified this way, as did 19 percent of the full
second generation, 13 percent of the third generation and 6 percent of
the immigrant generation. The third generation was most likely to
identify with American Italian. Fifty percent of the third generation
chose this designation, as did 25 percent of the full second, 24 percent
of the half second, and 13 percent of the first generation. The full
second generation can be associated with the identity Italian American,
since 47 percent of that group chose that identity. Thirty-eight
percent of the third generation chose the Italian American identity as
did 35 percent of the half second and 19 percent of the first generation. Not surprisingly the first generation was concentrated in the
Italian designation, with 63 percent of this generation in this
category. No third generation identified with Italy, and only 6 percent
of each of the second generations groups chose this identity.

Overall, the respondents were negative about changing their identifiable Italian surnames. Eighty-one, 89 percent, would not change their
names. Eight respondents, 9 percent, were exogamous women without

Italian names so the question did not apply to them. Only two respondents indicated they would change their names.

Interestingly, there was some evidence of names being changed from American back to Italian names. One man whose family had Americanized its name and three divorced exogamous women had changed back to their Italian names.

When asked about a feeling of closeness 79 percent (N=72) of the respondents indicated that they did feel a special closeness to other Italian Americans. Nineteen, 21 percent, did not feel close. Those who did not feel close frequently expressed a reluctance to choose Italian Americans as an exclusive group to be close with. For example one immigrant woman said, "I love all people, not just one group."

Of the 79 percent who did feel close 7 percent (N=5) felt a very strong sense of closeness, and 31 percent (N=22) felt a strong sense of closeness. Forty-one percent (N=30) felt a moderate sense of closeness, and 21 percent (N=14) felt a slight sense of closeness.

The question about how people react to meeting an Italian American for the first time elicited many spontaneous comments. This may be related to the fact that all the respondents had migrated to the area from elsewhere, and experienced meeting many new people of various backgrounds. Sixty-two respondents, 68 percent, felt they shared something in common with Italian Americans. One full second generation woman commented, ". . . there is a bond, things you can talk about. Like the family, the traditions. There is a warmth and a unity." A third generation man said, "Living here brings out something if I meet another Italian. I can recognize similarities from people I meet who've come here from elsewhere."

Eighteen respondents, 20 percent, felt that meeting an Italian American was like meeting anyone else. One younger immigrant woman noted, "Italian Americans are born here, they are Americans to me."

Only one person tried to avoid discussing a common background. The remaining ten respondents had responses other than the three given in the interview schedule. Most comments related to the other response indicated that the respondent judged each person met as an individual, rather than make any assumptions about the person. A half second generation woman said, "I see if I like the person as an individual."

On a more distant level respondents continued to identify with Italian Americans. Eighty, 88 percent, reported feeling pride when seeing the name of a successful Italian American. Generally comments were brief such as, "It's a credit." Four people did not notice Italian names, and five did not feel a sense of pride, and 2 could not decide how they felt.

The next question which asked if respondents were bothered when Italian names appear in connection with negative events brought a divided response. Overall 44 respondents, 48 percent, replied that it did bother them. An equal number replied it did not bother them. Two respondents replied they did not notice Italian names, and one person was undecided.

This question was designed to examine how the respondents felt about a negative identification of Italian Americans with organized crime.

The existence of this stereotype has been well documented (e.g., Gambino, 1977; Iorizzo and Mondello, 1980; La Gumina, 1973; Moquin, 1974). According to a recent study of the image of Italian Americans on television, the stereotype is being perpetuated (Lichter and Lichter, 1982).

Responses to the question indicated that respondents had strong reactions to this question. Twenty-eight people commented that the association of Italian names with criminal activities bothered them. One woman said, "Yes, [it bothers me] very much, it gives me a lump in my stomach [when I see it]. A third generation man stated, "I kid around a lot about the Mafia, but I feel bad about it." Another woman, who is second generation, said, "I feel a sense of shame." A young female respondent said, "We're used as a scapegoat, the media is very ignorant. They publicize things for a good story, they know it [Italians in crime] will sell."

The 12 respondents who were not bothered had fewer comments, which were generally brief. A male immigrant gave a typical response when he said, "You find it [crime] in all groups." Other comments indicated the negative image of Italian Americans had bothered them at one time, but not anymore. One full second generation man said, "It used to [bother me], it was a stigma. Now I see it as an individual, [involved in crime] not reflecting on us as a group."

The fifth question in this part of the scale asked if a person would vote for an Italian American if all other things were equal. Sixty-four respondents answered yes, 70 percent of the sample. Fourteen respondents, 15 percent, said no, while 10 were uncertain and 3

respondents had other responses. It should be noted that in the spontaneous responses 11 people stressed that they would choose an Italian
American only if the candidate were equal.

For the last question on the scale, which assessed whether the
respondents saw prejudice still existing in society, 37 respondents
answered yes, 41 percent, and 51 answered no, 56 percent. The remaining
three respondents were undecided. Responses for both yes and no indicated that respondents were aware of prejudice that had existed. Those
who felt prejudice still existed cited stereotypes which they believed
were still salient in terms of Italian Americans. For example a second
generation woman noted, ". . . there is still a slight stigma [to being
Italian American]. They feel we're loud, boisterous, and fat. There
are misconceptions. If you succeed people think you're with the Mob."

However, the higher response rate for believing prejudice had diminished may indicate that the barriers to identification with the larger
society are also diminishing. As a third generation woman said, "I
think it has declined and we aren't judged, like we used to be."`

Overall the respondents seemed to have definite feelings about
identificational ethnicity. They generally did not identify themselves
exclusively as Americans, and seemed opposed to changing the most
identifiable part of their heritage, their Italian surname.

The sense of identification extended to others from the ethnic group
with the majority expressing a feeling of closeness. However, the
feeling of closeness was not intense and most of the respondents felt a
moderate to slight closeness. There was an assumption of a common
background or a sense of peoplehood for over half the respondents when

they met someone of their ethnic group for the first time. While a sense of pride was admitted for those of the group who had achieved success, there were also negative feelings associated with the criminal stereotype of Italian Americans. The respondents also seemed inclined to vote for a member of their group if the person was on a par with other political candidates.

Finally, the perception of the respondents about the barrier of prejudice was examined. The group showed a slight tendency to believe that the barrier had dropped. This could indicate that evidence of identificational ethnicity might diminish in the future. However, given the emotional undertone to many of the spontaneous comments it is also possible that identificational ethnicity will continue in the future based on positive feelings rather than negative pressures from the larger society.

Analysis of the Identificational

Ethnicity Scale

The scores ranged from 1 to 11. The overall mean score was 7.2, and 2.5 was the standard deviation.

Overall, there were very few statistically significant differences between groups, as Tables 23 and 24 show. The significant declines occurred between the first and the half second generation, and the full second and the half second generation.

Apparently the respondents had a somewhat similar level of identificational ethnicity, despite differences in occupation, education, age, time in Arizona, the type of setting they were raised in, sex, and marital choice. This consistency may indicate that identificational

Table 23. Scottsdale Sample's Scores, Identificational Ethnicity Scale for Generation and Birth Cohort: One-Tail Probability (P), T-Value (T)*

Probability and T-Values

Generation	X**	First	Full Second	Half Second	Third
First (N=16)	7.9	——	P=.37 T=.32	P=.05[a] T=1.6	P=.11 T=1.2
Full Second (N=32)	7.9		——	P=.04[a] T=1.7	P=.18 T=.92
Half Second (N=17)	6.2			——	P=.15 T=-1.0
Third (N=24)	7.1				——

Probability and T-Values

Birth Cohort	X	1914-1929	1930-1945	1946-1960
1914-1929 (N=34)	7.1	——	P=.29 T=.05	P=.40 T=.26
1930-1945 (N=32)	7.4		——	P=.12 T=1.2
1946-1960 (N=19)	6.6			——

*11 points maximum score.
**The standard deviations and degrees of freedom for this scale are in Appendix E.
[a]Significant at the.05 level or less.

Table 24. Scottsdale Sample's Scores, Identificational Ethnicity Scale:
T-test, One-tail Probability*

Scottsdale Sample		X	s	T Value	Degree Freedom	1-Tail** Probability
OCCUPATION						
Blue Collar	(N=19)	7.3	2.2	.28	77	.43
White Collar	(N=60)	7.2	2.5			
EDUCATION						
High School	(N=34)	7.1	2.8	-.31	79	.37
College	(N=48)	7.3	2.4			
TIME IN ARIZONA						
0 to 6 Years	(N=42)	7.3	2.3	.28	89	.39
7 or More	(N=45)	7.1	2.7			
RAISED IN ITALIAN AMERICAN METROPOLIS						
Yes	(N=37)	7.3	2.2	.79	73	.21
No	(N=38)	6.8	2.9			
MALES/FEMALES						
Males	(N=56)	7.2	2.56	.18	89	.44
Females	(N=35)	7.3	2.54			
ENDOGAMOUS						
Yes	(N=30)	7.7	2.2	1.16	81	.12
No	(N=54)	7.0	2.5			

*11 points maximum score.
**No significant differences found.

ethnicity is a fairly strong component of ethnicity. The next section
is an analysis and interpretation of two scales relating to cultural
aspects of ethnicity.

Acculturation

In Chapter V two scales were presented which explored some cultural
dimensions of ethnicity. The IAFA scale assessed the retention of
cultural values regarding the family. The Cultural Ethnicity scale
assessed the respondent's attitudes about the preservation of Italian
cultural traits.   In the next scales other dimensions of cultural
distinctiveness for Italian Americans are presented to assess to some
degree the amount of acculturation that has taken place among Italian
Americans. The first scale measures the retention of language skills,
and food and musical preferences. The second scale measures the retention of religious traditionalism.

Development of the Food, Language and
Music Scale

The Food, Language, and Music scale was adapted from Crispino (1980:
48-50). The purpose of the scale was to measure aspects of cultural
behavior. The items used in the scale were the ability to prepare three
or more Italian dishes, cooking such Italian dishes, not including pizza
or spaghetti, three or more times per week, making pasta, speaking
Italian, and reading Italian. Each of the items was worth one point.

The scale used for Scottsdale combined the first two items, so that
cooking Italian food frequently was worth one point. Making homemade
pasta was not included, since the popularity of mechanical pasta
machines in recent years means this task no longer represents the test

of Italian cooking it once did. The ability to read and speak Italian, with some degree of proficiency, was ascertained. Each language skill was worth one point. Finally, the enjoyment of Italian music was added. While Crispino did not include this item, the appreciation of Italian music seemed reasonable since it was an integral part of the culture (Iorizzo and Mondello, 1980: 113). The items were worth one point each, for a total of four points.

Analysis of the Food, Language, and

Music Items

When asked about their ability to speak Italian 40 respondents, 46 percent, could not speak Italian at all. Another fourteen, 15 percent, could speak a limited amount of Italian, but not enough to receive a point for language use. Fluent Italian was spoken by 18 individuals, or 20 percent of the sample. Another 17 respondents, 19 percent of the sample, spoke Italian to a moderate degree. Several of the American born respondents mentioned studying Italian in school, rather than learning it at home.

Over half the sample, 53 individuals or 58 percent, could not read Italian. Eighteen respondents, 20 percent, could read it with ease. Another 12, 13 percent, could read well enough to translate Italian, although with some effort. The remaining eight respondents could only read a few words of Italian. As with speaking Italian some of the second generation respondents mentioned a loss of reading skills which they had when younger.

When asked about the frequency of eating Italian foods at home 70 respondents, 77 percent, were in the frequent use category. Four people ate Italian food once a month, 15 people, 16 percent, ate it infrequently and two respondents never ate Italian food. Spontaneous comments frequently showed the respondent's pride in fixing a particular dish. As one second generation man noted, "I cook my own sauce, like my mother." Those who did not eat Italian food often or at all sometimes specified dietary reasons for not doing so. One younger woman stated she seldom ate Italian food because, "I'm a vegetarian."

Many of the respondents, 62, or 68 percent, indicated that they liked Italian music. Most popular kinds of music were the opera which 24 respondents, 26 percent, liked and folk music liked by 23 respondents, or 25 percent of the sample.

Generally, these items did not elicit a strong reaction from the respondents. The following section on the scale will detail the overall reaction patterns to this measurement.

Analysis of the Food, Language, and
Music Scale

The following scales, shown in Tables 25 and 26 show several variables with significant decreases in the items which were measured. These statistically significant decreases in the cultural patterns of language, food, and musical preferences reflect some dimensions of acculturation for Italian Americans. There are statistically significant decreases in the mean scores between the first generation and all other generations. There are also decreases between the full second and the half second and third generation. The decrease between the half second and third generation is not statistically significant, however,

Table 25. Scottsdale Sample's Scores, Food, Language, Music Scale for
Generation and Birth Cohort: One-Tail Probability (P), T-
Value (T)*

			Probability and T-Values		
Generation	X**	First	Full Second	Half Second	Third
First (N=16)	3.5	———	P=.02[a] T=1.9	P=.0001[c] T=5.0	P=.0001[c] T=8.3
Full Second (N=32)	2.6		———	P=.03[a] T=1.9	P=.0005[b] T=3.5
Half Second (N=17)	1.8			———	P=.08 T=1.4
Third (N=24)	1.3				———

			Probability and T-Values		
Birth Cohort	X	1914-1929	1930-1945	1946-1960	
1914-1929 (N=34)	2.4	———	P=.01[a] T=2.1	P=.10 T=1.3	
1930-1945 (N=32)	1.8		———	P=.31 T=2.1	
1946-1960 (N=19)	2.0			———	

*4 points maximum score.
**The standard deviations and degrees of freedom for these variables
are in Appendix E.
[a]Significant at the .05 level or lower.
[b]Significant at the .01 level or lower
[c]Significant beyond the .0001 level.

Table 26. Scottsdale Sample's Scores, Food, Language, and Music Scale:
T-test, One-tail Probability*

Scottsdale Sample		$\bar{X}$	s	T Value	Degree Freedom	1-Tail Probability
OCCUPATION						
Blue Collar	(N=19)	2.5	2.0	1.40	77	.07
White Collar	(N=60)	2.0	1.1			
EDUCATION						
High School	(N=34)	2.2	1.7	.74	80	.23
College	(N=48)	2.0	1.1			
TIME IN ARIZONA						
0 to 6 Years	(N=42)	2.3	1.7	.07	85	.47
7 or More	(N=45)	2.2	1.1			
RAISED IN ITALIAN AMERICAN METROPOLIS						
Yes	(N=37)	1.9	1.6	-.32	73	.37
No	(N=38)	2.0	1.1			
MALES/FEMALES						
Males	(N=56)	2.0	1.1	2.09	89	.01[b]
Females	(N=35)	2.6	1.7			
ENDOGAMOUS						
Yes	(N=30)	3.0	1.6	3.9	81	.0005[b]
No	(N=54)	1.8	1.1			

*4 points maximum score.
[a]Significant at the .05 level.
[b]Significant at the .01 level.

is close to significance. Overall, the decline in mean scores between generations follows the straight line assimilation pattern, for this scale.

Those in the 1914 to 1929 cohort scored significantly higher on this scale than respondents in the 1930 to 1945 cohort. However, there was no significant difference between the 1914 to 1929 cohort and the 1946 to 1960 cohort, or between the 1930 to 1945 cohort and the 1946 to 1960 cohort.

As Table 26 shows, women scored higher on the scale than men did at a significant level. This was in the direction anticipated, as was the difference between those who were endogamous and those who were exogamous. As was the case for women, the difference was significant.

Neither occupation nor education showed a significant decline in the direction anticipated. The length of time spent in Arizona and being raised in an Italian American metropolis did not make a statistically significant difference in mean scores either, for this scale.

In general, the cultural items did produce more statistically significant changes between groups than the SBES and Identificational Ethnicity scales already discussed. This may be due to the fact that acculturation, or cultural assimilation, is one of the first types of assimilation to occur (M. Gordon, 1964: 77). Furthermore, for the European groups who migrated during the last period of immigration the process of acculturation was accelerated by strong pressures from American nativists who urged immigrants to discard their most obvious "foreign" traits (Carlson, 1975; Higham, [1955] 1975; Linkh, 1975).

Development of the Religious Ethnicity Scale

In Chapters III and V the religious cultural patterns of Italian Americans were discussed. It was pointed out that the items in the Sandberg scale did not apply to the Italian type of Catholicism. In the following scale an attempt was made to assess, to a limited degree, the adherance of the respondents to Italian religious traits. The effort is tentative for two reasons. First, the lack of an Italian Catholic church in the Phoenix metropolitan area, or even parishes with large numbers of Italian American parishioners, means that one cannot estimate if individuals would keep Italian religious traditions that would involve such parishes, such as the _festa_. Second, religious beliefs are not the central focus of this study, therefore the interview schedule did not contain an extensive section on this dimension of ethnicity.

Given the above limitations the following items were incorporated into a brief scale similar to the preceeding scale on other cultural items. The five items were each worth one point. A point was given if a person was Catholic, another point was given for a Catholic spouse. One point was given for church attendance. Since Italian Catholics, especially men, often do not attend church frequently it was decided not to give more points for frequent attendance. However, a person who identified as a Catholic but did not attend church at all did not receive a point. One point was given for a devotion to an Italian Catholic saint or for devotion to Mary. Another point was given an affirmative answer to the question, "Would you like to have an Italian Catholic Church here in Scottsdale?"

Analysis of the Religious Ethnicity Items

There were 69, 76 percent, respondents who were Catholics, as discussed in Chapter IV. Sixty-three percent (N=42) of the married respondents had Catholic spouses. One person attended church daily. Forty-one, 45 percent, attended church weekly. Fourteen, 15 percent, attended monthly or every other month. The remainder did not attend church on a regular basis.

Twenty-four respondents, 26 percent, expressed a devotion to, or faith in, Mary or a saint. Some respondents had more than one devotion. While the devotions were not included in the scale, it is of interest to note them. Sixteen people were devoted to Mary, seven to Saint Anthony, five to Saint Joseph, and four to Saint Jude. The remainder of the devotions were to a variety of saints.

When asked about having an Italian Catholic church in Scottsdale 33 people, 36 percent of the sample, said they would like such a church. However, a few individuals indicated that while they would like such a church they probably would not attend it regularly. As a third generation man said, "It would be nice to have the festivals, but I wouldn't go regularly." It would be necessary to have such a church to actually determine how many people would attend it.

Analysis of the Religious Ethnicity Scale

The Religious Ethnicity scale had scores which ranged from 0 to 5 points. The mean score was 2.7, with 1.7 the standard deviation. (See Tables 27 and 28).

There was not a significant difference in the mean scores of the first generation and the other generations, although the difference

Table 27. Scottsdale Sample's Scores, Religious Ethnicity Scale for Generation and Birth Cohort: One-Tail Probablity (P), T-Value (T)*

Probability and T-Values					
Generation	X**	First	Full Second	Half Second	Third
First (N=16)	2.7	------	P=.16 T=-1.0	P=.06 T=1.5	P=.10 T=1.3
Full Second (N=32)	3.2		------	P=.003[a] T=2.8	P=.005[a] T=2.6
Half Second (N=17)	1.8			------	P=.39 T=-.28
Third (N=24)	2.0				------

Probability and T-Values				
Birth Cohort	X	1914-1929	1930-1945	1946-1960
1914-1929 (N=34)	2.9	------	P=.21 T=.81	P=.001[a] T=3.2
1930-1945 (N=32)	2.5		------	P=.01[a] T=2.3
1946-1960 (N=19)	1.4			------

*5 points maximum score.
**The standard deviations and degrees of freedom for these variables are in Appendix E.
[a]Significant at the .01 level or lower.

Table 28. Scottsdale Sample's Scores, Religious Ethnicity Scale: T-
test, One-tail Probability*

Scottsdale Sample		X	s	T Value	Degree Freedom	1-Tail Probability
OCCUPATION						
Blue Collar	(N=19)	2.5	1.7	.23	77	.40
White Collar	(N=60)	2.6	1.7			
EDUCATION						
High School	(N=34)	2.4	1.7	-.24	79	.40
College	(N=48)	2.5	1.8			
TIME IN ARIZONA						
0 to 6 Years	(N=42)	2.3	1.8	-.75	89	.22
7 or More	(N=45)	2.6	2.5			
RAISED IN ITALIAN AMERICAN METROPOLIS						
Yes	(N=37)	2.6	1.6	.94	73	.16
No	(N=35)	2.2	1.8			
MALES/FEMALES						
Males	(N=56)	2.5	1.7	-.33	89	.37
Females	(N=35)	2.4	1.7			
ENDOGAMOUS						
Yes	(N=30)	3.3	1.5	3.14	81	.001[a]
No	(N=54)	2.2	1.6			

*5 points maximum score.
[a]Significant at the .01 level or less.

between the first and the half second generation is very close to significance. The full second generation had a mean score that was
significantly higher than the scores of the half second and third generations. No significant difference was exhibited between the scores of
the half second and the third generation.

Both the 1914 to 1929 and the 1930 to 1945 cohorts had mean scores
that were significantly higher than the scores of the 1946 to 1960
generation. The difference between the 1914 to 1929 and the 1930 to
1945 cohort was not statistically significant for this scale.
Apparently the younger respondents were not as religious as those in the
other cohorts. This may be due to changes in the Catholic church in
recent years.

The only other variable where a statistically significant difference
was found was the difference between those who married endogamously who
had a higher mean score than those who were married exogamously.

No statistically significant differences were found between the
other variables. Although there are indications of a declining Italian
Catholic religious tradition among the Scottsdale sample, as evidenced
by the statistically significant differences discussed, these differences need to be viewed with a certain amount of caution. In general
American Catholic religious behavior has exhibited a decline in traditional practices. In the decade between 1963 and 1974 Catholic church
attendance decreased, as did going to confession, and weekly visits to
church (Greeley, 1977: 127). Part of the decline in Italian religious
practices could be linked to a general decline in traditional religious
behavior for Catholics, and not just to assimilation.

Comparative Analysis of the Scales

The following discussion focuses on the variables analyzed in all

four scales in Chapter VI. An effort is made to distinguish between

those variables that show consistent evidence of differences between

groups and those variables that show few or no difference.

Generation is one variable which showed several statistically sig-

nificant decreases in mean scores for all four of the scales. The

differences between generations do not always exhibit what might be

termed a straight line decrease, however.

The first generation generally did not show significant differences

from the full second generation with the exception of the Food,

Language, and Music scale. However, there were significant differences

between the first and half second generation for all scales but the

Religious Ethnicity scale, although the difference was close to signifi-

cance. The first and third generation had significant differences on

the SBE scale and the Food, Language, and Music scale. However, these

two generations were not significantly different on the Identificational

and Religious Ethnicity scales.

The full second generation was significantly different from the half

second generation on all scales. With the exception of the Identifica-

tional Ethnicity scale, the same was true for the full second and the

third generation. However, the half second and the third generation

were fairly close, with no significant differences on the scales,

although the Food, Language, and Music scale was close to significance.

It appears that there is a leveling off in the decline in ethnicity

between these two groups.

Roche's study of behavioral ethnicity has already been discussed in this chapter. To recapitulate his findings, a statistically significant decline by generation was found for all generations he studied in Johnston. In Warwick he found a general decline in mean scores by generation, however, the difference between the first and second generation was not statistically significant (Roche, 1977: 104, 140). Crispino's Langauge and Food scale show a statistically significant decline between generations. The largest decline, 29 percentage points, is between the full second and half second generation. This is similar to the statistically significant declines in the Scottsdale sample (Crispino, 1980: 51-52). Both studies show the importance of generation in measurements of ethnicity.

Birth cohort shows statistically significant decreases in mean scores for two of the four scales. No significant changes were observed for the SBE scale or the Identificational Ethnicity scale. However there is a significant decline between the 1914 to 1929 and the 1930 to 1945 cohort on the Food, Language, and Music scale. The significant decreases for the Religious Ethnicity scale are between the 1914 to 1929 and the 1946 to 1960 cohort, and between the 1930 to 1945 and the 1946 to 1960 cohort.

Those who married endogamously had significantly higher mean scores than those who were exogamous for all scales but the Identificational Ethnicity scale. This seems to indicate that this variable is of some utility in studying ethnicity.

Women had scores which were significantly higher than the mean scores for men on both the SBE and Food, Language, and Music scales. As discussed in this chapter, Roche's (1977: 221) findings showed no effect of sex on behavioral ethnicity.

There was not a significant decline for any of the scales for either the occupational or educational groups. Similarly Roche (1977: 221-223) found that neither education nor upward occupational mobility appear to have a significant effect on behavior. Crispino's (1980: 50) scale on language and food maintenance showed a straight-line decline in language skills and dietary patterns, except for the highest levels of occupational status and educational attainment. The higher levels showed an unanticipated increase on the scale.

The length of the time spent in Arizona and being raised in an Italian American metropolis apparently did not have much impact in terms of these scales, for no significant differences were found for these two variables.

The overall implications of the results of the four scales presented in this chapter are discussed in the final chapter. The variables which were focused on for this summary will be reexamined in comparison with the findings on these variables for the three scales presented in Chapter V.

CHAPTER VII

A TEST OF THE MCKAY AND LEWINS' ETHNIC TYPOLOGY

This chapter contains a test of the typology developed by McKay and Lewins (1978: 412–427). The typology was presented in detail in Chapter II (pgs. 33 – 37). The following is a summary of the salient points of that discussion for analysis purposes.

McKay and Lewins point out the need for a conceptual clarification of some of the terminology used in discussing ethnicity. They focus on two areas of ambiguity in the literature, the use of the term ethnic group and the use of the term ethnic identity.

First, they note that the term ethnic group has been used to include individuals who may share similar demographic characteristics, but who do not necessarily have a sense of belonging to the ethnic group or have much interaction with their fellow ethnics (e.g., Abramson 1975; Greeley, 1974). McKay and Lewins argue that the term ethnic category more precisely identifies such aggregates. The term ethnic group should be reserved for use with individuals who interact with other individuals on the basis of belonging to a common ethnic group.

McKay and Lewins also note that the term ethnic identity has been used to represent two different types of identity. In reviewing the literature on ethnic identity they note that some researchers describe ethnic awareness (Driedger, 1975; Francis 1947). Ethnic awareness is present when a person is aware that they possess certain ethnic characteristics, but those characteristics are no more salient to the individual than other social characteristics which make up the individual. In contrast some researchers describe ethnic consciousness (Connor,

1972; Goering, 1971). Ethnic consciousness is more intense than ethnic awareness, and often forms the basis for an "us" versus "them" outlook in relation to other ethnic groups. Rather than being an identity which only partially defines the individual self, as is the case for an individual with ethnic awareness, the identity generated by ethnic consciousness becomes the primary self-identity for the individual.

Based on the above discussion McKay and Lewins developed a four-fold typology (1978: 418). (See Figure 2.) The typology is divided into two dimensions. The first dimension is called ethnic structuration, and is divided into groups and aggregates. Persons who are part of an ethnic aggregate do not involve themselves in meaningful interaction with fellow ethnics. However, persons in an ethnic group do engage in ethnic behavior through interaction with fellow ethnics.

The second dimension is ethnic identity which is divided into ethnic awareness and ethnic consciousness. Ethnic awareness is being aware one has an ethnic background, while ethnic consciousness is a stronger identification with the ethnic group. The division into these dimensions was made to facilitate a separate analysis of individual and group levels of ethnicity (van den Berghe, 1968).

Although McKay and Lewins do not give labels to each subtype, to facilitate the following discussion identifying names are given for each of the four cells. The first cell represents low identity and low interaction. This cell is called the minimal ethnicity cell. The second cell represents low identity and high interaction. This cell is called the moderate ethnicity cell. The third cell represents high identity and low interaction. This cell is called the marginal

ETHNIC STRUCTURATION

Ethnic Category (Low)		Ethnic Group (High)
(I) (Minimal Cell)	* * *	(II) (Moderate Cell)
Ethnic Awareness (Low)	* * * *	
[Examples] Polish Americans (Sandberg, 1974)	* * *	[Examples] St. Patrick's Day Marchers
"Ethnic Impact" (Greeley, 1974)	* * * * *	Ethnic Manipulators (Lyman and Douglass, 1973)
ETHNIC IDENTITY * * * * * * * * * * * * * * * *	* *	
(III) (Marginal Cell)	* * * *	(IV) (Maximum Cell)
[Examples] "Ethnic Orphans" (Feldstein and Costello, 1974)	* * * * * * *	[Examples] Hausa Traders (Cohen, 1969)
Basque Sheepherders (Douglass, 1973)	* * * *	Italian Catholics, Australia (Lewins, 1975)
Ethnic Consciousness (High)	* * * *	

Figure 2. McKay and Lewins' Typology of Ethnic Identification and Structuration

ethnicity cell. The fourth cell represents high identity and high interaction. This cell is called the maximum ethnicity cell.

The first cell represents individuals who belong to an ethnic category in terms of ethnic structuration or interaction. This means that while the individuals can be classified because they have an ethnic trait, such as a surname which was the basis for selection of respondents for this study, the individuals themselves do not have a sense of belonging to an ethnic group. The individuals in this group would have minimal ethnic interaction or no ethnic interaction, and a low level of ethnic awareness. These people might know that they have an ethnic trait, but that trait, or traits, is no more meaningful than a variety of other personal characteristics. This cell represents people who are either assimilated into the host society or are close to assimilation.

McKay and Lewins give the Polish-Americans studied by Sandberg in Los Angeles (1977) as an example of a group that would fit this cell. While not specified by McKay and Lewins there is another subtype that could fit into this cell. Greeley (1974: 310) points out that in the complex relation between ethnic identification and ethnic culture, some individuals may have a weak ethnic identification and a minimal knowledge of their ethnic group's history but still display cultural traits which distinguish them from their fellow Americans. Thus, these persons may not consider themselves ethnic and may not know much about the history of their ethnic group. However, the ethnic culture, in terms of attitudes and behavioral traits, still affects these individuals. Research by Fandetti and Gelfand (1978) on the relation between ethnicity and mental health confirms the presence of an ethnic cultural impact on individuals who do not express a strong ethnic identification.

The second cell includes individuals who interact with fellow ethnics, and so belong to an ethnic group. However, their ethnic identity is not strong enough to be considered ethnic consciousness. Actually the designation of high interaction for this cell is somewhat misleading. McKay and Lewins (1978: 420) note that,". . . the frequency and duration of this interaction [for this cell] varies. . . ." There can be people who only interact sporadically with fellow ethnics, perhaps for a specific ethnic celebration, such as St. Patrick's Day parade.

There can also be people in the second cell who interact with members of their ethnic group without a strong attachment to the group for reasons which are self-serving reasons. These people are classified as ethnic "manipulators" who use impression management in their interaction, and ethnic "brokers" or "entrepreneurs" who reap political or economic gains from their contact with their ethnic groups (e.g., Iorizzo, 1970; Lyman and Douglass, 1973).

The third category includes individuals who do not interact with fellow ethnics, but who do have an ethnic identity which can be termed ethnic consciousness. McKay and Lewins specify two types of ethnics in this category. There are those who are geographically isolated and so prevented from contact with their group, and those who despite their ethnic consciousness choose not to interact with members of their group. The latter group are labeled "ethnic orphans."

The fourth category includes individuals who are high on both ethnic interaction and ethnic consciousness. They are often involved in competitive situations involving ethnic groups. The competition can revolve around vested group interest involving political and economic issues (e.g., Farber and Gordon, 1982; Glazer and Moynihan, 1975). Or the competition can involve ideological differences (e.g., Lewins, 1975).

This four part typology is the basis for the types which were looked for in the Scottsdale sample. The following section explains how the types were looked for, and the results of the analysis that was the basis for testing the typology.

Testing the McKay and Lewins' Typology

The scores of the respondents on the ethnicity scales were used to examine the Scottsdale sample for evidence of individuals who might fall into the four categories.

The Structural Behavior and Identificational Ethnicity scales[1] from the Scottsdale study correspond closely to the two dimensions in the typology. The scales were each coded into a lower, middle, and upper group. Then a crosstabular analysis was done using the two scales, to examine what was produced by combining the scales. On the basis of the crosstabular analysis a new variable was computed that divided the respondents into four groups, corresponding to the four types. For example, if a score was low on both ethnic structural behavior and ethnic identity the respondent was placed in the minimal ethnicity cell. A score that was low on structural behavior but high to medium on

---

[1]These scales have a correlation of .36 that is significant beyond the .0001 level.

identity placed a respondent in the marginal ethnicity cell. Ideally only those respondents low on structural behavior but high on identity should be in this cell. The initial crosstabular analysis yielded only 2 respondents who fit this cell, so the range of scores was broadened to include enough respondents to permit this cell to be included in the statistical analysis for the cells.

However, it was necessary to see if the differences between the groups represented actual differences between different types or if the differences were merely artificial cut off points on a continuum. To examine this point the other five scales, the Italian American Family Attitude, Cultural Ethnicity, National Ethnicity, Religious Ethnicity and Food, Language, and Music scales from the study were used as a measure of ethnicity. A discriminant analysis demonstrated that the National Ethnicity, Religious Ethnicity, and Food, Language, and Music scales had the most discriminating power. Consequently those three scales were used in a series of t-tests to see if the mean score of those represented by each of the four identificational/behavioral types differed from the other three groups at a statistically significant level.

Analysis of the T-tests of the Typology

The results from the tests are show in Table 29. Overall the t-tests indicate that there are differences between the four cells at statistically significant levels. For the National Ethnicity scale only two differences in mean scores were not significant, and that was between the moderate and the marginal cells and the marginal and maximum cells. On the Food, Language, and Music scale there were also two

Table 29. One-tail Probability (P) and T Scores (T) Between Cells, Scottsdale Sample

Cells		X	I Minimal Cell	II Moderate Cell	III Marginal Cell	IV Maximum Cell
NATIONAL ETHNICITY						
Minimal Cell (N=19)	I	18.0	----	P=.03[a] T=1.92	P=.003[b] T=2.91	P=.001[b] T=3.16
Moderate Cell (N=31)	II	21.5		----	P=.23 T=.07	P=.05[a] T=1.66
Marginal Cell (N=21)	III	22.7			----	P=.13 T=1.13
Maximum Cell (N=21)	IV	24.8				
FOOD, LANGUAGE, AND MUSIC SCALE						
Minimal Cell (N=19)	I	1.3	----	P=.01[b] T=2.3	P=.004[b] T=2.77	P=.0001[c] T=5.14
Moderate Cell (N=31)	II	2.4		----	P=.39 T=-.27	P=.06 T=1.57
Marginal Cell (N=21)	III	2.2			----	P=.008[b] T=2.48
Maximum Cell (N=20)	IV	3.05				----
RELIGIOUS ETHNICITY						
Minimal Cell (N=19)	I	1.2	----	P=.004[b] T=2.75	P=.01[b] T=2.35	P=.0001[c] T=7.40
Moderate Cell (N=31)	II	2.4		----	P=.47 T=.05	P=.0001[c] T=3.52
Marginal Cell (N=21)	III	2.4			----	P=.003[b] T=2.90
Maximum Cell (N=21)	IV	3.9				----

[a]Significant at the .05 level or less.
[b]Significant at the .01 level of less.
[c]Significant beyond the .0001 level.

differences in mean scores that were not significant. The moderate ethnicity cell was not found to differ significantly from the marginal or the maximum ethnicity cells, although the difference between the maximum and moderate ethnicity cells (.06) did approach the .05 level of significance. For the Religious Ethnicity scale only one difference was found in mean scores that was not significant, it was between the marginal and moderate ethnicity cells.

The marginal ethnicity cell, judging from the above scores, is not clearly distinct from the moderate ethnicity cell. However, it is distinct from the maximum and minimum ethnicity cells. The minimal, moderate, and maximum ethnicity cells apparently are different enough to indicate that the division into separate types is justified.

Discriminant Analysis Classification

A discriminant analysis was used to further and assess the differences existing between the cells. (See Table 30.) One statistically significant function was derived which indicates a bipolar difference between the lowest and highest groups. Overall, 53.85 percent of the cases were classified correctly. An additional computation yielded a tau of .47, or a 47 percent improvement over random classification (Klecka, 1980: 51).

The classification of the cells also indicated a clear distinction between the minimal and maximum ethnicity cells and the moderate ethnicity cell. The classification of the marginal ethnicity cell is less clear, with most of that cell being classified in the moderate ethnicity cell. Sixty-three percent of the minimum ethnicity cell was classified correctly as was 65 percent of the maximum ethnicity cell and

Table 30. Discriminant Analysis of McKay and Lewins' Ethnic Typology, Scottsdale Sample

DISCRIMINANT FUNCTION

Eigen Value	Percent of Variance	Canonical Correlation	Wilks'* Lambda	Chi Square	Degrees of Freedom	Significance
.60	98	.61	.62	41.5	9	.0000[a]

GROUP MEANS (GROUP CENTROIDS)

Group	Function
1	-1.2
2	- .01
3	.06
4	1.09

CLASSIFICATION RESULTS

Actual Group	Number of Cases	Predicted Group Membership			
		1	2	3	4
Minimal Ethnicity I	19	12 63%	5 26%	1 5%	1 5%
Moderate Ethnicity II	31	5 16%	20 64%	2 6%	4 13%
Marginal Ethnicity III	21	4 19%	9 43%	4 19%	4 19%
Maximum Ethnicity IV	20	0 0%	7 35%	0 0%	13 65%

Percent of "Grouped" cases correctly classified: 53.85
Tau=.47, [a] 47% improvement over chance

[a]Significant beyond the .00001 level. *Wilks' lambda is an inverse measure of residual discrimination. It is converted into a chi-square test of significance. This is an indirect test of the statistical significance of the function that (1) indicates if there are statistically significant differences between the groups used in the function and (2) if the first function derived is statistically significant.

64 percent of the moderate ethnicity cell. In contrast only 19 percent of the minimal ethnicity cell was correctly classified.

An examination of the group means, or group centroids, for the discriminant function provides a further indication that the marginal and the moderate cells are closely related. The group mean for the minimal ethnicity cell was -1.2, while the group mean for the maximum ethnicity cell was 1.09. The group mean for the marginal ethnicity cell was -.01 and for the moderate ethnicity cell the group mean was .06.

Based on the t-test scores and the discriminant analysis clear evidence does not exist in the Scottsdale sample for the type of marginal ethnicity delineated by McKay and Lewins' ideal types for this cell. They delineated individuals who were high on ethnic identity but low on ethnic interaction. McKay and Lewins included two different types in the marginal cell. The first are those physically isolated from their ethnic group, and apparently physical isolation, despite the geographically dispersed nature of the city, is not a problem for respondents in the Scottsdale sample who wish to interact with fellow ethnics. The second type is the "ethnic orphans" who choose not to interact with members of their ethnic group because they wish to assimilate, but are prevented from doing so by the large society or because they may have an abstract pride in their ethnic group, but reject actual contact with members of the group. It is possible that "ethnic orphans" may be individuals, given the above description, who would be likely to change their names, as part of their desire to assimilate, or refuse to participate in a study on their ethnic group.

It seems likely that individuals who would closely fit the description of the ideal type marginal ethnics were not included in the Scottsdale sample. Therefore, while the marginal ethnicity cell is examined further in this chapter, it should be kept in mind that it does not represent the ideal type designated by McKay and Lewins, and it is possibly a subtype of the moderate ethnicity cell. The latter point is returned to at the conclusion of this chapter.

A further assessment of the results of the t-test and discriminant analysis is presented at the end of the chapter for all cells.

Description of the Scottsdale Cells

The following discussion focuses on some of the characteristics of the respondents who are represented in the four cells. (see Table 31.) The information provided should prove useful for prediction purposes for those who decide to further test the McKay and Lewins typology for a sample similar to that drawn in Scottsdale.

Minimal Ethnicity Cell

The percentage of exogamous respondents was higher for this cell, 22 percent (N=12), than for the endogamous respondents, 13 percent (n=4).

The first generation and full second generation were close in their percentages represented in this cell with 13 percent (N=2), and 16 percent (N=5) respectively. The third generation had a slightly higher representation, with 21 percent (N=5) of this group in this cell. The half second generation had a higher percentage than the other generations, with 35 percent (N=6) of that generation represented in the minimal ethnicity cell.

Table 31. Percentage of Selected Variables in Cells

Variables		Cell I (Minimal) N=19	Cell II (Moderate) N=31	Cell III (Marginal) N=21	Cell IV (Maximum) N=20
ENDOGAMOUS					
Yes	(N=30)	13%	27%	20%	40%
No	(N=54)	22%	41%	24%	13%
GENERATION					
First	(N=16)	13%	25%	12%	50%
Full Second	(N=34)	16%	37%	19%	28%
Half Second	(N=17)	35%	23%	35%	6%
Third	(N=24)	21%	42%	29%	8%
BIRTH COHORT					
1914 to 1929	(N=34)	21%	32%	18%	29%
1930 to 1945	(N=32)	13%	44%	31%	12%
1946 to 1960	(N=19)	42%	21%	16%	21%
OCCUPATION					
Blue-Collar	(N=19)	16%	37%	21%	26%
White-Collar	(N=60)	22%	37%	22%	20%
EDUCATION					
High School	(N=34)	23%	29%	26%	21%
College	(N=48)	19%	38%	25%	17%
RAISED IN ITALIAN AMERICAN METROPOLIS					
Yes	(N=37)	19%	43%	22%	16%
No	(N=38)	26%	29%	29%	16%

For birth cohort the 1946 to 1960 cohort was most strongly represented, with 42 percent (N=8) of that cohort in the cell. Twenty-one percent (N=7) of the 1914 to 1929 cohort was in the minimal ethnicity cell, while only 13 percent (N=4) of the 1930 to 1945 cohort was in the cell.

In terms of occupational groups the white-collar group had a higher percentage, 22 percent (N=13), than the blue-collar group, 16 percent (N=3), had in the minimal ethnicity cell.

For educational groups there was a slightly higher percentage of the high school educated respondents, 19 percent (N=9) in the cell.

Those raised in an Italian American metropolis had a somewhat lower percentage in this cell 19 percent (N=7), than those American born respondents who were raised elsewhere, 26 percent (N=10).

The most outstanding characteristics in terms of the minimal ethnicity cell are apparently the distinct representations of the half second generation and the youngest birth cohort.

Although it was expected that some evidence could be found of Greeley's ethnic impact type for this cell, it was not possible to do so for this sample. A separate discriminant analysis was performed which divided the sample into five groups, with the possible ethnic impact group designated as group five. However, this group appeared in the cell one group in a higher percentage, 37 percent, than in the fifth cell where only 25 percent fell.

Moderate Ethnicity Cell

The endogamous respondents had a lower percentage, 27 percent (N=8), in this cell than the percentage, 41 percent (N=22) of exogamous respondents.

The percentage of the first generation, 25 percent (N=4) and the half second generation, 23 percent (N=4) was similar. The full second generation had a higher percentage, 37 percent (N=12) in the moderate ethnicity cell. The third generation had an even higher percentage of 42 percent (N=10).

The youngest cohort had the smallest percentage, 21 percent (N=4), in the cell. The 1914 to 1929 cohort had the next highest representation with 32 percent (N=11), while the 1930 to 1945 cohort was the most clearly represented in this cell with 44 percent (N=11).

The blue collar and white-collar groups had an identical percentage in the moderate ethnicity cell, with both groups having 37 percent of their groups in the cell.

For educational groups the college educated group had a higher percentage, 38 percent (N=18), than did the high school group with 29 percent (N=10) of their group in the cell.

Those who were raised in an Italian American metropolis had higher percentage, 43 percent (n=16), in the cell than did those raised elsewhere who had 29 percent (N=11) of their group in the moderate ethnicity cell.

The most outstanding characteristics of the moderate ethnicity cell are apparently the distinct representations of the exogamous respondents, the middle birth cohort, and those raised in an Italian American metropolis. Also, the college educated respondents have a clear representation.

The scales were not expected to reveal information about those who interact with their ethnic group, at least in part, for self-interests. However, a question was incorporated in the interview schedule that was designed to gain some information about this type. The question asked when appropriate was, "What is the ethnic background of your clientele." Four respondents mentioned having Italian American clients, but none of the respondents belonged to an Italian organization. They all mentioned that they did get at least a few clients who first contacted them because of seeing an Italian name.

The lack of evidence of such types as ethnic brokers or manipulators in the Scottsdale sample does not mean that such types do not exist in the community. Evidence has been gathered, through participant observation research from 1975 to 1984, that suggests some individuals seem to have self-serving reasons for involvement in the local Italian American community.

Marginal Ethnicity Cell

Twenty percent (N=6) of the endogamous respondents were in this cell, as were 24 percent (N=13) of the exogamous respondents.

In terms of generations the half second generation had the highest percentage, 35 percent (N=6), followed by the third generation, with 29 percent (N=7), and the full second generation with 19 percent (N=6). The first generation had the lowest representation with 12 percent, (N=2), of that generation in the cell.

The 1930 to 1945 cohort was the most strongly represented birth cohort, with 31 percent (N=10), in this cell. The 1946 to 1960 cohort had 16 percent (N=3) of its members in this cell, and the 1914 to 1929 cohort had 18 percent (N=6) of its members in the cell.

The representation of blue-collar and white-collar workers was similar. Twenty-one percent (N=4) of the blue collar workers and 22 percent (N=13) of the white collar workers were represented in this cell. The percentage of educational groups was also similar. Twenty-six percent (N=9) of the high school educated respondents were present as were 25 (N=12) percent of the college educated respondents.

A somewhat higher percentage of those who were not raised in an Italian American metropolis were present in this cell, 29 percent (N=11) compared to 21 percent (N=8) of those raised in an Italian American metropolis.

Overall, this cell does not have representations of variables that are as distinct as for the other two cells already examined. The half second generation is the most distinct group in this cell.

Maximum Ethnicity Cell

A distinctly higher percentage of endogamous respondents, 40 percent (N=12), was found in this cell than the percentage, 13 percent (N=8), of exogamous respondents.

The first generation was the generation mostly clearly represented in this cell, with 50 percent (N=8) of that generation present, followed by the full second generation, with 28 percent (N=9). The half second and third generation clearly had lower percentages. There were 6 percent of the half second (N=1) and 8 percent (N=2) of the third generation in cell four.

The oldest birth cohort had the highest percentage for the cohorts in this cell. Twenty-nine percent (N=10) of the 1914 to 1929 cohort was in this cell. The 1930 to 1945 cohort was represented by a 12 percent (N=4) of that cohort, with the 1946 to 1960 cohort having a higher percentage, 21 percent (N=4), of that group in the maximum ethnicity cell.

The blue-collar respondents had a slightly higher representation in this cell than did the white-collar respondents. Twenty-six percent (N=5) of the blue collar group was in the maximum ethnicity cell compared to 20 percent (N=12) of the white-collar cell. The differences between educational groups were also small. Those with a high school education had 21 percent (N=7) of their group in this cell, while those with a college education had 17 percent (N=8) of their group present.

Both those raised in an Italian American metropolis (N=6) and those American born respondents raised elsewhere (N=6) had 16 percent of their respective groups in this cell.

The first, or immigrant, generation is the group that is clearly represented in this cell. Endogamous respondents are also fairly well represented, although not as clearly as the first generation. In contrast the half second and third generations are rather weakly represented in this cell.

Conclusion

The data presented indicate that McKay and Lewins' typology can be used as a basis for studying divisions within the Scottsdale sample. There is a division into at least three clear subgroups within the sample, and these groups seem to fit within the cells of the ethnic typology. The t-tests indicate statistically significant differences between the mean scores on the ethnicity scales for the minimal, moderate, and maximum ethnicity cells. The separation of the marginal ethnicity cell is not as clear, a point that will be returned to.

The discriminant analysis also indicated a separation between the minimal and maximum ethnicity cells. However, the separation between the moderate and marginal ethnicity cells was not distinct. This inability to discriminate between the moderate and marginal ethnicity cells seems to be related to an overlap between the two groups.

The cell that is designated "marginal ethnicity" for the Scottsdale sample seems to be a subtype of the moderate ethnicity cell, characterized by a somewhat lower behavior ethnicity. However, the level of identificational ethnicity is sufficiently high to help statistically distinguish this group from the minimal ethnicity cell. It is possible that this lower level of structural behavior characterizes those types in the moderate cell that McKay and Lewins describe as having sporadic interaction with their ethnic group. For the Scottsdale sample there seems to be a fairly wide range of both ethnic identity and ethnic structuration, to use McKay and Lewins' terms, in the moderate ethnicity and marginal ethnicity cells.

215

Another question emerges in relation to McKay and Lewins' typology. Their description of ethnics to be found in the maximum ethnicity cell was of people likely to have a "we" versus "them" mentality, and who are also likely to have their ethnicity the primary focus of their lives. Furthermore, it was the members of this cell who were likely to become engaged in conflict with other ethnic groups. However, the Scottsdale Italian American community is not currently involved, nor has it been involved, in ethnic conflict. Therefore, can the Scottsdale respondents in the maximum ethnicity cell be considered as really representative of the type of ethnics McKay and Lewins describe?

It is believed that the respondents in the maximum ethnicity cell can, in fact, be correctly classified as an example of a latent manifestation of the types in this cell. Some examples should serve to illustrate this point. A serendipitous confirmation of the level of ethnicity for one respondent in the maximum ethnicity cell occurred after the compilation of the scores. A local classified newspaper carried a public service announcement of the formation of an Italian American organization in the larger Phoenix area. In an effort to keep informed of local Italian American activities the group was contacted for more information. During a conversation with the organizer of the new organization it was discovered that this person had been one of the respondents in the Scottsdale study. Apparently this individual was willing to take a public role as an Italian American.

A check of other respondents showed that while only 12 percent of the respondents belonged to local Italian American organizations, 73 percent (N=8) of those club members were in the maximum ethnicity cell.

The remaining club members, 27 percent (N=3) were in the moderate ethnicity cell. The number in the maximum ethnicity cell seems relevant because the clubs represent the most visible and active form of Italian American ethnicity in the larger Phoenix area. These clubs can be seen as those groups which would potentially be likely to become engaged in "we" versus "them" behavior, since the groups are organized around the common bond of ethnicity and are known within the community as representative of Italian American culture.

It is possible to envision a situation when those in the maximum ethnicity cell, particularly those who belong to clubs, could change from a latent to active status in terms of their ethnicity. The reaction of the respondents to the question on the Identificational scale that assessed the individual's feelings about Italian Americans being connected with negative events indicated a strong emotional reaction, as was discussed in Chapter VI (pgs. 176 - 177). If the local media consistently focused on such negative events, it is possible that there would be a reaction from the local Italian American clubs. And it is possible that the individuals who would initially become involved in such a confrontation would fit into the maximum ethnicity cell. Therefore, although the respondents in the maximum ethnicity cell are not currently engaged in ethnic conflict, it seems that this group could represent a group with a latent potential for the type of ethnic activity described by McKay and Lewins.

The McKay and Lewins typology apparently represents at least three distinct groups within the Scottsdale sample. This typology can be useful in assisting researchers to be more precise in their description of ethnic groups. Further research will be necessary to uncover clearer evidence of the characteristics of some of the subtypes, such as the person affected by ethnic impact, the self-serving ethnic, and the ethnic orphan.

In terms of those respondents who fit into the cells, it is apparent that for some variables the respondents are not dispersed throughout the four cells, but clustered in one or more cells. Generation is one variable that shows clear signs of clustering. The half second generation has its highest representations, 35 percent each, in the minimal ethnicity and marginal ethnicity cells. The third generation is concentrated, 42 percent, in the moderate ethnicity cell, as is the full second generation with 37 percent of its group. The first generation is clearly, 50 percent, in the maximum ethnicity cell.

There is also a division between the birth cohorts. The youngest cohort was 42 percent of its members in the minimal ethnicity cell, while the 1930 to 1945 cohort was 44 percent of its members in the moderate ethnicity cell. The 1914 to 1929 cohort also has its highest percentage, 32 percent, in the moderate ethnicity cell.

Endogamous respondents are clustered in the maximum ethnicity cell, 40 percent, while exogamous respondents are clustered, 41 percent, in the moderate ethnicity cell. Both of the occupational and educational groups have their strongest representation in the moderate ethnicity cell. Those raised in an Italian American metropolis also have a strong representation in this cell. Although the moderate ethnicity and the marginal ethnicity cells were not combined for this analysis, if they were the percentages under discussion would change with most variables concentrated in the expanded moderate ethnicity cell.

These findings and the others presented in this chapter should enable some predictions in the future regarding how samples similar to the Scottsdale sample might be distributed into the various cells.

CHAPTER VIII

SUMMARY AND CONCLUSIONS

This chapter presents an overview of the findings, that were previously presented for this study in Chapter V and VI, on the seven
scales representing ethnicity. The independent variables and their
contribution to the analysis are discussed. An overview of the
Scottsdale Italian American community is presented, and the implications
of ethnicity in an emergent setting are considered. Finally, some
conclusions are presented about the extent to which ethnicity may still
be important to white ethnics in American society.

An Overview of the Findings

The variables which were used to assess the respondent's Italian
American ethnicity can be subdivided into two broad groups. The first
group of variables are the centrifugal variables that include generation, birth cohort, occupation, and education, and represent those
variables that respond to the centrifugal push of influences toward the
larger society. The second group of variables are the centripetal
variables that include marriage patterns, being raised in an Italian
American community, and length of time lived in an ethnic community, and
represents those variables that respond to the centripetal pull of
influences from the Italian American community (Farber and Gordon,
1982).

Findings on the Centrifugal Variables

Table 32 displays the findings on generation and birth cohort, the
first two centrifugal variables to be examined, for the seven scales

Table 32. Summary: Generation and Birth Cohort Findings, All Scales in the Scottsdale Study

Variables	Italian American Family Attitude	Cultural Ethnicity	National Ethnicity	Behavioral Ethnicity	Identificational Ethnicity	Religious Ethnicity	Food Language Music
GENERATION[1]							
1. First / Full Second	n.s.*	n.s.	n.s.	n.s.	n.s.	n.s.	Decrease .02[a]
2. First / Half Second	Decrease** .05[a]	n.s.	n.s.	Decrease .004[b]	Decrease .05[a]	n.s. .06	Decrease .0001[c]
3. First / Third	Decrease .002[b]	n.s.	n.s.	Decrease .02[a]	n.s.	n.s.	Decrease .0001[c]
4. Full Second / Half Second	Decrease .01[b]	Decrease .03[a]	n.s.	Decrease .01[b]	Decrease .04[a]	Decrease .003[b]	Decrease .03[a]
5. Full Second / Third	Decrease .002[b]	Decrease .04[a]	n.s.	n.s.	n.s.	Decrease .005[a]	Decrease .0001[c]
6. Half Second / Third	n.s.	n.s.	n.s.	n.s.	n.s.	Decrease .005[a]	n.s. .08
BIRTH COHORT[2]							
7. 1914-1929 / 1930-1945	n.s.	n.s.	n.s.	n.s.	n.s.	n.s.	Decrease .01[b]
8. 1914-1929 / 1946-1960	Decrease .03[a]	n.s.	n.s.	n.s.	n.s.	Decrease .001[b]	n.s.
9. 1930-1945 / 1946-1960	Decrease .01[b]	n.s.	n.s.	n.s.	n.s.	Decrease .01[b]	n.s.

[a]Significant at the .05 level or beyond. [b]Significant at the .01 level or beyond. [c]Significant beyond the .0001 level. *n.s. = Not Significant. **Decrease = Decrease in the Direction Anticipated. [1]First Generation N=16, Full Second Generation N=32, Half Second Generation N=17, Third Generation N=24, [2]1914 Birth Cohort N=32, 1930 Birth Cohort N=34, 1946 Birth Cohort N=19.

used in the Scottsdale study: the Italian American Family Attitude scale (IAFA), Cultural, National, Identificational, and Religious Ethnicity scales, the Structural Behavior Ethnicity scale (SBES), and the Food, Language, and Music scale.

The Food, Language, and Music scale shows a clear decline by generation, although the decrease in mean scores between the half second and the third generation are almost but not quite. (.08), statistically significant. The pattern of differences varies on the other six scales. For example, findings for the National Ethnicity scale show no statistically significant differences among the generations. This may indicate an area of agreement regarding the attitudes underlying the National Ethnicity scale.

The findings and interpretations of the findings are discussed below by rows in Table 32.

Row 1: The first generation shows one significant difference between it and the full second generation. This difference is on the Food, Language, and Music scale. The lack of differences between the immigrant generation and the full second generation may be related to the high percentage, (70 percent, N=11), of post World War II migrants, discussed in Chapter IV, in the Scottsdale sample. These more contemporary immigrants may be closer to the full second generation in attitudes and behavior than the earlier Italian immigrants would have been to the full second generation. The presence of a high percentage of recent Italian migrants in Scottsdale is apparently a reflection of the increased number of Italian migrants to America since the relaxation of immigration restrictions in 1965. At first the newest stream of Italian immigration flowed to still existing Italian American enclaves. However, the presence of relatively new immigrants in a western Sunbelt community like Scottsdale indicates that these immigrants may, like a certain proportion of the general Italian American population, be dispersing throughout the nation. It has been suggested that the presence of a new immigrant generation provides ties to Jewish values and practices that may stem the potential loss of Jewish identity among the younger generations of Jewish Americans (Gordon and Mayer, 1983). It will be of interest to see if new Italian immigrants who may now be present in Italian American communities throughout the nation, such as Scottsdale, have an influence on the ethnicity of this white ethnic group.

Row 2: The first generation is distinct from the half second generation on the Italian American Family Attitude (IAFA) scale, the Structural Behavior Ethnicity scale (SBES), and the Identificational Ethnicity scale. Further, the difference between the two generations is close to significance (.06) on the Religious Ethnicity scale.

Row 3: Interestingly the first generation is not as significantly different from the third generation as it is from the half second generation, although there is no evidence of a resurgence of ethnicity for the third generation (Goering, 1970; Hansen, 1952). There is a significant difference on the IAFA and the SBES scales as was the case for the first and the half second generation. However, there is no significant difference between the first and the third generation on the Identificational and Religious Ethnicity scales.

Row 4: Another clear distinction between generations occurs between the full second and the half second generation. The expected decline is present and is statistically significant for all but the cultural and national ethnicity scales. Crispino's (1980) sample, as mentioned, showed similar findings.

These findings suggest that those who have one immigrant parent and one native-born parent represent a significant departure from the experience of those with two immigrant parents. Other studies also report differences between these two generations. Half second generation individuals are able to convert their education into earning power better than full second generation individuals can. Furthermore, for the half second generation individuals it is those with a foreign-born father and native-born mother who succeed the most (Chiswick, 1977; Martin and Poston, 1977; Martin et al., 1980). Martin, Poston, and Goodman (1980) suggest that the reason for the higher success of half second individuals with a foreign-born father is because the fathers were successful in two ways. First, these immigrants were successful in migration to America, and second, they were successful in finding a native-born mate. So, the children of such a marriage have successful fathers and mothers who are already socialized into the host culture.

In the Scottsdale sample 82 percent (N=14) of the half second generation had foreign-born fathers. Since a foreign-born father contributes the most to differences between generations in other studies (e.g., Martin et al., 1980), it is possible that the high percentage of half second generation respondents with foreign-born fathers in the Scottsdale sample accounts for the differences exhibited by this generation.

Row 5: The full second and the third generation actually exhibit less differences on the scales than the differences between the full second generation and the half second generation. The full second and the third generation do not have statistically significant differences on the National Ethnicity, SBES, and Identificational Ethnicity scales. Apparently the third generation, for the Scottsdale sample, is closer to the full second generation than the half second generation is.

Row 6: Having one native-born Italian American parent does seem to make the half second generation more like the third generation where both parents are native-born. The scales show some evidence of this tendency, since there is only one significant difference between these two generations on the scales. The exception is the Religious Ethnicity scale, where the difference is significant at the .005 level. On the Food, Language, and Music scale the difference is close to significance at the .08 level. Generally, there is a leveling off of the decline in ethnicity between these two generations.

The differences in the three birth cohorts were not always clearly in the direction of decreasing ethnicity for the younger cohorts. In fact, for four of the seven scales there were no significant decreases. Those scales were the Cultural, National, SEBS, and Identificational Ethnicity scales. None of the remaining three scales showed a clear significant decline from one cohort to the next.

Row 7: The only statistically significant decrease in scores between the 1914 to 1929 and the 1930 to 1945 cohort occur for the Food, Language, and Music scale. These two cohorts appear to be similar in this respect.

Row 8: Two statistically significant differences are observed between the oldest (1914 to 1929) and youngest (1946 to 1960) cohorts. These differences are reported for the IAFA scale and the Religious Ethnicity scale.

Row 9: The same statistically significant differences on the IAFA and the Religious Ethnicity scale are reported between the 1930 to 1945 and the 1946 to 1960 cohorts.

The lack of many clear differences among the cohorts may be related to the social changes that have occurred regarding being ethnic. It was not until after World War II that Italian Americans as an ethnic group showed widespread evidence of upward mobility (e.g., Lieberson, 1980; Lubell, 1952; Vecoli, 1978). Those in the 1914 cohort were between 16 and 31 years old by this time, and had grown up in an era when there was still considerable prejudice toward white ethnics (e.g., Krickus, 1976). In contrast members of the 1930 to 1945 cohort were in their teen years or younger as Italian Americans became upwardly mobile. In 1946 to 1960 cohort grew up in an era with even fewer costs associated with being ethnic, and in fact may see some advantages to being an ethnic (Gans, 1979: 15).

As anticipated, those who were upwardly mobile through having white-collar occupations and at least some college education showed an overall trend toward a somewhat decreased ethnicity. (See Table 33.) However,

Table 33. Summary: Occupation and Education Findings, All Scales in the Scottsdale Study

Variables	Italian American Family Attitude	Cultural Ethnicity	National Ethnicity	Behavioral Ethnicity	Identificational Ethnicity	Religious Ethnicity	Food Language Music
OCCUPATION[1]							
Blue-Collar	Decrease* .01[a]	n.s.**	n.s.	n.s.	n.s.	n.s.	n.s.
White-Collar							
EDUCATION[2]							
High School or Less	Decrease .01[a]	n.s.	n.s.	n.s.	n.s.	n.s.	n.s.
1 Year College or More							

[a]Significant at the .01 level. *Decrease in the direction anticipated. **n.s. = Not Significant.
[1]Blue-Collar N=19, White-Collar N=60. [2]High School N=34, College N=48.

the decrease was significant only for the IAFA scale. No statistically significant differences were found for any of the other scales between blue-collar and white-collar respondents or between those with a high school education, or less, and those with at last some college education.

This failure to find sharp ethnic differences between the more mobile and more traditional respondents may indicate the presence of symbolic ethnicity, an emergent ethnicity that is a voluntary rather than an ascribed status (Gans, [1962] 1982), among the upwardly mobile members of the Scottsdale sample. Although this type of ethnicity is discussed later in this chapter, it can be mentioned here that symbolic ethnicity tends to be found among younger, upwardly mobile ethnics (Gans, 1979). Indeed, some observers of ethnicity have been suggested that it is poverty and not affluence that erases ethnic differences (Enloe, 1973: 33).

Findings on Centripetal Variables

The variables presented in Table 34 represent those variables which refer to respondent's ties to the Italian American ethnic community in particular having lived in an Italian American metropolis in terms of a viable enclave and marrying endogamously.

The first variable examined is whether or not being raised in an Italian American metropolis contributes to a higher sense of ethnicity. Table 34 shows that such an upbringing does apparently make a difference, but only on two of the scales, the IAFA and the National Ethnicity scale. This finding on being raised in an Italian American metropolis indicates that there is some contribution to ethnicity that comes from

Table 34. Summary: Respondent's Ties to Italian American Community, Findings All Scales in the Scottsdale Study

Variables	Italian American Family Attitude	Cultural Ethnicity	National Ethnicity	Behavioral Ethnicity	Identificational Ethnicity	Religious Ethnicity	Food Language Music
TIES TO ITALIAN AMERICAN COMMUNITY							
Raised in an Italian American Metropolis[1]							
Yes							
No	Decrease* .04[a]	n.s.**	Decrease .03[a]	n.s.	n.s.	n.s.	n.s.
Endogamous[2]							
Yes							
No	n.s.	Decrease .005[b]	n.s.	Decrease .0001[c]	n.s.	Decrease .0001[c]	Decrease .001[b]
Years in Arizona[3]							
0 to 6	n.s.	n.s.	n.s.	n.s.	n.s.	n.s.	n.s.
7 +	n.s.	n.s.	n.s.	n.s.	n.s.	n.s.	n.s.

[a] Significant at the .05 level or beyond. [b] Significant at the .01 level or beyond. [c] Significant beyond the .0001 level. *Decrease = Decrease in the direction anticipated. **n.s. = Not Significant. [1] Raised in Italian American Metrololis Yes N=37, No N=38. [2] Endogamous N=30, Exogamous N=54. [3] Years in Arizona 0 to 6 N=42, 7 + N=45.

living in an area that can support a fairly vigorous and extensive ethnic community. However, the contribution is not strong enough to make a difference on most of the scales. The lack of differences on the scales suggests that white ethnics who are raised in nonethnic areas, as these ethnics increasingly disperse out of their enclaves in eastern and midwestern urban areas, may retain some sense of ethnicity.

Apparently, choosing to marry within one's ethnic group is indicative of a strong sense of ethnicity. Those who are endogamous have mean scores that are higher on several scales than means for exogamous respondents. The difference in scores between the groups are not significant for the IAFA, National Ethnicity, and Identificational Ethnicity scales. However, they are statistically significant for the other three scales, the SBES, Food, Language, and Music scale, and the Religious Ethnicity scale.

The significant differences in the two marital groups indicates that if exogamy continues to increase, Italian Americans may diminish in their sense of ethnicity. However, the findings for the three scales on which there is no difference by endogamy (IAFA, Identificational Ethnicity, and National Ethnicity) suggest that a core of ethnicity persists among those who are exogamous.

The pull of ethnicity that emerges once a person has been socialized into an ethnic group apparently does not diminish easily (e.g., Allport, 1958; M. Gordon, 1978). Living in a nonethnic community like Scottsdale does not seem to cause an automatic decline in ethnicity. Tendencies in other studies are similar: Roche's (1977: 150) respondents did not show a change in ethnicity due to the amount of time spent in a suburb.

But, unlike Scottsdale, Johnston was an ethnic suburb and both communities in Rhode Island that he studied are closer to ethnic enclaves than is Scottsdale.

Summary Analysis of the Centrifugal and

Centripetal Variables

To determine which of the centrifugal and centripetal variables discussed (generation, birth cohort, education, occupation, endogamy, being raised in an Italian metropolitan area, and living in an Italian community) is most powerful in separating the respondents into distinct groups, a discriminant analysis was performed.

The scores of the respondents on all seven scales were combined into an overall ethnicity score. The composite score was divided into high, medium, and low groups. Two statistically significant functions were derived (See Table 35). Only two variables contributed to the first function. Generation contributed the most to the function with a standardized discriminant function coefficient, analogous to a beta weight, of .99. Endogamy also contributed to the first function, although in a lesser amount, with a standardized discriminant function coefficient of .06.

The second function is weaker in its ability to separate the groups, as the lower Eigen value and the associated canonical correlation indicate. Further, the larger Wilks' lambda in the second function indicates that less discriminating power is left in this function. Again generation and endogamy contribute to this function, but in a reverse order. Generation contributes .13 and endogamy contributes .99 to the second discriminant function. The other centripetal and centrifugal

Table 35. Discriminant Functions for the Scottsdale Study Centrifugal
and Centripetal Variables

Eigen Value	Percent of Variance	Canonical Correlation	Wilks'* Lambda	Chi Square	Degrees of Freedom	Significance
		"GENERATION" FUNCTION (1)				
.17	76.3	.38	.80	18.4	4	.001[a]
		"ENDOGAMY" FUNCTION (2)				
.05	23.6	.22	.95	4.5	1	.03[B]

[a]Significant beyond the .01 level.
[b]Significant beyond the .05 level.
*Wilks' lambda is an inverse measure of residual discrimination. It
is converted into a chi-square test of significance. This is an
indirect test of the statistical significance of the function that (1)
indicates if there are statistically significant differences between the
groups used in the function and (2) if the function to be devrived is
statistically significant.

variables did not contribute to the first or second function. The first function is labeled "Generation" since this variable contributed the most to the function, while the second function is labeled "Endogamy."

This findings on the importance of generation in the first, more powerful, function seems to support the findings just discussed. These findings seem to indicate that most differences on the seven scales used to measure ethnicity for the Scottsdale sample can be found among the generation groups.

Female/Male Differences

The final variable to be discussed does not fit into the centripetal or centrifugal categories. The differences between the sexes were examined to see if men or women were higher in ethnicity. The assumption that women would be more ethnic than men was based on the traditional role of the Italian woman that centered on the home and family.

An examination of the scales showed variations between men and women, but these variations were not always in the direction anticipated. Women had mean scores that were significantly higher (.01 level) than men's scores for both the SBES and the Food, Language, and Music scale. However, for the National Ethnicity scale men had a significantly higher (.03 level) mean score. For the remaining four scales (IAFA, Cultural Ethnicity, Religious Ethnicity, and Identificational Ethnicity scales) there were no significant differences between the sexes.

A particularly unexpected finding was the lack of scores that were significantly higher for women on the IAFA and the Religious Ethnicity scales. The importance of the family and church in the role of the traditional Italian woman would suggest that women would be likely to score significantly higher on the family and religious scales, but this was not the case for the Scottsdale sample.

The lack of significant differences between the women and men on the IAFA and Religious Ethnicity scales, when coupled with the high percentage of women in the Scottsdale sample in the two younger age cohorts, suggest an explanation of Krause's (1978) results on Italian American female college students. The young, upwardly mobile women of this ethnic group may be a manifestation of the ideal of a "woman of seriousness" among younger Italian American women (D'Andrea, 1983; Gambino, 1974). According to D'Andrea (1983: 62-63) the traditional Italian role required that a woman be alert and practical in advancing the interests of her family; this was an active role that encouraged a positive self-identity. Although the home bound aspect of the role is no longer salient, the other dimensions of the role of a woman of seriousness may have prepared Italian American women to deal with modern society. To ascertain if the ideal is, in fact, still influential will provide an interesting area for future research.

In general the lack of the expected significant differences among many of the variables indicates that many of the divisions in the Scottsdale community that were anticipated are not present. The findings seem to indicate a fairly cohesive set of attitudes, behavior, and feelings among the respondents in this sample.

The next section is a description of the Italian American community of Scottsdale that emerged from the combined findings of this study. It is supplemented by the participant observation findings from research on the Scottsdale Italian American community started in 1975.

The Italian Americans of Scottsdale

The outlines of the Italian American community of Scottsdale,
Arizona are still unclear. The movement of Italians and Italian Americans to the "West's most Western town" did not really begin until after
World War II. This movement was hardly more than a trickle in the early
post-war years. It began to grow in the 1960s and 1970s, and appears to
be continuing into the 1980s.

Organizational Involvement

In a sense, the Italian Americans in this Sunbelt community can be
considered an immigrant community. They are the first of their ethnic
group to move to Scottsdale in fairly large numbers. They entered a
community which, while not hostile to the development of an ethnic
subcommunity, was not conducive to the development of such a community
either. Scottsdale has too few ethnic institutions to attract Italian
American newcomers and introduce them to the existing community.

One type of organization in Scottsdale that has some potential for
at least initially attracting Italian Americans to the existing
community is the local Italian club. However, the club generally is not
visible. Several problems were observed in early years of the
Scottsdale Italian club that prevented the establishment of a permanent
headquarters which would give the club visibility. The club formed in
1974 as an offshoot of an Italian club in Phoenix. Both clubs are
chapters of a national organization, the Sons of Italy. The national
organization discouraged the club from purchasing a site to build a
clubhouse, or buying an existing building citing many chapters in the
East that had difficulty in keeping their existing clubhouses open.

Another problem in establishing a headquarter was the fact that, despite a core of loyal members, club membership was generally transitory. This turnover in membership made it difficult to get the financial commitment necessary to build or buy a clubhouse.

During the nine years the club has been in existence, the cost of property in Scottsdale has increased, and the population of the city, and the club members, has shifted to new areas in the northern part of Scottsdale. This has meant that some of the earlier "bargains" are now out of financial range. Any future "bargains" are likely to be in the older part of the city, distant from the majority of the member's homes.

Given the small percentage of the Scottsdale Italian American sample belonging to an Italian club locally (only 12 percent) even having a clubhouse would probably not result in a rapid increase in members. However, 21 percent of the sample (n=19) indicated they attend club activities even though they are not members, and an additional 22 percent, (N=20) indicated that they had thought of joining a local Italian American club. So it seems reasonable to assume that a visible club could attract some Italian Americans to their social events, ethnic celebrations, and community service efforts. While these individuals may not join an ethnic club they would become involved, although peripherally, with the existing organized Italian American community.

Since many of the Italian Americans in the sample (76 percent) are Catholic, an Italian American parish could be another asset in building a sense of community. However, at present none of the local Catholic churches has a sufficient number of Italian Americans to support the celebration of a _festa_. Nor do any of the churches have an order of Italian priests or nuns to encourage _italianita_ in a parish.

Yet, since the Italian American community is relatively new, it is possible that a focal point or points may emerge. Within the last five years sporadic celebrations of the traditional St. Joseph's feast have been held by various clubs and some of the local churches (Polson, 1979). If this celebration coalesces into a major, permanent _festa_, it would serve to foster a sense of community among the local Italian Americans. The club still has the potential to establish a permanent location, or perhaps become widely known through the celebration of an ethnic festival or holiday. For example, one local Italian American club in the larger Phoenix area plans to concentrate its activities on Columbus Day. Or, the club could become known for its fund raising efforts for the March of Dimes. The Scottsdale chapter of the Sons of Italy is trying to become visible through their booth in Scottsdale's Festival of Nations and participation in the March of Dimes fund raising events in the larger Phoenix area.

Currently, Italian Americans are visible in the Scottsdale community mainly through the establishment of numerous Italian restaurants, pizza places, and delicatessens following the influx of post World War II migrants to the Sunbelt. Many establishments are opened by individuals who were in the food business in their original communities (e.g., Scottsdale Daily Progress, 1980a; 1980b). As Paine (1978: 49) noted in an article about ethnic foods in the larger Phoenix area, "Of all the ethnic groups in town, the Italians seem to be the most food-oriented."

While the stores and delicatessens provide a source of structural ethnic behavior for the community, this behavior does not stimulate much interaction among Italian Americans. However, if the community were to coalesce more, the stores and restaurants could serve as informal information and meeting centers, as they do in other ethnic communities.

Friendship Ties

Despite the fact that many of the respondents, 46 percent, have lived in Scottsdale for only six or fewer years many of the respondents report having friends with an Italian background. Forty-three percent of all friends reported are Italian or Italian American. However, only 11 percent of the respondents have Italian American friends in Scottsdale from "back home." Apparently there is not a major chain migration of friends, and the majority of the Italian American friendships are formed in Scottsdale.

When asked with whom they spent their leisure time 41 respondents, 45 percent, indicate their time is spent with other Italian Americans, or with Italian Americans and other ethnic groups. The remaining 49 respondents, or 54 percent, report no one ethnic group predominates in terms of the respondent's leisure time activities.

Ethnic friendships seem to be a salient feature of ethnic inter- action within the Scottsdale Italian American community. While friend- ship ties are not as numerous as those often found in traditional Italian American working class enclaves (e.g., Palisi, 1966a), apparently nonfamilial primary relations with members of one's ethnic group are widespread in a diffuse Sunbelt setting.

Family Ties

The data analyzed for the Scottsdale sample indicate the continuing importance of the family to these Italian American respondents.

Actually almost two thirds (64 percent) of the Scottsdale respondents have relatives in the Phoenix metropolitan area, or Valley of the Sun as it is known locally. Even when adult children living independently are excluded, about half (52 percent) have "family" in the area. The families gather to celebrate holidays, birthdays, and other occasions. Many gather for traditional weekly dinners, or just to enjoy each other's company. As reported in Chapter IV, daily or weekly contact among relatives is the norm for 60 percent of the respondents within relatives locally.

In addition, ninety-one percent of the respondents keep in close contact with their relatives living elsewhere. Most respondents keep in contact with their family members out of the area by mutual visiting patterns and frequent phone calls.

Respondents were asked how important it was to them to feel a sense of emotional closeness to their relatives who were not a part of their immediate household. The majority of the respondents replied it was either "very important" 47 percent, or "important," 35 percent. This question was one that elicited many strong spontaneous comments. Those who saw closeness as important sometimes saw it as a basic element in their lives. One older woman who lived alone in Arizona due to health reasons, but kept in close contact with her family said, "I would die without my family." Several others qualified their response of very important or important by specifying those relatives to whom they felt most close. Still others noted that their feelings of closeness changed as they matured. One third generation woman noted, "One of the reasons I came here was I felt too sheltered by my family, too close . . . I've grown enough to handle that closeness now."

Those respondents who mentioned their mixed feelings about relatives (11 percent) indicated the problems they saw in being overly close. As a third generation respondent put it, "I miss them at times, but then I talk to my sisters and hear the hassle of all the relatives, and I'm glad to be here. But I miss them more than not when you add it all up."

The 7 percent who responded that they did not feel close to their families often mentioned breaking ties with their families before they moved to Arizona. As one man commented, "We were all close knit at one time, but we drifted away gradually."

As the analysis of the IAFA scale in Chapter V demonstrated, the respondents generally have retained many of the traditional Italian attitudes regarding the family. There is a lessening of the impact of these attitudes for the third generation. However, not all of the values presented in the scale are rejected, and on some of the items there is no significant change by generation in adherence to the value. Finally, for one item the third generation shows a significantly higher mean score than does the full second generation. This finding suggests a return by the third generation to the traditional value of placing one's family before work.

However, not only the third generation but also upwardly mobile Italian Americans show a lessening of adherence toward traditional family values. Furthermore, the youngest birth cohort and those raised outside of an Italian American metropolitan area also indicate a decline in adherence to traditional family values.

Apparently the absolute primacy of the Italian family is now being questioned. The extent of the questioning does not appear to be strong enough, however, to precipitate a prediction that the Italian American family is being undermined. Rather, there generally seems to be a shift from a high level of agreement on the items to a more moderate level of agreement. There is also some evidence of a stress on extending some traditional values, such as including boys in customary family protection.

Possibly, family ties among the Italian Americans of Scottsdale will increase as the community matures. Twenty-four percent of the respondents indicate that their relatives are planning to move to Arizona, and consequently even more families may be united locally. If one views the current Scottsdale residents as analogous to immigrants, then perhaps the generation of Italian Americans born and raised in Scottsdale will have more kin contacts, as families grown and stabilize, than the "immigrant" generation of Scottsdale Italian Americans (cf. Palisi, 1966a).

Patterns Exhibited by the Scottsdale

Italian American Community

The Scottsdale Italian American community exhibits varying levels of ethnic identity and conduct. The McKay and Lewins (1978) typology, discussed in Chapter VII, is useful for considering these levels. In the minimal ethnicity cell, Cell I, is found 21 percent of the Scottsdale respondents who have an overall low level of ethnicity. At least some of the respondents in this cell can be considered assimilated, while those who are higher in their overall scores have a low level of Italian American ethnicity that will persist.

Cell II, moderate ethnicity, has 34 percent of the respondents. These moderate ethnics are probably the most representative of the modern, upwardly mobile, suburban ethnics. Their ethnicity is situational to some extent, and represents one facet of their lives. Still it is salient enough a feature of their personal lives to distinguish these respondents from those respondents in the minimal ethnicity cell. It is believed that respondents in this cell represent emergent symbolic ethnicity.

The respondents in Cell III, marginal ethnicity, as noted in Chapter VII do not fit the McKay and Lewins' ideal type for this cell. Based on the t-tests for this cell, respondents in this cell are close to the moderate ethnicity cell. It seems possible that these respondents may also represent symbolic ethnicity represented by Cell II. Twenty-three percent of the respondents are in this cell.

Those in Cell IV, the maximum ethnicity cell, do exhibit a strong ethnicity for the Scottsdale sample. For these respondents even a nonethnic setting like Scottsdale does not appear to diminish their focus on their ethnic identity and behavior as a major emphasis in their selfhood. Approximately 22 percent of the sample fits into the characteristics of this cell.

Overall, respondents in the Scottsdale sample are characterized by a moderate level of ethnicity when moderate and marginal ethnicity cells are combined, which seems justified by the results of the statistical analyses in Chapter VII. (See Table 36 for the combined cells.)

Some exceptions to the concentration in the combined moderate ethnicity cell do emerge, however. The youngest birth cohort, 1946 to 1960, does have its highest concentration in the minimal ethnicity cell. This may indicate that a substantial number of the younger cohort have a fairly low level of ethnicity, although over half of the cohort is found in the moderate and maximum ethnicity cells. The first or immigrant generation is clearly concentrated in the maximum ethnicity cell (50 percent).   Those who are endogamous also have 40 percent of their group in this cell, although an additional 47 percent of their group is in the moderate ethnicity cell.

The pattern of continued ethnic salience in Scottsdale is similar to findings in other suburban settings. Both Sandberg (1977) and Roche (1977) in their respective studies of white ethnic groups in suburban communities conclude that ethnic identity and behavior can be maintained in such settings. Roche notes that attitudinal ethnicity, "that general attitudinal orientation by which an individual perceives himself as part of an ethnic group" (Gabriel, 1973: 12), is similar in both an ethnically homogeneous and ethnically mixed suburb. However, structural ethnic behavior, that usually links the individual to the ethnic group (Roche, 1977: 75), does decline in the mixed suburb (Roche, 1977: 220). Sandberg points out that the original Los Angeles Polish community pioneered new interactive patterns, based on the telephone and auto, that allowed the community to develop as the ethnic group became

Table 36. Percentage of Selected Variables in Cells, Scottsdale Sample

Variables		CELL I Minimal Ethnicity (N=19)	CELL II Moderate (Combined) Ethnicity (N=52)	CELL IV Maximum Ethnicity (N=20)
ENDOGAMOUS				
Yes	(N=30)	13%	47%	40%
No	(N=54)	22%	65%	13%
GENERATION				
First	(N=16)	13%	37%	50%
Full Second	(N=34)	16%	56%	28%
Half Second	(N=17)	35%	59%	6%
Third	(N=24)	21%	71%	8%
BIRTH COHORT				
1914 to 1929	(N=34)	21%	50%	29%
1930 to 1945	(N=32)	13%	75%	12%
1946 to 1960	(N=19)	42%	37%	21%
OCCUPATION				
Blue—Collar	(N=19)	16%	58%	26%
White—Collar	(N=60)	22%	58%	20%
EDUCATION				
High School	(N=34)	23%	56%	21%
College	(N=48)	19%	64%	17%
RAISED IN ITALIAN AMERICAN METROPOLIS				
Yes	(N=37)	19%	65%	16%
No	(N=26)	26%	58%	16%

upwardly mobile. He holds that a new, less intense form of ethnicity emerged in Los Angeles that continues to influence the lives of Polish Americans (1977: 73).

The Italian community that is emerging in Scottsdale gives evidence that Italian American ethnicity exists in this Sunbelt suburb. The evidence of ethnic behavior is not strong, although this has the potential to change as the community matures. While the Scottsdale community does not parallel the totality of an ethnic enclave, it does indicate that the population shift to the Sunbelt has not resulted in the eradication of ethnicity for those Italian Americans who have moved. Nor do the findings indicate that the Italian Americans who moved were already alienated from their ethnicity.

Reevaluation of Straight-Line Assimilation

The straight-line assimilationist perspective takes the view that ethnicity in its truest form is found in the immigrant generation. Some examples serve to illustrate this point. Steinberg (1977: 45) describes ethnicity for Europeans as authentic as long as immigrants continued to migrate to America because the immigrant generation, ". . . personified their [European] ethnicity in the purest form." Crispino (1980: 34) in discussing the operational procedures for the study of Italian Americans of Bridgeport notes that in using the straight-line theory for his research the first generation is regarded as the ". . . statistical baseline" to assess how far other generations have moved from being "Italian." Crispino specifically states that for the study "The abandonment of traditional values and life styles is accepted as evidence that the assimilation process has and is occurring for contemporary Italian Americans" (1980: 34).

These examples point out that the straight-line view supports a fairly rigid perception of ethnicity. The immigrant culture is seen as the Gibraltar of ethnicity. Any evidence of change from this bastion of "pure" culture is taken as evidence of assimilation. In a somewhat mixed metaphor, as generations appear that are successively removed from the immigrant generation, then the "real" ethnic culture erodes in a straight-line fashion.

However, given the historical realities of the period of mass migration, it would be surprising to find that the ethnic culture of the second and later generations had not been modified. It seems as if the most stringent interpretation of the straight-line assimilationist view is in fact setting up a "straw man" so that one could hardly fail to find evidence of assimilation.

The period of mass European migration to America was during a period of rapid social and technological change for the society. America was in the process of changing, as was discussed in Chapter III, from an agricultural to an industrial society. The new immigrant groups were, for the most part, fully exposed to this rapidly changing society since they migrated to the burgeoning industrial centers. It seems inescapable that the immigrant generation, and their children and grandchildren, would be influenced by these rapid social changes. To add to the dynamics of social change was the pressure from the host society for immigrants and their children to assimilate.

Furthermore, while the "pure" immigrant culture was being modified in America even for the immigrant generation, the "pure" European culture was being modified for the brethren of the immigrants who remained in Europe. If one were to take the values, attitudes, and behaviors of the immigrant generation of the Italian culture that were described in Chapter III and examine contemporary Italians for evidence of them, it may be that one would come to the conclusion that modern Italians are not really Italian.

A brief summary of the social changes in Italy since the period of mass emigration should serve to enhance this point. Italy changed from a relatively backward agricultural society with an emergent industrial sector to a society that by the 1970s was dominated by the industrial and service sectors of the economy. Changes in the economic sectors have led to the decline of the peasantry as a working class and large middle class have emerged (Acquaviva and Santuccio, 1976: 34-35, 87).

Profound changes were to affect the Italian family system, although it remains a central institution in modern Italy (e.g., Acquaviva and Santuccio, 1976: 109; Nichols, 1973: 227-240). The feminist movement emerged in Italy in the late 1800s, primarily in Northern Italy (Bortolotti [1963] 1972). However, it was not to have much influence until the Unione Donne Italiane (Union of Italian Women), formed in 1945 as a result of the Partisan fight against the Nazis in World War II, and other Italian feminist groups grew in strength in the late 1960s. By the early 1970s the feminist movement took hold in Southern Italian areas like Sicily (Birnbaum, 1980), and began having an impact on the life styles and values of the Southern Italian women (Stella, 1979).

Changing attitudes toward family planning also affect the Italian family. In 1951 Italian fertility was at a historical minimum nation-wide. While fertility had begun to increase in Northern and Central Italy by 1961, fertility continued to decline in the South. Early in the 1970s divorce became legal, and it withstood a repeal attempt in 1974 (Livi-Bacci, 1977). These changes, declining fertility, divorce, and the feminist movement, are some of the most important changes that have had a direct impact on the traditional Italian family system.

Contemporary Italian journalists and intellectuals write about such issues as the "children of the plentiful Sixties" who were influenced by rock music and student movements. They also write about the influence of the mass media, acceptance of an open market economy, and the emergence of Italian haute cuisine (Chiaberge, 1983; Sartori, 1984; Weaver, 1983; Zincone, 1983).

Considering the preceeding brief sketch of some, though certainly not all, of the changes in Italy one would hardly expect contemporary Italian men and women, particularly middle-class, college educated, urban Italians, to be identical in values, attitudes, and behavior to their peasant grandparents. So it is curious that some social scientists expect modern Italian Americans to be like their grandparents.

It might be more salient to ask how alike are contemporary Italians and Italian Americans in relation to traditional values. This kind of question was asked in relation to Japanese Americans. Iga (1966) studied Japanese, Japanese Americans, and Americans in relation to hypothesized Japanese values. The Japanese Americans were found to fall between the Japanese and Americans, and showed significant differences from Americans on several of the values.

In general the straight-line assimilation perspective seems to lack flexibility in dealing with the possibility of changes in ethnic home-land cultures. Some adherents of the perspective have attempted to modify it while at the same time holding to the view that European ethnics are on the path to irreversible and total assimilation. Herbert Gans is perhaps the most influential of these theorists. Gans (1979) acknowledges that the array of Europeans from the period of mass migra-tion has not vanished into a "melting pot." Instead, Gans notes that the mosaic image used by Greeley (1974) is more relevant today than the melting pot image (1979: 2).

Additionally, Gans does not stress the immigrant culture as being the only representative of ethnic culture. He focuses, as do several others (e.g., Berger, 1960; Kornblum, 1974; Wrong, 1972; Yancey et al., 1976), on ethnicity as a working class phenomenon. According to this argument, ethnicity has persisted in working class neighborhoods because it was similar to the life style of that class. However, the upward mobility of ethnics into the middle-class reduces ethnicity and furthers the straight-line process of assimilation.

Still, Gans feels compelled to deal with the emergent ethnicity of the middle-class and third generation white ethnics that does not fit the notion of working-class ethnicity. He notes that, while third generation ethnics are often cut off from ethnic secondary groups and ethnic culture, this generation persists in seeing itself as ethnic.

The type of ethnicity that the third, and possibly the fourth, generation has adopted is labeled symbolic ethnicity (Gans, 1979: 13). This ethnicity is seen as abstracted from close involvement with functioning ethnic groups. Individuals seek symbols of ethnicity they can identify with from the ethnic culture, although they may have little direct involvement with the ethnic group. Gans is uncertain about the ultimate future of symbolic ethnicity; it may vanish as remaining ethnics are rendered in subcultural melting pots. Or, symbolic ethnicity may persist for several generations because of some of the benefits that enhance ethnicity in contemporary America. Ethnicity has become an acceptable social "anchor" to stabilize people in a highly mobile society, as the Scottsdale Italian Americans illustrate. It also is, currently, a fairly safe way of standing out in a crowd. But despite these benefits, Gans recognizes that ethnic scapegoating is still a salient element in American society. He (1982: 237) speculates that symbolic ethnicity might even by turned into an ethnic resurgence if the scapegoating of European ethnics were to ever increase in intensity.

It has been suggested that Gans implicitly views symbolic ethnicity in a negative manner (Waxman, 1981). It is clear that other scholars from the straight-line perspective view this type of ethnicity in a negative light. For example, Alba (1981) sees symbolic ethnicity as a minimal ethnicity that primarily consists of some identificational symbols chosen by individuals to add ethnic "spice" to their personal identity. Alba holds that the ethnic symbols differ according to individual preferences, so that the basis for ethnic group cohesion disappears. Symbolic ethnicity represents, therefore, ". . . an ethnicity in disarray." (Alba, 1981: 96). Although Stein and Hill (1977) acknow-ledge that white ethnics have attitudes toward food, health, and mental illness that represent a "hidden" dimension of ethnicity they, like Alba, stress the voluntaristic aspect of contemporary ethnic identity. Steinberg (1981) rejects symbolic ethnicity as a viable form of ethnic expression. Stressing the immigrant culture as the essential ethnic culture, he holds that symbolic ethnicity lacks depth. "It [ethnicity in American society today] consists mainly of vestiges of decaying cultures that have been so tailored to middle-class patterns that they have all but lost their distinctive qualities" (Steinberg, 1981: 63).

Based on the above discussion, it seems that the straight-line assimilation perspective may not be flexible enough to provide a useful perspective on American ethnicity in the 1980s, since the emphasis is on the erosion of an immigrant culture. The next section explores the perspective known as modified pluralism as a more useful perspective on contemporary ethnicity.

Reevaluation of Modified Pluralism

The modified pluralism perspective holds that while acculturation and assimilation have taken place in American society for European ethnics, new ethnic cultures and identities also emerged that allowed American ethnic cultures to develop and continue (e.g., Glazer and Moynihan, [1963] 1971; M. Gordon, 1964; Greeley, 1974). Thus attention is focused on the dynamic and flexible elements in ethnicity. To use the modified pluralism approach in research means moving away from a "survivalistic framework" that looks for pure Old World cultural elements (Stern, 1978) toward an orientation that regards ethnicity as dynamic, and at least partly subjective. The perspective allows the researcher to look for evidence of changes in ethnicity, without assuming that the changes are ipso facto a sign of a loss of ethnicity.

Max Weber ([1922] 1965: 306-308) gave an early, but still useful perspective on ethnicity. Weber stressed that ethnic groups were based on subjective belief in a common ancestry, termed abstammungverwandschaft. The belief in a common ancestry can be based on shared physical traits, culture, memories of emigration from a "mother" country or community, or memories of being colonized.

Weber ([1922] 1965) stated that attachment to a community can survive after the actual community is no longer in existence. This idea seems particularly relevant for today's younger ethnics who might not have had direct contact with the immigrant generation.

The ethnogenesis model, a modified pluralism model discussed in Chapter II, offers a useful perspective for interpreting contemporary ethnicity. Instead of primarily focusing on assimilation, it is also possible to look for evidence of retained immigrant traits, and an American ethnic culture. Ethnicity is viewed ". . . not as a residual social force that is slowly and gradually disappearing, . . . [but] a dynamic, flexible social mechanism that can be...transformed and transmuted to meet changing situations" (Greeley, 1974: 301).

There is certainly evidence of cultural assimilation for Italian Americans, with the decline in the Italian language one of the most obvious examples. There is also evidence of the immigrant culture that survives as exemplified by the processions honoring particular saints that are still held in some cities, or the presence of bocce courts.

There is also evidence of an Italian American culture. Howard Blane (1977) found evidence of the emergence of an Italian American drinking pattern among third generation males. Ulin ([1958] 1975) identified changes in the Italian family system among the suburban Italian Americans he studied. Valletta ([1968] 1975) traced the changes in the expression of traditional Italian values throughout three generations. Krause (1978) explored the differences among Italian, Jewish, and Slavic American women. Fandetti and Gelfand (1976, 1978) examined Italian American and other white ethnic groups. They found differences between them in attitudes relating to mental health and care for the elderly. Cohler and Lieberman (1979) studied changing personalities for aging Italian, Irish, and Polish-American men and women. Finally, Zborowski (1969) showed that Italian Americans responded more openly to pain than did Irish American and Anglo Saxon patients.

There is also evidence of change in Italian American ethnic culture. The immigrant generation, for the most part, came to America with strong regional identifications, since Italy was just emerging as a modern nation during the height of immigration to America. Thus, for many immigrants a sense of being Italian, as opposed to a regional identification, was forged in America. Their descendants generally do not think of themselves as Calabrese Americans, Sicilian Americans, or Ligurian Americans, but as Italian Americans. The green, white, and red symbol of Italy may have more meaning now in America than it did a century ago (Greeley, 1977; Rolle, 1972).

Yet, because ethnicity has a flexible and dynamic component this homogenization of disparate regional identities into an Italian American identity may be changing. Within the last ten years in the San Francisco Bay Area seven new Italian regional organizations have been formed. These organizations attract not only the immigrant generation, but also included some members from the second and third generation (Canepa, 1984). Nor has there been a major influx of new immigrants to the San Francisco Bay Area, as has been the case for other Italian enclaves, (Martinelli, 1976), that could account for the growth of these regional organizations.

The ethnogenesis model seems useful for analyzing the Scottsdale sample. The sample shows evidence of assimilation in some areas, such as the decreases by generation and birth cohort for the IAFA scale, the Religious Ethnicity scale, and the Food, Language, and Music scale. There is, however, some retention of values from the immigrant generation in the emphasis on family ties, for example. The building of a bocce court in a Scottsdale park and the growth of Italian food stores also carries implications of holdovers from the immigrant generation. Finally, efforts to celebrate the feast day of St. Joseph indicates an immigrant tradition.

On the whole, the Scottsdale sample does not provide clear evidence of straight-line assimilation even for the scales (the IAFA, Religious Ethnicity, and Food, Language, and Music scales) where some straight-line assimilation can be observed. There is little or no evidence of assimilation trends for other scales such as the Identificational Ethnicity, National Ethnicity, and Cultural Ethnicity scales.

Rather the findings suggest the emergence of a uniquely Italian American culture. Evidence for this emergence comes from the overall Italian American or American Italian identity expressed by most of the respondents, and the feelings of closeness and common background shared with fellow Italian Americans. The support for the Cultural Ethnicity scale indicates a desire to see the cultural heritage continued, while the support for the National Ethnicity scale indicates a moderate feeling of Italian American peoplehood. The circle of Italian American friends that many respondents have cultivated in Scottsdale also indicates a tie to fellow Italian Americans.

Consistent with the emergence position, the Scottsdale sample also shows some evidence of a changing emphasis in terms of ethnic values and attitudes. It is possible that the emphasis on extending the protection of the family to include both boys and girls may be representative of a new Italian American value. Additionally, the emphasis on placing the family before one's job among the younger generation could indicate a reemergence of a traditional value that is once again salient. There is also evidence of the emergence of symbolic ethnicity for the respondents in the moderate and marginal ethnicity cell.

Symbolic ethnicity is basically compatible with the modified pluralism apporach. For Isajiw (1978) ethnicity that is symbolic is not a poor substitute for the "real" ethnicity of the immigrant generation. Instead it is a "new" ethnicity formed by and perpetuated by the sophisticated technological culture that has emerged in North America. In rapidly industrializing societies the demand for labor has served to bring together peoples from a variety of ethnic ancestries. Their holistic ethnic cultures from rural economies could not survive in a componential urban technological society. However, a new form of ethnicity that functioned in a modern technological society has developed. This new form of ethnicity is also componential, ". . . it is a phenomenon of identification with selected ethnic cultural patterns. . . . The `new ethnicity'. . . has adapted itself to the technological culture" (Isajiw, 1978: 36).

The symbolic ethnicity found among the upwardly mobile Italian Americans in the emergent ethnic community of Scottsdale seems to fit Isajiw's notion of a new type of ethnicity. The findings do not indicate an ethnicity in "disarray" as critics have characterized symbolic ethnicity. In general there is an overall agreement by the various subgroups regarding ethnicity, as represented by the lack of significant differences on many of the scales. There is strong support for interpreting the date as showing a persistent identificational, national, and cultural ethnicity. Family values are still important, although there is evidence of a decline in adherence to some of these values. There is also a decline in ethnic structural behavior, some Old World cultural traits, and religious ethnicity. However, overall there is more evidence of continuity than of disagreement.

A flexible approach to understanding the Italian American community of Scottsdale, in light of the findings presented, seems to come the closest to explaining this community. The next section deals with the question of whether or not the emergent Italian American ethnicity is part of a general ethnic revival in the United States.

Reevaluation of the Ethnic Revival Question

Newman (1973: 182) suggests both pluralism and assimilation have the most utility as concepts when they are viewed as dual aspects of the same process of group relationships. There can be simultaneously, both a movement toward assimilation and evidence of pluralism within the same group.

This duality may be the crux of the debate (discussed in Chapters I and II) that centers around the question of whether or not there has been an ethnic revival for white ethnics. As the testing of McKay and Lewins typology for the Scottsdale sample has demonstrated, there may be more than one pattern in relation to ethnicity and assimilation present in a given community. It seems possible that recognizing this can aid in understanding the debate. There is no doubt that a certain percentage of the white ethnics have become assimilated except for some vestigial identification, such as surname. This group is represented for the Scottsdale sample by some of the respondents in the minimal ethnicity cell.

In contrast are the respondents in the maximum ethnicity cell, to whom ethnicity is very important. This type doubtlessly is represented in other ethnic communities by those who are visibly involved in ethnic conflict over issues such as territory and political power. Whether the high level of ethnicity for this group is new and represents a revival, or has been in existence continuously but was not recognized, or is merely a self serving excuse for ethnic conflict cannot be answered by looking at the Scottsdale sample, since this community has not been involved in ethnic conflict.

The respondents in the moderate ethnicity cell seem to represent what may be an increasingly salient form of ethnicity for future generations, symbolic ethnicity. Interestingly, Gans ([1962] 1982) observes that what some labeled an ethnic revival may actually have been the recognition of the emergence of symbolic ethnicity, when it began to emerge as a "numerically significant pattern" (Gans, [1962] 1982: 236).

This seems like a reasonable explanation for some of the confusion over an ethnic revival. Observers may well have been examining at least three different patterns of assimilation and ethnicity, as designated by the minimal, moderate, and maximum cells of the typology studied in Scottsdale.

Conclusion

The complexities of ethnic research have many dimensions if contemporary ethnicity is to be understood. It is useful to take a flexible approach to the study of ethnicity, and to be familiar with the ethnic group and type of community under study.

If the view is taken that a new expression of ethnicity may be emerging, and coexisting with other expressions of ethnicity, then one can take the view that modern ethnicity is not a diminished version of earlier ethnicity but a dynamic, albeit different, form of ethnicity.

More research needs to be done in emergent ethnic communities throughout the Sunbelt, and in suburban areas in the East and Midwest. The time is also ripe for attention to be focused on fourth generation white ethnics and people of mixed ethnic ancestry.

It seems apparent after reviewing the findings from this study that ethnicity is more durable that many observers suspected. Ethnicity has survived despite upward mobility in education, and occupation. It also seems to continue to have some salience for the younger ethnics and those of at least the third generation. Although the exact form it will take cannot be predicted, it seems reasonable to project a future with viable ethnic groups.

REFERENCES

References

Abramson, Harold J.
   1973   Ethnic Diversity in Catholic America. New York: Wiley.
   1975   "The religioethnic factor and the American experience:
             another look at the three-generational hypothesis."
             Ethnicity 2:163-177.

Acquaviva, Sabino and Mario Santuccio
   1976   Social Structure in Italy Crisis of a System. Translated
             by Colin Hamer. Boulder, Colorado: Westview.

Acocella, Nicholas
   1979   "How do we vote?" Attenzione 1 (August):20-21.

Adams, Bert
   1971   "Isolation, function and beyond: American kinship in the
             1960s. Pp. 163-186 in Decade Review of Family Research
             and Action. Minneapolis: National Council of Family
             Relations.

Aiello, Stephen
   1979   "Italian Americans and education." Italian Americana
             2:224-231.

Alba, Richard
   1976   "Social dissimilation among American Catholic national-
             origin groups." American Sociological Review 42:1030-
             1046.
   1981   "The twlight of ethnicity among American Catholics of
             European ancestry." The Annals 454:86-97.

Alba, Richard and Ronald Kessler
   1979   "Patterns of interethnic marriage among American
             Catholics." Social Forces 57:1124-1140.

Alba, Richard and Mitchell Chamlin
   1983   "Ethnic identification among whites." American
             Sociological Review 48:240-247.

Allport, Gordon
   1958   The Nature of Prejudice. New York: Doubleday Anchor
             Books.

Babbie, Earl R.
   1973   Survey Research Methods. Belmont, California: Wadsworth.

Balch, Emily Greene
   1911   Our Slavic Fellow Citizens. New York: Charities.

Banfield, Edward G.
1958   The Moral Basis of a Backward Society. New York: The
            Free Press.

Barth, Frederik (ed.)
1969   Ethnic Groups and Boundaries. Boston: Little, Brown.

Barton, Josef J.
1975   Peasants and Strangers. Italians, Rumanians, and Slovaks
            in an American City, 1890-1950. Cambridge, Massachusetts:
            Harvard University Press.

Barzini, Luigi
1964   The Italians. New York: Atheneum.

Bell, Rudolph M.
1979   Fate and Honor, Family and Village. Demographic and
            Culture Change in Rural Italy Since 1800. Chicago:
            University of Chicago Press.

Berger, Bennett
1960   Working Class Suburbs. Berkeley, California: University
            of California Press.

Berkson, Isaac
1920   Theories of Americanization: A Critical Study, With
            Special Reference to the Jewish Group. New York:
            Columbia University Press.

Birnbaum, Lucia Chiavola
1980   "Earth mothers, godmothers, and radicals: The inheritance
            of Sicilian-American women." Marxist Perspectives 3:128-
            141.

Blalock, Hubert M.
1979   Social Statistics (Revised Edition). New York: McGraw-
            Hill.

Blane, Howard T.
1977   "Acculturation and drinking in an Italian American
            community." Journal of Studies on Alcohol 38:1324-1346.

Borhek, J. T.
1970   "Ethnic group cohesion." American Journal of Sociology,
            76:33-46.

Bortolotti, Franca Pieroni
[1963]   Alle Origini del Movimento Femminile in Italia, 1848-1892.
1972   Turin, Italy: Reprints Einaudi.

Bugelski, B. R.
1971   "Assimilation through intermarriage." Social Forces
            40:148-153.

Burgess, M. Elaine
1978   "The resurgence of ethnicity: Myth or reality?" Ethnic
            and Racial Studies 1:265-285.

Burns, Robert K., Jr.
1963   "The circum-Alpine culture area: A preliminary view."
            Anthropological Quarterly 36:130-155.

Briggs, John W.
1978   An Italian Passage. Immigrants to Three American Cities,
            1890-1930. New Haven: Yale University Press.

Campisi, Paul
1948   "Ethnic family patterns: The Italian family in the United
            States." American Journal of Sociology 53:443-449.

Canepa, Andrew
Forth-   "Review of Dino Cinel, from Italy to San Francisco: The
coming   immigrant experience." Il Caffe'.

Carlson, Robert
1975   Quest for Conformity: Americanization Through Education.
            New York: Wiley.

Chiaberge, Riccardo
1983   "How we are changing; a silent revolution is taking place
            in the attitudes and values of Italians." Notizie dall'
            Italia, July 10:1-3.

Child, Irwin Long
[1943]   Italian or American? The Second Generation in Conflict.
1970   New York: Russell and Russell.

Chiswick, B. R.
1977   "Sons of immigrants: Are they at an earnings
            disadvantage?" American Economic Review Papers and
            Proceedings 67:376-380.

Chapman, Charlotte Gower
1971   Milocca, a Sicilian Village. Cambridge: Schenkman.

Cohen, Abner
1969   Custom and Politics in Urban Africa. Berkeley,
            California: University of California Press.

Cohler, Bertram and Morton Lieberman
1979   "Personality changes across the second half of life:
            Findings from a study of Irish, Italian, and Polish
            American men and women." Pp. 227-245 in Donald Gelfand
            and Alfred Kutzik (eds.) Ethnicity and Aging. New York:
            Springer.

Colburn, David and George Pozzetta (eds.)
1979   America and the New Ethnicity. Port Washington, New York:
            Kennikat.

Cole, Stewart and Mildred Wiese Cole
1954   Minorities and the American Promise. New York: Harper
            and Brothers.

Connor, Walker
1972   "Nation-building or nation-destroying?" World Politics
            24:319-355.

Cordasco, Francesco (ed.)
1975   Studies in Italian American Social History. Totowa, New
            Jersey: Rowman and Littlefield.

Cordasco, Francesco and Eugene Bucchioni (eds.)
1974   The Italians, Social Backgrounds of an American Group.
            Clifton, New Jersey: Augustus M. Kelley.

Cornelisen, Ann
1977   Women of the Shadows. The Wives and Mothers of Southern
            Italy. New York: Vintage.

Covello, Leonard
1967   The Social Background of the Italo-American School Child.
            A study of the Southern Italian Family Mores and Their
            Effect on the School Situation in Italy and America.
            Leiden, The Netherlands: E. J. Brill.

Crispino, James
1980   The Assimilation of Ethnic Groups: The Italian Case. New
            York: Center for Migration Studies.

Cronbach, Lee
1951   "Coefficient Alpha and the internal structure of tests."
            Psychometrika 16:297-331.

Cronin, Constance
1970   The Sting of Change; Sicilians in Sicily and Australia.
            Chicago: The University of Chicago Press.

D'Andrea, Veneita-Marie
  1983   "The social role identity of Italian-American women: An
              analysis and comparison of families and religious
              experience." Pp. 61-68 in Richard Juliani (ed.), The
              Family and Community Life of Italian Americans. New York:
              American Italian Historical Association.

Danesino, Angelo
  1960   "Contrasting personality patterns of high and low achievers
              among college students of Italian and Irish descent.
              Ph.D. dissertation, Western Reserve University.

Dashefsky, Arnold (ed.)
  1976   Ethnic Identity in American Society. Chicago: Rand
              McNally.

DeConde, Alexander
  1971   Half Bitter, Half Sweet. An Excursion Into Italian
              American History. New York: Scribner's.

DeVos, George and Lola Romanucci-Ross
  [1975]   Ethnic Identity, Cultural Continuities and Change (Second
  1982   Edition). Chicago: University of Chicago Press.

Dingley, F. L.
  1890   "Italian emigration." Pp. 211-234 in Special Consular
              Reports, European Emigration. Washington, D.C.: U.S.
              Government Printing Office.

Di Stasi, Lawrence
  1981   Mal Occhio (Evil Eye), The Underside of Vision. San
              Francisco: North Point.

Dore, Grazia
  1974   "Some social and historical aspects of Italian emigration
              to America." Pp. 7-32 in Francesco Cordasco and Eugene
              Bucchioni (eds.), The Italians: Social Backgrounds of an
              American Group. Clifton, New Jersey: Agustus M. Kelley.

Douglass, William
  1973   "Lonely lives under the big sky." Natural History 82:28-
              38.

Drachsler, Julius
  1920   Democracy and Assimilation: The Blending of Immigrant
              Heritages in America. New York: Macmillan.

Driedger, Leo
  1975   "In search of cultural identity factors: A comparison of
              ethnic students." Canadian Review of Sociology and
              Anthropology 12(2):150-162.

Edwards, G. Franklin (ed.)
1968   E. Franklin Frazier on Race Relations. Selected Writings.
            Chicago: The University of Chicago Press.

Eisenstadt, S. N.
1956   From Generation to Generation. Glencoe, Illinois: The
            Free Press.

Emerson, Ralph Waldo
[1845]   Essays and Poems of Emerson. New York: Harcourt Brace.
1921

Enloe, Cynthia
1973   Ethnic Conflict and Political Development. Boston:
            Little, Brown and Company.
1980   Ethnic Soldiers, State Security in Divided Societies.
            Athens, Georgia: The University of Georgia Press.

Ericksen, Julia, William Yancey and Eugene Ericksen
1979   "The division of family roles." Journal of Marriage and
            the Family 41:302–313.

Erikson, Erik H.
1959   "Identity and the life cycle." Pp. 1–171 in George
            Klein (ed.), Psychological Issues. New York:
            International Universities Press.

Etzioni, Amitai
1959   "The ghetto—A re-evaluation." Social Forces March
            37:255–262.

Fairchild, Henry Pratt
1925   Immigration. New York: Macmillan.

Fandetti, Donald and Donald Gelfand
1976   "Care of the aged, attitudes of white ethnic families."
            The Gerontologist 16:544–549.
1978   "Attitudes towards symptoms and services in the ethnic
            family and neighborhood." American Journal of
            Orthopsychiatry 48:477–485.
1983   "Middle-class white ethnics in suburbua: A study of
            Italian-Americans." Pp. 111–125 in William McCready
            (ed.), Culture, Ethnicity, and Identity: Current Issues
            in Research. New York: Academic.

Farber, Bernard
1977   "Social context, kinship mapping, and family norms."
            Journal of Marriage and the Family 39:227–240.
1981   Conceptions of Kinship. New York: Elsevier.

266

Farber, Bernard, Leonard Gordon, and Albert J. Mayer
1979   "Intermarriage and Jewish identity." Ethnic and Racial
            Studies 2:222-230.

Farber, Bernard and Leonard Gordon
1982   "Accounting for Jewish intermarriage: An assessment of
            national and community studies." Contemporary Jewry 6:47-
            75.

Feagin, Joe R.
1978   Racial and Ethnic Relations. Englewood Cliffs, New
            Jersey: Prentice-Hall.
1984   Racial and Ethnic Relations (Second Edition). Englewood
            Cliffs, New Jersey: Prentice-Hall.

Feldstein, Stanley and Lawrence Costello (eds.)
1974   The Ordeal of Assimilation: A Documentary History of the
            White Working Class. Garden City, New Jersey: Doubleday.

Femminella, Frances X.
1983   "The ethnic ideological trends of Italian-Americans." Pp.
            109-120 in Richard Juliani (ed.), The Family and Community
            Life of Italian Americans. New York: American Italian
            Historical Association.

Femminella, Francis X. and Jill Quadagno
1976   "The Italian American family." Pp. 61-87 in C. Mindel and
            R. Habenstein (eds.), Ethnic Families in America. New
            York: Elsevier.

Fischer, Claude S.
1982   To Dwell Among Friends: Personal Networks in Town and
            City. Chicago: University of Chicago Press.

Fishman, Joshua
1983   "Language and ethnicity in bilingual education." Pp. 127-
            137 in William McCready (ed.), Culture, Ethnicity, and
            Identity. New York: Academic.

Foerster, Robert F.
[1919]   The Italian Emigration of Our Times. New York: Russell
1968   and Russell.

Francis, Emerich K.
1947   "The nature of the ethnic group." American Journal of
            Sociology 52:393-400.

Frazier, E. Franklin
1953   "Theoretical structure of sociology and sociological
            research." The British Journal of Sociology 4:293-311.

267

Fucilla, Joseph G.
1949   Our Italian Surnames. Evanston, Illinois: Chandler's
            Inc.

Gabriel, Richard
1973   Ethnic Factors in Urban Politics. New York: M.S.S.
            Information Corporation.

Gallo, Patrick
1974   Ethnic Alienation, the Italian-Americans. Cranbury, New
            Jersey: Fairleigh Dickinson University Press.

Gambino, Richard
1974   Blood of My Blood. New York: Doubleday.
1977   Vendetta. New York: Doubleday.

Gans, Herbert
[1962]   The Urban Villagers. (Expanded edition). New York: The Free
1982   Press.
1979   "Symbolic ethnicity: The future of ethnic groups and
            cultures in America." Ethnic and Racial Studies 2:1-20.

Gardner, Allen (Publication Manager)
1980   Foresight Eighty. Phoenix: Western Savings and Loan.

Geertz, Clifford
1968   "The integrative revolution: primordal sentiments and
            civil politics in the new states." Pp. 105-157 in C.
            Geertz (ed.), Old Societies and New States. New York:
            Free Press.

Gelfand, Donald E. and Donald V. Fandetti
1980   "Suburban and urban white ethnics: Attitudes towards care
            of the aged." The Gerontologist 20:588-594.

Gesualdi, Louis J.
1983   "A documentation of criticisms concerning amoral familism."
            Pp. 129-133 in Richard N. Juliani (ed.), The Family and
            Community Life of Italian Americans. New York: American
            Italian Historical Association.

Giovanni, Maureen J.
1978   "A structural analysis of proverbs in a Sicilian village."
            American Ethnologist 5:322-333.

Glazer, Nathan
1954   "Ethnic groups in America: From national culture to
            ideology." Pp. 161-164 in Morroe Berger, Theodore Abel
            and Charles Page (eds.), Freedom and Control in Modern
            Society. New York: D. Van Nostrand.

Glazer, Nathan and Daniel P. Moynihan
   [1963]   Beyond the Melting Pot: The Negroes, Puerto Ricans,
   1971   Italians, and Irish of New York City. Cambridge: MIT
               Press.
   1979   "Why ethnicity." Pp. 29-44 in David Colburn and George
               Pozzetta (eds.), America and the New Ethnicity. Port
               Washington: New York: Kennikat.

Glazer, Nathan and Daniel Moynihan (eds.)
   1975   Ethnicity: Theory and Experience. Cambridge: Harvard
               University Press.

Gleason, Philip
   1982   "American identity and Americanization." Pp. 57-143 in
               William Peterson, Michael Novak, and Philip Gleason
               (eds.), Concepts of Ethnicity. Cambridge: Harvard
               University Press.

Glick, Paul and Arthur Norton
   1979   "Marrying, divorcing, and living together in the U.S.
               today." Population Bulletin 32:28-37.

Gluckman, Max G.
   1940   "The analysis of a social situation for modern Zululand."
               African Studies 14:1-13.

Goering, John
   1971   "The emergence of ethnic interests: A case of
               serendipity." Social Forces 49:379-384.

Gordon, Leonard
   1973   "Progress in Phoenix: A multicultural analysis." Pp. 3-5
               in W. Noyes (ed.), The Multi-Ethnic Society. Tucson,
               Arizona: The University of Arizona Press.
   1979   "Social issues in post cybernetic age arid area cities."
               Pp. 24-45 in Albert J. Mayer and L. Gordon (eds.), Urban
               Life and the Struggle To Be Human. Dubuque:
               Kendall/Hunt.

Gordon, Leonard and Albert Mayer
   1983   "The effects of U.S. generation on religio-ethnic
               identity: Evidence from the national Jewish population
               survey." Humboldt Journal of Social Relations 10:143-162.

Gordon, Milton
1964   Assimilation in American Life: The Role of Race,
               Religion, and National Origins. New York: Oxford Press.
1978   Human Nature, Class, and Ethnicity. New York: Oxford
               Press.

Gramsci, Antonio
1957   "The southern question." Pp. 28-51 in A. Gramsci (ed.),
               The Modern Prince and Other Writings. New York:
               International Publishers.

Greeley, Andrew
1969   Why Can't They Be Like Us? America's White Ethnic Groups.
               New York: E. P. Dutton.
1974   Ethnicity in the United States. New York: Wiley.
1976   Ethnicity, Denomination, and Inequality. Beverly Hills,
               California: Sage.
1977   The American Catholic. New York: Basic Books.

Handlin, Oscar
1941   Boston's Immigrants, 1780-1865: A Study in Acculturation.
               Cambridge: Harvard University Press.

Hansen, Marcus
1952   "The third generation in America." Commentary 14:492-500.

Harney, Robert and J. Vincenza Scarpaci (eds.)
1981   Little Italies in North America. Toronto: The
               Multicultural History Society of Ontario.

Harris, Chauncey and Edward Ullman
1945   "The nature of cities." The Annals of the American
               Academy of Political and Social Science 245:7-17.

Hawley, Amos
1971   Urban Society. New York: The Ronald Press.

Herberg, Will
1955   Protestant, Catholic, and Jew. Garden City, New York:
               Anchor.

Higham, John
[1955]   Strangers in the Land: Patterns of American Nativism,
1975   1860-1925. New York: Atheneum.

Huber, Rina
1977   From Pasta to Pavlova; a Comparative Study of Italian
               Settlers in Sidney and Griffith. St. Lucia, Queensland:
               University of Queensland Press.

Hull, C. Hadlai and Norman Nie
1981   SPSS Update 7-9, New Procedures and Facilities. New York:
            McGraw-Hill.

Ianni, Francis
1957   "Residential and occupational mobility as indices of the
            acculturation of an ethnic group [The Italo-American
            colony in Norristown, Pennsylvania]." Social Forces
            36:65-72.
1961   "Italo-American teenagers." Annals 338:70-78.
1977   "Familialism in the South of Italy and in the U.S." Pp.
            103-110 in S. M. Tomasi (ed.), Perspectives in Italian
            Immigration and Ethnicity. New York: Center for
            Migration Studies.

Iga, Mamoru
1969   "Changes in value orientation of Japanese Americans." Pp.
            107-108 cited in Harry Kitano (ed.), Japanese Americans,
            the Evolution of a Subculture. Englewood Cliffs, New
            Jersey: Prentice Hall.

Iorizzo, Luciano
1970   "The padrone and immigrant distribution." Pp. 43-76 in S.
            M. Tomasi and M. H. Engel (eds.), The Italian Experience
            in the United States. New York: Center for Migration
            Studies.

Iorizzo, Luciano and Salvatore Mondello
1971   The Italian Americans. New York: Twayne.
1980   The Italian Americans (Revised Edition). Boston: Twayne.

Isajiw, Wsevold
1975   "The process of maintenance of ethnic identity: The
            Canadian context." Pp. 129-139 in Paul Mingus (ed.),
            Sounds Canadian: Languages and Cultures in Multi-Ethnic
            Society. Toronto: Peter Martin Associates.
1978   "Olga in Wonderland: Ethnicity in a technological
            society." Pp. 29-39 in Leo Driedger (ed.), The Canadian
            Ethnic Mosaic, a Quest for Identity. Toronto: McClelland
            and Stewart.

Johnson, Colleen Leahy
1978   "The maternal role in the contemporary Italian American
            family." Pp. 234-244 in Betty D. Caroli, Robert Harney
            and L. Tomasi (eds.), The Italian Immigrant Woman in North
            America. Toronto: The Multicultural History Society of
            Ontario.
1982   "Sibling solidarity: Its origin and functioning in
            Italian-American families." Journal of Marriage and
            Family 44:155-167.

Johnson, G. Wesley, Jr.
1982   Phoenix, Valley of the Sun. Tulsa, Oklahoma: Continental
            Herritage.

Juliani, Richard
1981   "The Italian community of Philadelphia." Pp 85-104 in
            Robert Harney and Vincenza Scarpaci (eds.), Little Italies
            in North America. Toronto: The Multicultural History
            Society of Ontario.

Kallen, Horace
[1915]   Culture and Democracy in the United States. New York:
1924   Boni and Liveright.

Kennedy, Ruby Jo Reeves
1944   "Single or triple melting pot? Intermarriage trends in
            New Haven." American Journal of Sociology 49:331-339.
1952   "Single or triple melting pot? Intermarriage in New
            Haven, 1870-1950." American Journal of Sociology 58:56-
            59.

Kinton, Jack, (ed.)
1977   American Ethnic Revival: Group Pluralism Entering
            America's Third Century. Aurora, Illinois: Social
            Science and Sociological Resources.

Kish, Leslie
1949   "A procedure for objective respondent selection within the
            household." Journal of the American Statistical
            Association 44:380-387.

Klecka, William R.
1981   Discriminant Analysis. Beverly Hills, California: Sage.

Kohn, Melvin L.
1977   Class and Conformity. Chicago: University of Chicago
            Press.

Korbin, Frances and Calvin Goldscheider
1978   The Ethnic Factor in Family Structure and Mobility.
            Cambridge, Massachusetts: Ballinger.

Kornblum, William
1974   Blue Collar Community. Chicago: University of Chicago
            Press.

Kourvetaris, George and Betty Dobratz
1976   "An Empirical test of Gordon's ethclass hypothesis among
            three ethnoreligious groups." Sociology and Social
            Research 361:39-53.

272

Krase, Jerome
1978   "Italian-American female college students: A new
            generation connected to the old." Pp. 246-251 in Betty B.
            Caroli, Robert Harney and Lydio Tomasi (eds.), The Italian
            Immigrant Woman in North America. Toronto: The
            Multicultural History Society of Ontario.

Krause, Corinne Azen
1978   Grandmothers, Mothers, and Daughters: An Oral History
            Study of Ethnicity, Mental Health and Continuity of Three
            Generation of Jewish, Italian and Slavic-American Women.
            New York: The Institute on Pluralism and Group Identity.

Krickus, Richard
1976   Pursuing the American Dream. White Ethnics and the New
            Populism. Bloomington: Indiana University Press.

La Gumina, Savatore J. (ed.)
1973   Wop! A Documentary History of Anti-Italian Discrimination
            in the United States. San Francisco, California:
            Straight Arrow Books.

Lazerwitz, Bernard
1978   "An approach to the components and consequences of Jewish
            identification." Contemporary Jewry 4:3-8.

Lee, Rose Hum
1949   "The decline of Chinatown in the United States." American
            Journal of Sociology 54:422-432.

Lewins, Frank
1975   "Ethnicity as a process: Some considerations of Italian
            Catholics." Australian and New Zealand Journal of
            Sociology 11:15-17.

Lichter, Richard and Linda Lichter
1982   "Italian-American characters in television entertainment."
            Report prepared for the Commission for Social Justice,
            Order of Sons of Italy.

Lieberson, Stanley
1962   "Suburbs and ethnic residential patterns." American
            Journal of Sociology 67:673-681.
1980   A Piece of the Pie—Blacks and White Immigrants Since
            1880. Berkeley: University of California Press.

Linkh, Richard
1975   American Catholicism and European Immigration 1900-1924.
            New York: Center for Migration Studies.

Lipjhart, Arendt
1968   The Politics of Accommodation. Berkeley, California:
            University of California Press.

Livi-Bacci, Massimo
1977   A History of Italian Fertility During the Last Two
            Centuries. Princeton, New Jersey: Princeton University
            Press.

Lopata, Helena Znaniecki
1976   "The Polish American Family." Pp. 15-40 in Charles Mindel
            and Robert Habenstein (eds.), Ethnic Families in America.
            Patterns and Variations. New York: Elsevier.

Lopreato, Joseph
1967   Peasants No More, Social Class and Social Change in an
            Underdeveloped Society. San Francisco: Chandler.
1970   Italian Americans. New York: Random House.

Lubell, Samuel
1952   The Future of American Politics. New York: Harper and
            Brothers.

Lyman, Stanford
1973   The Black American in Sociological Thought. New York:
            Capricorn Books

Lyman, Stanford and William Douglass
1973   "Ethnicity: Strategies of collective and individual
            impression management." Social Research 40:344-365.

Lynch, Richard E.
1978   Winfield Scott. Scottsdale, Arizona: City of Scottsdale
            (Arizona Bicentennial Commemorative Publication).

McKay, James and Frank Lewins
1978   "Ethnicity and the ethnic group: A conceptual analysis
            and reformulation." Ethnic and Racial Studies 1:412-427.

McLemore, S. Dale
1980   Racial and Ethnic Relations in America. Boston: Allyn
            and Bacon.

MacDonald, John S.
1963   "Migration versus non-migration: Regional migration
            differentials in rural Italy." Pp. 491-498 in Proceedings
            of the International Population Conference, 1961. London:
            UNESCO.

MacDonald, John and Leatrice MacDonald
1964   "Chain migration, ethnic neighborhood formation, and
            social networks." Milbank Memorial Fund Quarterly 42:82–
            97.

Mangano, Antonio
[1917]   Sons of Italy: A Social and Religious Study of the
1972   Italians in America. New York: Russell and Russell.

Mahoney, Ralph
1957a   "Our Italian-American heritage." Chapter Two. Arizona
            Days and Ways Magazine 18:25–29.
1957b   "Our Italian-American heritage." Chapter Three. Arizona
            Days and Ways Magazine 25:20–24.

Martin, Walter and Dudley Poston, Jr.
1977   "Differentials in the ability to convert education into
            income: The case of the European ethnics." International
            Migration Review 11:215–231.

Martin, Walter, Dudley Poston, Jr., and Jerry Goodman
1980   "Converting education into income and occupational
            status." Pacific Sociological Review 23:297–313.

Martinelli, Phylis Cancilla
1977   "Italy in Phoenix." Journal of Arizona History 18:319–
            340.
1978   "Italian immigrant women in the Southwest." Pp. 324–340
            in Betty Boyd Caroli, Robert Harney and Lydio Tomasi
            (eds.), The Italian Immigrant Woman in North America.
            Toronto: Multicultural History Society of Toronto.
1981   "Pioneer paesani: The Italians of Globe, Arizona." Paper
            presented at the Annual Conference of the AIHA, St. Paul,
            Minnesota.
1983   "Beneath the surface: Ethnic communities in Phoenix,
            Arizona." Pp. 181–192 in William McCready (Ed.), Culture,
            Ethnicity and Identity, Current Issues in Research. New
            York: Academic.

Masnick, George and Mary Jo Bane
1980   The Nation's Families: 1960–1990. Boston: Aburn House.

Masuda, Mimoru, Gary H. Matsumoto and Gerald Meredith
1970   "Ethnic identity in three generations of Japanese
            Americans." The Journal of Social Psychology 81:199–207.

Mathews, Jay
1982   "Darker side of sunny West probed in suicide study."
            Arizona Republic January 3:AA5.

Miller, Roy A., Jr.
1974   "Are familists amoral: A test of Banfield's amoral
            familism hypothesis in a south Italian villlage."
            American Ethnologist 1:515-537.

Miller, Roy A., Jr. and Marie Gabriella Miller
1978   "The golden chain: A study of the structure, function,
            and paterning of comparatico in a south Italian village."
            American Ethnologist 5:116-136.

Monticelli, Guiseppe L.
1970   "Italian emigration: Basic characteristics and trends
            with special reference to the post-war years." Pp. 3-22
            in S. M. Tomasi and M. H. Engel (eds.), The Italian
            Experience in the United States. New York: Center for
            Migration Studies.

Moquin, Wyane, Charles Van Doren, and Francis Ianni (eds.)
1974   A Documentary History of the Italian Americans. New York:
            Praeger.

Moss, Leonard
1974   "The passing of traditional peasant society in the South."
            Pp. 147-170 in Edward Tannenbaum and Emiliana Noether
            (eds.), Modern Italy: A Topical History Since 1861. New
            York: New York University Press.

Moss, Leonard and Walter H. Thomson
1959   "The south Italian family: Literature and observation."
            Human Organization 18:35-41.

Myrdal, Gunnar
[1944]   An American Dilemma. New York: Harper and Row.
1962

Nelli, Humbert
1983   From Immigrants to Ethnics: The Italian Americans. New
            York: Oxford University Press.

Newman, William
1973   American Pluralism. A Study of Minority Groups and Social
            Theory. New York: Harper and Row.

Nichols, Peter
1973   Italia, Italia. Modern Italy and the Contemporary
            Italians. Boston: Little, Brown.

Nie, Norman C., Hadlai Hull, Jean Jenkins, Karin Steinbrenner and Dale
    Bent
1975   Statistical Package for the Social Sciences (Second
            Edition.) New York: McGraw-Hill.

Nordlinger, Eric
1972   Conflict Regulation in Divided Societies. Cambridge:
            Harvard University Centre for International Affairs.

Novak, Michael
1973   The Rise of the Unmeltable Ethnics: Politics and Culture
            in the Seventies. New York: Macmillan.

O'Brien, Thaddeus
1972   "Attitudes of suburbian Italian Americans toward the Roman
            Catholic Church." Ph.D. dissertation, Department of
            Education, University of Chicago.

Okamura, Jonathan Y.
1981   "Situational Ethnicity." Ethnic and Racial Studies 4:452-
            465.

Paine, Doris
1978   "Cooks tour of the Valley's ethnic markets." Phoenix
            13:48-50.

Palisi, B. J.
1966a   "Ethnic generation and family structure." Journal of
            Marriage and Family 28:49-50.
1966b   "Ethnic patterns of friendship." Phylon 27:217-225.

Parenti, Michael J.
[1962]   Ethnic and Political Attitudes: A Depth Study of Italian
1975   Americans. New York: Arno Press.

Park, Robert
1926   "Our racial frontier on the Pacific." Survey Graphic
            66:57-85.
1949   Race and Culture. New York: The Free Press of Glencoe.

Parsons, Talcott
1966   "Full citizenship for the Negro American? A sociological
            problem." Pp. 709-754 in Talcott Parsons and Kenneth B.
            Clark (eds.), The Negro American. Boston: Houghton
            Mifflin.

Patterson, Orlando
1977   Ethnic Chauvinism: The Reactionary Impulse. New York:
            Stein and Day.

Petersen, William
1982   "Concepts of Ethnicity." Pp. 1-26 in William Petersen,
            Michael Novak and Philip Gleason (eds.), Concepts of
            Ethnicity. Cambridge: The Belknap Press of Harvard
            University Press.

Pleck, Joseph
1979   "Men's family work: Three perspectives and some new
             data." The Family Coordinator 28:481–488.

Polson, Dorothee
1979   "St. Joseph feast has Sicilian flavor." The Arizona
             Republic, March 28:Section FD, p. 1.

Pozzetta, George
1974   "Foreigners in Florida: A study of immigration promotion,
             1865–1910." Florida Historical Quarterly LIII:164–180.

Proacci, Guiliano
1970   History of the Italian People. New York: Harper and Row.

Radin, Paul
[1935]   The Italians of San Francisco: Their adjustment and
1970   acculturation. San Francisco: R. & E Research.

Rieseman, David
1957   "The suburban dislocation." Annals of the American
             Academy of Political and Social Sciences 314:123–147.

Roche, John P.
1977   "Ethnic attitudes and ethnic behavior: Italian Americans
             in two Rhode Island suburban communities." Ph.D.
             dissertation, University of Connecticut

Roff, Margaret Clark
1974   The Politics of Belonging: Political Change in Sabah and
             Sarawak. Oxford: Oxford University Press.

Rolle, Andrew F.
1968   The Immigrant Upraised: Italian Adventurers and Colonists
             in an Expanding America. Norman, Oklahoma: University of
             Oklahoma Press.

Rolle, Andrew F.
1972   The American Italians: Their History and Culture.
             Belmont, California: Wadsworth.

Ross, Edward
[1914]   The Old World in the New. New York: The Century Co.
1965

Ross, Heather and Isabel Sawhill
1975   Time of Transition: The Growth of Families Headed by
             Women. Washington, D.C.: Urban Institute.

Royce, Anya Peterson
1982   Ethnic Identity: Strategies of Diversity. Bloomington,

Royce, Anya Peterson
1982   Ethnic Identity: Strategies of Diversity. Bloomington,
            Indiana: Indiana University Press.

Russo, Nicholas J.
1970   "Three generation of Italians in New York City: Their
            religious acculturation." Pp. 195-211 in Silvano Tomasi
            and Madeline Engel (eds.), The Italian Experience in the
            United States. New York: Center for Migration Studies.

Ryan, Joseph (ed.)
1973   White Ethnics—Life in Working Class America. Englewood
            Cliffs, New Jersey: Prentice Hall, Inc.

Sandberg, Neil C.
[1974]   Ethnic Identity and Assimilation: The Polish-American
1977   Community. Case Study of Metropolitan Los Angeles. New
            York: Praeger Press.

Salomone, A. William
1974   "Statecraft and ideology in the Risorgimento." Pp. 27-52
            in Edward Tannenbaum and Emiliana P. Noether (eds.),
            Modern Italy: A Topical History Since 1861. New York:
            New York University Press.

Sartori, Carlo
1984   "Italian television viewers' habits are undergoing
            sweeping changes." Notizie dall' Italia 12:2-3.

Scanzoni, John
1975   Sex Roles, Life Styles, and Childbearing: Changing
            Patterns in Marriage and the Family. New York: The Free
            Press.

Scarpaci, J. Vincenza
1981   "Observations on an ethnic community: Baltimore's Little
            Italy." Pp. 105-122 in Robert Harney and J. Vincenza
            Scarpaci (eds.), Little Italies in North America.
            Toronto: The Multicultural History Society of Ontario.

Scelsa, Joseph
1983   "Italian-American women: Their families and American
            education, systems in conflict." Pp. 169-172 in Richard
            Juliani (ed.), The Family and Community Life of Italian
            Americans. New York: American Italian Historical
            Association.

Scherini, Rose Doris
1976   "The Italian American community of San Francisco: A
            descriptive study. Ph.D. dissertation, University of
            California, Berkeley.

279

Schiavo, Giovanni
[1934]   The Italians in America Before the Civil War. New York:
1975   Arno

Schnall, David J.
1975   Ethnicity a Suburban Local Politics. New York: Praeger
          Publishers.

Scottsdale Daily Progress
1980a   "Top pizza chef brings talents to Valley." Night Beat,
          May 30:6.
1980b   "Scottsdale restaurant has New York roots." Night Beat,
          July 11:8.

Shils, Edward
1957   "Primordal, personal, sacred, and civil ties." British
          Journal of Sociology 8:130-145.

Smith, Dennis Mack
1959   Italy: A Modern History. Ann Arbor: University of
          Michigan.

Stein, Howard and Robert Hill
1977   The Ethnic Imperative: Examining the New White Ethnic
          Movement. University Park, Pennsylvania: Pennsylvania
          State University Press.

Steinberg, Stephen
1981   The Ethnic Myth: Race, Ethnicity, and Class in America.
          New York: Antheneum Press.

Stella, Simonetta Piccone
1979   Ragazze del Sud. Rome, Italy: Editori Riuniti.

Stern, Stephen
1972   "Ethnic folklore and the folklore of ethnicity." Western
          Folklore 36:7-32.

Tannenbaum, Edward R. and Emiliana P. Noether (eds.)
1974   Modern Italy: A Topical History Since 1861. New York:
          New York University Press.

Thomas, William J. and Florian Znaniecki
[1918]   The Polish Peasant in Europe and America. New York:
1958   Dover.

Thomlinson, Ralph
1969   Urban Structure. New York: Random House.

Thornton, Arland, Duane Alwin, and Donald Camburn
1983   "Sex-role attitudes and attitude changes." American
          Sociological Review, 48:211-227.

Tomasi, Lydio
1972   The Italian-American Family: The Southern Italian
              Family's Process of Adjustment to an Urban America. New
              York: Center for Migration Studies.

Tomasi, Silvano M.
1970   "The ethnic church and the integration of Italian
              immigrants in the United States." Pp. 163-194 in S. M.
              Tomasi and Madeline H. Engel (eds.), The Italian
              Experience in The United States. New York: Center for
              Migration Studies.

Turner, Frederick Jackson
1920   The Frontier in American History. New York: Henry Holt.

Ulin, Richard
[1958]   The Italo-American Student in the American Public School:
1975   A Description and Analysis of Differential Behavior. New
              York: Arno.

U.S. Bureau of the Census
1904   "Special Reports, 313, Occupations." Twelfth Census.
              Washington, D.C.: U.S. Government Printing Office, pp.
              225-227.
1962   General Social and Economic Characteristics, Arizona.
              1960 Census. Washington, D.C.: U.S. Government Printing
              Office.
1973a   Characteristics of the Population, Arizona. 1970 Census.
              Washington, D.C.: U.S. Government Printing Office.
1973b   "1970 Census of the Population: National Origin and
              Language." Vol. 2, Table 10, June, 1973. Washington,
              D.C. U.S. Government Printing Office.
1980a   Current Population Reports, Geographic Mobility: March
              1975 to March 1979. Washington, D.C.: U.S. Government
              Printing Office.
1980b   Census of Population and Housing: Summary Tape File 3A
              (Arizona) [machine readable data file]. Washington, D.C.:
              U.S. Bureau of the Census.
1981a   Census of Population and Housing, Arizona. Final
              Population and Housing Unit Counts, March, 1981.
              Washington, D.C.: U.S. Government Printing Office.
1981b   Social and Labor Force Characteristics of White Persons:
              1980 Phoenix, Arizona SMSA. Washington, D.C.: U.S.
              Government Printing Office.
1982a   General Population Characteristics Part 4, Arizona. 1980
              Census of the Population. Washington, D.C.: U.S.
              Government Printing Office.
1982b   Census of Population and Housing: Summary Characteristics
              for Government Units and Standard Metropolitan Statistical
              Areas, Arizona. September, 1982. Washington, D.C.: U.S.
              Government Printing Office.

1983a   Ancestry of the Population by State: 1980 Census of
Population Supplementary Report. April, 1983.
Washington, D.C.: U.S. Government Printing Office.
1983b   Census Tracts, Phoenix, Arizona SMSA. June, 1983.
Washington, D.C.: U.S. Government Printing Office.

U.S. Commissioner-General of Immigration
1904   Annual Report. Washington, D.C.: U.S. Government
Printing Office.

Uyeki, Eugene S.
1960   "Correlates of ethnic identification." American Journal
of Sociology 65:468–474.

Valletta, Clement
[1968]   A Study of Americanization in Cameta: Italian–American
1975   Identity Through Three Generations. New York: Arno.

van den Berghe, Pierre
1968   "Ethnic membership and cultural change in Guatemala."
Social Forces 46:514–522.
1970   Race and Ethnicity. New York: Basic Books.
1981   The Ethnic Phenomenon. New York: Elsevier.

Vander Zanden, James
1972   American Minority Relations (Third Edition). New York:
The Ronald Press.

Varbero, Richard A.
1975   "The politics of ethnicity: Philadelphia's Italians in
the 1920's." Pp. 164–183 in Francesco Cordesco (eds.),
Studies in Italian American Social History. Essays in
Honor of Leonard Covello. Totowa, New Jersey: Rowman and
Littlefield.

Vecoli, Rudolph J.
1969   "Prelates and peasants, Italian immigrants and the
Catholic church." Journal of Social Science 2:271–268.
1978   "The coming of age of the Italian–Americans: 1945–1974."
Ethnicity 5:119–147.

Velikonja, Joseph
1970   "Italian immigrants in the United States in the sixties.
Pp. 23–40 in M. H. Engel and S. M. Tomasi (eds.), The
Italian Experience in the United States. New York:
Center for Migration Studies.

Wagoner, Jay
1983   Early Arizona: Prehistory to the Civil War. Tucson:
University of Arizona Press.

Warner, W. Lloyd and Leo Srole
   1945   The Social Systems of American Ethnic Groups. New Haven:
                Yale University Press.

Waxman, Chaim
   1981   "The fourth generation grows up: The contemporary
                American Jewish community." Annals 454:70-85.

Weaver, William
   1983   "Report from Italy: What's cooking?" Attenzione 5:12.

Weber, Max
   [1922]   "Ethnic Groups." Pp. 305-309 in Talcott Parsons (ed.),
   1965   Theories of Society, Foundations of Modern Sociological
                Theory. Vol. 1. New York: The Free Press.

Weed, Perry
   1973   The White Ethnic Movement and Ethnic Politics. New York:
                Praeger.

Welkowitz, Joan, Robert Ewen, and Jacob Cohen
   1976   Introductory Statistics for the Behavioral Sciences. New
                York: Academic.

Wenk, Michael, S. M. Tomasi, and Geno Baroni (eds.)
   1972   Pieces of a Dream, the Ethnic Worker's Crisis with
                America. New York: Center for Migration Studies.

Whyte, William F.
   [1943]   Street Corner Society: The Social Structure of an Italian
   1981   Slum. Chicago: University of Chicago Press.

Williams, Phyllis
   [1938]   South Italian Folkways in Europe and America, a Handbook
   1969   for Social Workers, Visiting Nurses, School Teachers, and
                Physicians. New York: Russell and Russell.

Wilson, Maggie
   1983   "Scottsdale." Arizona Highways 59:2-21.

Winch, Robert, Scott Greer and Rae Blumberg
   1967   "Ethnicity and the extended family in an upper middle
                class suburb." American Sociological Review 32: 265-272.

Wirth, Louis
   1928   The Ghetto. Chicago: The University of Chicago Press.

Wrobel, Paul
   1979   Our Way. Family, Parish and Neighborhood in a Polish-
                American Community. Notre Dame, Indiana: University of
                Notre Dame Press.

Wrong, Dennis
1972   "How important is social class." Pp. 297-309 in Irving
           Howe, (ed.), The World of the Blue Collar Worker. New York:
           Quadrangle.
Wytrwal, Joseph
1961   America's Polish Heritage. Detroit: Endurance.

Yancey, William, Eugene Ericksen and Richard Juliani
1976   "Emergent ethnicity: A review and reformulation."
           American Sociological Review, June 41:391-394.

Zangwill, Israel
1909   The Melting Pot. New York: Macmillan.

Zborowski, Mark
1969   People in Pain. San Francisco: Jossey-Bass.

Zincone, Rosaria
1983   "The empty cradles." Notizie dall' Italia 9:1-2.

APPENDIX A

MAPS

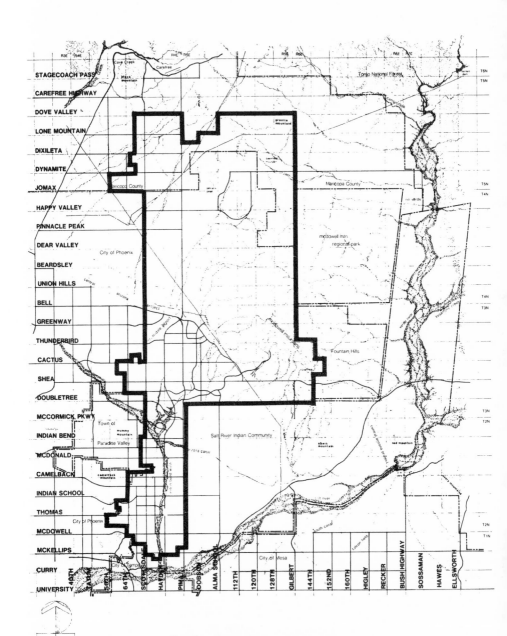

Map 1. Scottsdale, Arizona 1984

Courtesy of the City of Scottsdale, Arizona.

Trentino
Veneto
Lombardy
Piedmont
Venezia-Giulia
Liguria
Tuscany
Emilia-Romagna
Umbria
Marches
Lazio
Abruzzi-Molise
Apulia
Campania
Basilicata
Calabria
Sicily

.... Region of High Emigration, 1861 to 1914

**** Region of Meduim Emigration, 1861 to 1914

(Source, MacDonald, 1963)

Map 2. Regional Areas of Italy

APPENDIX B

LETTER AND SAMPLE INTERVIEWS

ARIZONA STATE
UNIVERSITY_____ TEMPE, ARIZONA 85281

DEPARTMENT OF SOCIOLOGY

By way of introduction, my name is Phylis Cancilla Martinelli and I am doing research on the migration of Italian Americans to Arizona. For the last few years I have been doing historical research on Italians in Arizona.

However, I noticed that most people of Italian ancestry that I met were recent migrants from other states. A brief check of census figures showed that from 1940 to 1970 the Italian American population increased 500% in Arizona. During the same time period the general population in Arizona only grew 250%. Given this kind of rapid growth pattern I believe it is important to know about people of Italian ancestry who are moving to Arizona.

The project I am starting now will explore the identity, origins, and opinions of Italian Americans. Since there is no Italian neighborhood to go to for contacting people, I am contacting households through the mail.

Let me assure you that any information given to me is confidential. None of it will be released in any way that would permit the identification of the individual interviewed or that person's family. Cooperation is, of course, voluntary. However, I hope you will seriously consider taking part in this study.

I will be calling your household in the near future. If you have any questions before then, please call the sociology department at Arizona State University, 965-3546.

Most Sincerely,

Phylis Cancilla Martinelli

* *

Phylis Cancilla Martinelli taught sociology part-time at San Francisco Community College and San Francisco State University. Moving to Arizona in 1975 she continued teaching part-time at Scottsdale and Mesa Community Colleges, and Arizona State University. She began research on the Italian community of Phoenix and won the Leonard Covello Award for her efforts in 1977. Currently she is in the doctoral program at Arizona State University. Her teaching areas now include courses on white ethnic groups and the Italian-American experience.

* *

SAMPLE NUMBER _____

(Interviewer: Record All Additional Comments)

Before we begin, I would like to assure you that all information
you give is completely confidential and that none of it will be
released in any way that would permit identification of you or your
family. Your participation is, of course, voluntary. You may
decline to answer any question.

1. How long have you lived in the Scottsdale area?

   _____ MONTHS   (ONLY IF LESS THAN ONE YEAR)

   _____ YEARS

   (   ) LIVES IN SCOTTSDALE ONLY PART OF THE YEAR
        (For how many years?) _____

2. Where were you brought up?   (What city and state?)
   (RECORD MULTIPLE RESPONSES)

   _____ (CITY OR TOWN AND STATE, IF U.S.)

   _____ (REGION (E.G. SICILY, LIGURIA IF ITALY)

   _____ (COUNTRY IF NOT U.S. OR ITALY)

3. In what year were you born? _____

4. (INTERVIEWER: CHECK ONE)

   (   ) MALE
   (   ) FEMALE

5. Are you single, married, divorced, widowed, separated, or what?

   (   ) SINGLE, NEVER MARRIED (GO ON)
   (   ) MARRIED
   (   ) DIVORCED
   (   ) WIDOWED
   (   ) SEPARATED
   (   ) OTHER _____

6. Have you ever had any children or adopted any children?

   (   ) YES (How many?) _____
   (   ) NO   (GO ON)

ONLY CHILD
---

7. Does your child live at home with you now?   (Even only part time?)

   ( ) YES (GO ON)
   ( ) NO

8. Where does your child live now?   (RECORD CITY AND STATE)

   _____

9. Is the child male or female?

   ( ) MALE   ( ) FEMALE

10. When was (he/she) born?   (What month and year?)

   _____ MONTH _____ YEAR

MORE THAN ONE CHILD
---

11. Are any of your children living with you now?   (Even part time?)

   ( ) YES (How many?) _____
   ( ) NO   (GO ON)

12. Would you tell me the month and year each child was born, and if
    the child is male or female. Let's start with the oldest.

   _____ Mo. _____ Yr.   ( ) MALE   ( ) FEMALE
   (Space was given for additional children)

13. Now I'd like to ask you about your children who are not living at
    home. Would you tell me the month and year each child was born, if
    the child is male or female, and where the child is living now.
    Let's start with the oldest. (RECORD CITY, STATE, IF U.S., OR
    COUNTRY IF NOT U.S.)

   _____ Mo. _____ Yr.   ( ) MALE   ( ) FEMALE

   _____

(Space was given for additional children)

14. Why did you move here? (Read off choices). Because:

   (   )   MY FAMILY DECIDED TO MOVE HERE
   (   )   I VACATIONED HERE
   (   )   JOB OR BUSINESS OPPORTUNITY
   (   )   RELATIVE MOVED HERE FIRST
   (   )   FRIEND MOVED HERE FIRST
   (   )   I WAS HERE (OR HUSBAND WAS) DURING THE SERVICE
   (   )   HEALTH REASONS
   (   )   COLLEGE
   (   )   CLIMATE
   (   )   OTHER _____

15. Where did you live right before you moved here? (What city and state?)

_____

16. How long did you live there? _____ YEARS

_____ MONTHS ONLY IF LESS THAN ONE YEAR

17. Thinking of the number of Italian Americans where you lived before moving here, would you say there were: (INTERVIEWER READ CHOICES)

   (   )   ALL OR MOSTLY ITALIANS
   (   )   SOME ITALIANS AND OTHER GROUPS
   (   )   FEW ITALIANS, THEY WERE A SMALL GROUP
   (   )   ALMOST NO ITALIANS, ONLY INDIVIDUALS, NO GROUP
   (   )   NONE AT ALL

18. In terms of the number of Italian Americans in the part of Scottsdale you live in now, would you say there are (READ OFF CHOICES)

   (   )   ALL OR MOSTLY ITALIANS
   (   )   SOME ITALIANS AND OTHER GROUPS
   (   )   FEW ITALIANS, THEY ARE A SMALL GROUP
   (   )   ALMOST NO ITALIANS, ONLY INDIVIDUALS, NO GROUP
   (   )   NONE AT ALL

19. If you could move back to (INTERVIEWER, GIVE STATE RESPONDENT LIVED IN BEFORE ARIZONA) without causing financial loss, would you move?

   (   )   YES   (   )   NO   (   )   UNSURE

| ABOUT FAMILY |

20. Now I would like to ask you some questions about your family. Where was your father born?

( ) U.S. (RECORD CITY AND STATE)

_____

( ) ITALY (RECORD CITY AND REGION)

_____

( ) COUNTRY (IF NOT U.S. OR ITALY)

_____

21. Where was his father born? (Your grandfather)

( ) U.S. (RECORD CITY AND STATE)

_____

( ) ITALY (RECORD CITY AND REGION)

_____

( ) COUNTRY (IF NOT U.S. OR ITALY)

_____

22. Where was his mother born? (Your grandmother)

( ) U.S. (RECORD CITY AND STATE)

_____

( ) ITALY (RECORD CITY AND REGION)

_____

( ) COUNTRY (IF NOT U.S. OR ITALY)

_____

23. Where were his grandparents born? (Your great-grandparents)

( ) U.S. (RECORD CITY AND STATE)

_____

( ) ITALY (RECORD CITY AND REGION)

_____

( ) COUNTRY (IF NOT U.S. OR ITALY)

_____

24. About when (what year) did the first member of your father's family come to the United States? (What would be your best guess?)

_____

25. What is the highest grade or year your father finish in school?

_____ (GRADE OR YEAR FINISHED IN REGULAR SCHOOL)

_____ (YEAR FINISHED IN COLLEGE)

26. What is, or was, your father's occupation? (What kind of work does (did) he do? (RECORD MULTIPLE RESPONSES)

_____

_____

27. Where was your mother born?

( ) U.S. (RECORD CITY AND STATE)

_____

( ) ITALY (RECORD CITY AND REGION)

_____

( ) COUNTRY (IF NOT U.S. OR ITALY)

_____

28. Where was her father born? (Your grandfather)

( ) U.S. (RECORD CITY AND STATE)

_____

( ) ITALY (RECORD CITY AND REGION)

_____

( ) COUNTRY (IF NOT U.S. OR ITALY)

_____

29. Where was her mother born? (Your grandmother)

( ) U.S. (RECORD CITY AND STATE)

_____

( ) ITALY (RECORD CITY AND REGION)

_____

( ) COUNTRY (IF NOT U.S. OR ITALY)

_____

30. Where were her grandparents born? (Your great-grandparents)

( ) U.S. (RECORD CITY AND STATE)

_____

( ) ITALY (RECORD CITY AND REGION)

_____

( ) COUNTRY (IF NOT U.S. OR ITALY)

_____

31. About when (what year) did the first member of your mother's family
    come to the United States? (What would be your best guess?)

_____

32. What is the highest grade or year your mother finished in school?

_____ (GRADE OR YEAR FINISHED IN REGULAR SCHOOL)

_____ (YEAR FINISHED IN COLLEGE)

33. What is (or was) your mother's occupation?   (What kind of work does or did she do?)   (RECORD MULTIPLE RESPONSES)

_____

_____

34. Now I would like to know a little about your brothers and sisters. Would you tell me the month and year each of your brothers and sisters were born. I would also like to know the nationality of their spouse if they are married? (RECORD NATIONALITY) Let's start with the oldest.

| ( )   RESPONDENT IS AN ONLY CHILD |

NATIONALITY

_____ Mo. ____ Yr.   ( ) Bro/Sis ( )   ( ) Married   _____

(Space Was Provided for Additional Siblings)

35. (ASK ONLY IF MARRIED.) What is the ethnic background (nationality) of your (Husband/Wife)?

( ) ITALIAN
( ) ITALIAN AMERICAN
( ) ITALIAN AMERICAN AND OTHER _____
( ) OTHER _____

| LOCAL RELATIVES |

36. Does your (Husband/Wife) have relatives in Scottsdale or nearby (like Phoenix, Tempe, Mesa, Glendale, etc.)?

( ) YES   ( ) NO

37. Which family member(s) does your (husband/wife) have living here? (RECORD MULTIPLE RESPONSES)

( ) GRANDPARENT(S)   (SPECIFY WHICH ONE, E.G., MOTHER'S FATHER)

_____

( ) MOTHER
( ) FATHER
( ) SISTER(S) (SPECIFY: OLDEST OR PLACE IN SIBLING RANKING)

_____

( ) BROTHER(S) (SPECIFY: E.G., OLDEST OR PLACE IN SIBLING RANKING)

_____

297

37. CONTINUED

    (   ) AUNT(S) (SPECIFY: E.G., MOTHER'S SISTER)

_____

    (   ) UNCLE(S) (SPECIFY: E.G., MOTHER'S BROTHER)

_____

    (   ) NIECE(ES) (SPECIFY RELATIONSHIP, E.G., OLDER SISTER'S DAUGHTER)

_____

    (   ) COUSIN(S) (SPECIFY RELATIONSHIP E.G., MOTHER'S SIDE OR FATHER'S)

_____

38. Do you have any relatives in the Scottsdale area or a nearby area (like Phoenix, Tempe, Mesa, Glendale, etc.)?

    (   ) Yes   (   ) No (GO ON)

39. Which family member(s) (relatives) do you have living here? (RECORD MULTIPLE RESPONSES AND NOTE RELATIONSHIPS)

    (   ) GRANDPARENT (SPECIFY WHICH ONE)

        (   ) MOTHER'S MOTHER
        (   ) MOTHER'S FATHER
        (   ) FATHER'S MOTHER
        (   ) FATHER'S FATHER

    (   ) FATHER

    (   ) MOTHER

    (   ) SISTER(S) (SPECIFY: OLDER, MIDDLE, OR OTHER PLACE IN SIBLING RANK)

    (   ) BROTHER(S) (SPECIFY: OLDER, OR OTHER PLACE IN SIBLING RANK)

    (   ) AUNT(S) (SPECIFY RELATIONSHIP: E.G., MOTHER'S OLDEST SISTER)

    (   ) UNCLE(S) (SPECIFY RELATIONSHIP, E.G., FATHER'S YOUNGEST BROTHER)

    (   ) NIECES(ES) (SPECIFY RELATIONSHIP, E.G., OLDEST SISTER'S DAUGHTER)

39. CONTINUED

( ) NEPHEW(S) (SPECIFY RELATIONSHIP, E.G., YOUNGER BROTHER'S SON)

( ) COUSIN(S) (SPECIFY RELATIONSHIP, E.G., MOTHER'S SIDE/FATHER'S SIDE)

40. Now I would like to know about when (what year) your relatives moved here. Let's start with the first to move. (CONTINUE FOR ALL RELATIVES. IF A FAMILY MOVED TOGETHER, E.G., AUNT, UNCLE, AND CHILDREN, RECORD ONLY ONCE. IF A FAMILY OR INDIVIDUAL MOVED HERE AND THEN LEFT, ALSO NOTE THAT. RERECORD IF THERE WAS A RETURN LATER.)

WHO MOVED _____ YR. MOVED _____ ( ) STAY/LEFT ( )

(SPACE WAS PROVIDED FOR ADDITIONAL RELATIVES)

41. How often do you actually see your relatives who live here? (START WITH ONE FAMILY OR INDIVIDUAL, CONTINUE FOR ALL MENTIONED)

_____

( ) DAILY, EVERY FEW DAYS
( ) WEEKLY
( ) MONTHLY
( ) ONCE OR TWICE A YEAR
( ) NEVER

(SPACE WAS PROVIDED FOR ADDITIONAL RELATIVES.)

42. Do all the members of your family, who do not live in your home, get together?

( ) YES   ( ) NO

43. What are the occasions for which your family gets together? (RECORD MULTIPLE RESPONSES)   (READ CHOICES)

( ) BIRTHDAYS
( ) HOLIDAYS (EASTER, THANKSGIVING, CHRISTMAS
( ) ANNIVERSARY
( ) RELIGIOUS EVENTS (BAPTISM, FIRST COMMUNION, CONFIRMATION)
( ) FAMILY DINNERS (OR SUNDAY DINNERS)
( ) OTHER _____

44. How important to you is a feeling of closeness (emotional) between family members, that is relatives not living together. Would you say it is <u>very important, important, you have mixed feelings, it is not important,</u> or <u>you would prefer not to be close.</u>

    ( ) VERY IMPORTANT
    ( ) IMPORTANT
    ( ) HAVE MIXED FEELINGS
    ( ) NOT IMPORTANT
    ( ) PREFER NOT TO BE CLOSE

RELATIVES NOT IN THE SCOTTSDALE AREA

45. (ASK ONLY IF RESPONDENT HAS BROTHER(S) AND SISTER(S) WHO ARE <u>NOT</u> <u>ALREADY ACCOUNTED</u> FOR IN THE SCOTTSDALE AREA.

    Where (does/do) your (brother/brothers) and/or (sister/sisters) who do not live here, live now? (RECORD CITY AND STATE OR COUNTRY IF NOT U.S.)

    _____

    _____

46. Which of your relatives who do not live here do you have the most contact with, and where do they live? (RECORD CITY AND STATE)

    _____

    _____

47. What kind of contact do you have with them? (<u>READ CHOICES</u>)

    ( ) THEY VISIT HERE
    ( ) I VISIT THEM
    ( ) TELEPHONE
         ( ) WEEKLY
         ( ) MONTHLY
         ( ) OCCASIONALLY
    ( ) LETTERS
         ( ) WEEKLY
         ( ) MONTHLY
         ( ) OCCASIONALLY

48. Do you have any relatives who are thinking of moving here?

    ( ) YES   ( ) NO   ( ) UNSURE

49. Which relatives are thinking of moving here? (E.G., AUNT, COUSIN) (SPECIFY RELATIONSHIP)

_____

_____

FRIENDSHIP

50. Now I want to ask some questions about your friends. Are your best friends mostly from work, your neighborhood, relatives, or elsewhere (ASK WHERE IF ELSEWHERE)

( ) WORK
( ) NEIGHBORHOOD
( ) RELATIVES
( ) ELSEWHERE _____

51. What is the ethnic background (nationality) of your five best friends? (FILL IN)

_____

(Space was left for list of five friends.) _____

52. Would you say that your friends today are different in terms of ethnic background (nationality) than friends you had when you lived in _____(NAME THE STATE RESPONDENT LIVED IN BEFORE MOVING TO ARIZONA)

( ) YES   ( ) NO

53. How are they different, would you say you had more Italian American friends before, had more ethnic friends before, or would you say you have more Italian American friends here or more ethnic friends here?

( ) MORE ITALIAN AMERICAN FRIENDS BEFORE
( ) MORE ETHNIC FRIENDS BEFORE
( ) MORE ITALIAN AMERICAN FRIENDS HERE
( ) MORE ETHNIC FRIENDS HERE
( ) OTHER _____

54. Do you know of any Italian Americans like friends, neighbors, or acquaintances thinking of moving here from where you lived before?

( ) YES   ( ) NO

55. How many would you say are thinking of moving here? (RECORD NUMBER)

_____

56. Thinking of the ethnic background of the people you spend most of your leisure time with, would you say they are mostly <u>Italian,</u> <u>Italian American,</u> <u>Italian Americans</u> <u>and</u> <u>other groups,</u> <u>another</u> <u>ethnic</u> (nationality) <u>group,</u> or a <u>mixed group</u>?

( ) ITALIAN
( ) ITALIAN AMERICAN
( ) ITALIAN AMERICAN AND OTHER _____
( ) ANOTHER GROUP
( ) MIXED

ORGANIZATIONS

57. Do you currently belong to any clubs, lodges, unions, church groups, or other organizations?

( ) YES   ( ) NO

58. Which ones do you belong to?

_____

_____

59. (ASK ONLY IF NOT APPARENT) Are any of these Italian American organizations)

( ) YES   ( ) NO

60. (ASK FOR ITALIAN AMERICAN ORGANIZATIONS) Why did you join (INSERT NAME OF ORGANIZATION) (<u>READ CHOICES</u>)

( ) TO MEET OTHER ITALIAN AMERICANS
( ) TO KEEP IN CONTACT WITH MY CULTURE
( ) BECAUSE FRIENDS BELONG
( ) BECAUSE RELATIVES BELONG
( ) OTHER _____

61. Do any of the organizations which are not Italian American clubs that you belong to have many members who are Italian American?

( ) YES   ( ) NO

62. Which organization(s) has Italian Americans?

_____

_____

63. How often would you say you attend the Italian American club meetings (and/or meetings of the organization(s) with many Italian Americans). (INTERVIEWER ONLY PUT DOWN THE APPROPRIATE LETTER: A = EVERY MEETING, B = MOST MEETINGS, C = FAIR NUMBER, D = FEW, E = NEVER) (RECORD MULTIPLE RESPONSES)

ATTEND   ORGANIZATION

_____   _____

_____   _____

64. Did you belong to any Italian American organizations where you lived before?

( ) YES   ( ) NO

65. Have you ever thought about joining an Italian American organization here in the Scottsdale/Phoenix area?

( ) YES   ( ) NO   ( ) DOESN'T KNOW OF ANY LOCAL CLUBS

ETHNICITY

66. Can or could your parents speak Italian or a dialect?

( ) YES, BOTH PARENTS
( ) NO, BOTH PARENTS
( ) YES, MOTHER
( ) YES, FATHER

67. Do you speak Italian or a dialect? Or can you understand Italian or a dialect? (RECORD MULTIPLE RESPONSES)

( ) YES, ITALIAN
( ) NO, ITALIAN
( ) YES, DIALECT
( ) NO, DIALECT
( ) YES, BOTH
( ) NO, BOTH (GO ON)
( ) UNDERSTAND, BUT CANNOT SPEAK (GO ON)

68. How well do you speak (Italian, dialect, both) (READ CHOICES)

( ) FLUENTLY
( ) MODERATELY
( ) LIMITED (Few Words)
( ) SPOKE AT ONE TIME, HAVE NOT USED RECENTLY

69. Can you read Italian?

( ) YES   ( ) NO

70. How well can you read Italian? (READ CHOICES)

( ) CAN READ NEWSPAPER, FOR EXAMPLE, EASILY
( ) CAN GET THE GENERAL IDEA, BUT NOT READ WORD FOR WORD
( ) CAN ONLY READ A LIMITED AMOUNT OF WORDS

71. (IF RESPONDENT HAS CHILDREN) Can your (child/children) speak Italian or understand Italian?

( ) YES SPEAK
( ) YES UNDERSTAND
( ) NO

72. Have you ever visited Italy? Or do you plan to visit Italy?

( ) YES
( ) NO
( ) PLAN TO VISIT

73. Did you (do you plan to) visit Italy to visit relatives, for business, as a tourist, or for other reasons (RECORD MULTIPLE RESPONSES)

( ) VISIT RELATIVES
( ) BUSINESS
( ) AS A TOURIST
( ) OTHER _____

74. What is your religious preference? (READ CHOICES)

( ) CATHOLIC
( ) PROTESTANT (DENOMINATION) _____
( ) JEWISH
( ) MORMON
( ) NONE
( ) OTHER_____

75. (IF MARRIED) What is your (husband/wife's) religious preference?

( ) CATHOLIC
( ) PROTESTANT (DENOMINATION) _____
( ) JEWISH
( ) MORMON
( ) NONE
( ) OTHER_____

76. (IF HAS RELIGION) Which of the following statements best describes your church (or temple) attendance (READ CHOICES)

( ) DAILY, OR NEARLY EVERY DAY
( ) WEEKLY
( ) MONTHLY

76. CONTINUED

   (   ) EVERY TWO OR THREE MONTHS
   (   ) I GO FOR IMPORTANT HOLIDAYS
   (   ) I BELIEVE, BUT I AM NOT A CHURCH GOER

77. (ONLY IF CATHOLIC, OTHERWISE GO ON). Do you have a devotion to (faith in) a particular saint or Mary?

   (   ) YES   (   ) NO (GO ON)

78. Who are you devoted to (which saint or Mary)? (RECORD RESPONSES)

_____

_____

79. Would you like to have an Italian Catholic Church here in Scottsdale? (That is a church with Italian Catholic religious traditions like processions for saints and other celebrations)

   (   ) YES   (   ) NO

80. Do you (or your husband/wife) shop in an Italian food store?

   (   ) YES   (   ) NO (GO ON)

81. How often would you say you shop at an Italian food store? (READ CHOICES)

   (   ) WEEKLY
   (   ) EVERY COUPLE OF WEEKS (EVERY OTHER MONTH)
   (   ) MONTHLY
   (   ) EVERY COUPLE OF MONTHS (EVERY OTHER MONTH)
   (   ) EVERY SIX MONTHS
   (   ) ONCE A YEAR

82. Is Italian food cooked at home? (READ CHOICES)

   (   ) DAILY, OR MOST OF THE TIME
   (   ) ONCE A WEEK
   (   ) EVERY OTHER WEEK
   (   ) MONTHLY
   (   ) SELDOM
   (   ) NEVER

83. Do you subscribe to any magazine, journals, or newspapers written for Italians or Italian Americans?

   (   ) YES   (   ) NO (GO ON)

84. Which ones do you get?   (RECORD MULTIPLE RESPONSES)

_____   _____

_____   _____

85. Is there any kind of Italian music you enjoy?

( ) YES   ( ) NO (GO ON)

86. What kind of Italian music do you enjoy? (READ CHOICES)

( ) OPERA
( ) CLASSICAL
( ) FOLK MUSIC (LIKE THE TARANTELLA, O SOLE MIO, ETC.)
( ) RELIGIOUS
( ) INDIVIDUAL SINGER OR COMPOSER _____
( ) CURRENT POPULAR ITALIAN MUSIC
( ) OTHER _____

87. How do you think of yourself? (READ CHOICES)

( ) ITALIAN
( ) ITALIAN AMERICAN
( ) AMERICAN ITALIAN
( ) AMERICAN
( ) REGIONAL IDENTITY (LIKE SICILIAN OR GENOVESE)
( ) OTHER _____

88. Do you feel any special sense of closeness to Italian Americans?

( ) YES   ( ) NO (GO ON)

89. How close would you say you feel to Italian Americans? (READ
    CHOICES)

( ) A SLIGHT SENSE OF CLOSENESS
( ) A MODERATE SENSE OF CLOSENESS
( ) A STRONG SENSE OF CLOSENESS
( ) A VERY STRONG SENSE OF CLOSENESS

90. When you meet an Italian American for the first time, how do you
    feel? (READ CHOICES)

( ) I ASSUME WE HAVE SOMETHING IN COMMON
( ) IT IS JUST LIKE MEETING ANYONE ELSE
( ) I TRY TO AVOID TALKING ABOUT MY ITALIAN BACKGROUND
( ) I HAVE ANOTHER FEELING (RECORD RESPONSE) _____

91. How important (did/do) your parents feel (it was/it is) for you to marry an Italian American? (READ CHOICES)

( ) VERY IMPORTANT
( ) IMPORTANT
( ) NOT IMPORTANT
( ) THEY (PREFERRED/PREFER) I WOULD NOT MARY AN ITALIAN AMERICAN
( ) OTHER _____

92. Before you were married (IF SINGLE Now for you) was (is) finding an Italian American (Husband/Wife) something you thought (think) about?

( ) YES   ( ) NO

93. (IF HAS CHILDREN) How important (was it/will it be) to you to see your (child/children) marry an Italian American? (READ CHOICES)

( ) VERY IMPORTANT
( ) IMPORTANT
( ) NOT IMPORTANT
( ) I PREFER THEY WOULD NOT MARY AN ITALIAN AMERICAN

94. (ASK IF CATHOLIC) How important (was it/will it be) to you to see your (child/children) marry a Catholic? (READ CHOICES)

( ) VERY IMPORTANT
( ) IMPORTANT
( ) NOT IMPORTANT
( ) I PREFER THEY WOULD NOT MARRY A CATHOLIC

95. (ASK IF HAS UNMARRIED CHILDREN) Do you think they will actually marry a Catholic?
( ) YES   ( ) NO   ( ) UNSURE

OCCUPATION

96. What do you do for a living? _____

_____

97. Has this always been your like of work?

( ) YES (GO ON)

98. What other kinds of work have you done? (RECORD MULTIPLE RESPONSES)

_____

_____

99. What is the ethnic background of most of the people you work with?

( ) ITALIAN AMERICAN
( ) OTHER _____
( ) MIXED, (NO ONE GROUP PREDOMINATES)
( ) DO NOT KNOW

100. (IF IT APPLIES TO OCCUPATION) What is the ethnic background of your clientele?

( ) ITALIAN AMERICAN
( ) OTHER _____
( ) MIXED, NO ONE GROUP PREDOMINATES
( ) DO NOT KNOW

101. Most of us have a variety of people whose services we use, like a doctor, dentist, insurance agent, mechanic, barber, etc. Are any of the people you use Italian American?

( ) YES   ( ) NO   (GO ON)

102. Which services are performed for you Italian Americans?

_____   _____

_____   _____

STEROTYPES

103. If you thought it would help you socially or professionally would you change your Italian name?

( ) YES   ( ) NO

104. How do you feel about people who have changed their Italian names? (READ CHOICES)

( ) IT'S ALL RIGHT WITH ME
( ) I DON'T LIKE IT
( ) I HAVE NO OPINION

105. Some people think that Italian Americans face prejudice and discrimination. Would you agree with them?

( ) YES   ( ) NO   (GO ON)

106. Do you think there is more prejudice toward Italian Americans here in Arizona, in your old area, or is it about the same?

( ) HERE
( ) OLD AREA
( ) ABOUT THE SAME

107. Do you ever feel proud when you see someone with an Italian name do well, or succeed for example in sports, business or entertainment?

    ( ) YES
    ( ) NO
    ( ) NEVER NOTICE ITALIAN NAMES

108. Does it bother you when Italian names appear in connection with criminal activities or other negative events?

    ( ) YES
    ( ) NO
    ( ) NEVER NOTICE ITALIAN NAMES

109. Are you now a member of any political party, or do you favor any political party?

    ( ) YES   ( ) NO (GO ON)

110. Which party would that be? (DO NOT READ OFF CHOICES)

    ( ) DEMOCRAT
    ( ) REPUBLICAN
    ( ) INDEPENDENT
    ( ) OTHER _____

111. If during an election you had to choose between two people you thought had equal ability, with no real political differences, and one was Italian American and the other was not, would you vote for the Italian American?

    ( ) YES
    ( ) NO
    ( ) OTHER _____

112. Now I would like to read some statements to you to get your reaction to them. As I read each one could you tell me your response according to the following scale.

1	2	3	4	5	6
STRONGLY AGREE	AGREE	MILDLY AGREE	MILDLY DISAGREE	DISAGREE	STRONGLY DISAGREE

_____ 1. Children show respect for their parents by being obedient and not talking back. C*

_____ 2. The family is all you really have because friends can come and go. B

_____ 3. The public schools should teach more about the contributions of Italian people to America. A

112. CONTINUED

1	2	3	4	5	6
STRONGLY AGREE	AGREE	MILDLY AGREE	MILDLY DISAGREE	DISAGREE	STRONGLY DISAGREE

_____ 4. We don't need stronger organizations to express the views of Italian Americans. A

_____ 5. Your job should come first, even if it has come before your family. C

_____ 6. Girls should be supervised more closely than boys, even when they are teenagers. C

_____ 7. An Italian neighborhood is a friendlier place to live. A

_____ 8. One way a parent shows love for a child is by setting strict standards for the child. B

_____ 9. I feel more comfortable with Italian American people. A

_____ 10. If a woman decides to work outside the home she should find a job that will interfere with her family as little as possible. C

_____ 11. We don't need to know the history of the Italian people. A

_____ 12. A person who puts their trust in their family is better off than someone who puts their trust in outsiders. B, F

_____ 13. I would be willing to give money to preserve the Italian tradition. A

_____ 14. When a person does something wrong, it reflects on the whole family. F

_____ 15. Our children should learn Italian dance and music. A

_____ 16. The father is the head of the family, and the mother is the heart of the family. B, D

_____ 17. You can be for your own people first and still be a good American. A

_____ 18. A well kept home is the symbol of a sound family. D

_____ 19. It is too bad that the Italian tradition is not being carried on by many of our young people. A

112. CONTINUED

1	2	3	4	5	6
STRONGLY AGREE	AGREE	MILDLY AGREE	MILDLY DISAGREE	DISAGREE	STRONGLY DISAGREE

_____ 20. Italian American families are warmer and express more feelings than other families. B

_____ 21. If you're in trouble, you cannot count on Italian people to help you. A

_____ 22. A person should be willing to put the needs of their family ahead of their own needs. B

_____ 23. Our children should learn to speak Italian. A

_____ 24. A person has a duty to help their relatives. B

*Letters refer to source for the statement. Many statements are modified from the original source.

A Sandberg (1977)
B C. Johnson (1978)
C Crispino (1980)
D Gambino (1974)
E Bell (1978)

EDUCATION

113. Could you tell me which of the following statements in closest to your parent's attitude about you going on for a college education. (READ CHOICES)

( ) I WAS NOT ENCOURAGED TO GO TO COLLEGE (BUT TOLD TO WORK OR GET MARRIED
( ) GOING TO WORK WAS JUST AS ACCEPTABLE AS GOING TO COLLEGE
( ) I WAS ENCOURAGED TO GO TO COLLEGE
( ) OTHER _____

114. For your education from grammar school through (including) high school, did you go to public, parochial, or private schools?

( ) PUBLIC ELEMENTARY (K - 8TH GRADE)
( ) PUBLIC HIGH SCHOOL
( ) PAROCHIAL ELEMENTARY
( ) PAROCHIAL HIGH SCHOOL
( ) PRIVATE ELEMENTARY
( ) PRIVATE HIGH SCHOOL

115. Are your children going (Did your children go) to public, parochial, or private schools? (Generally, not for each child)

    (   )   PUBLIC ELEMENTARY
    (   )   PUBLIC HIGH SCHOOL
    (   )   PAROCHIAL ELEMENTARY
    (   )   PAROCHIAL HIGH SCHOOL
    (   )   PRIVATE ELEMENTARY
    (   )   PRIVATE HIGH SCHOOL

116. What is the highest grade or year you finished in school?

    _____ (GRADE OR YEAR FINISHED IN REGULAR SCHOOL)

    _____ (YEAR FINISHED IN COLLEGE)

117. Could you estimate the annual combined income of your household (that is income from wages and salaries, rental income, interest, and any other money income received by all the people in the household who are related to you).

    (What would be your best guess?)

    (   )   UNDER $10,000
    (   )   10,000 to 15,000
    (   )   15,000 to 20,000
    (   )   20,000 to 30,000
    (   )   40,000 to 50,000
    (   )   50,000 to 60,000
    (   )   60,000 AND OVER

118. Finally, do you know of anyone who is of Italian heritage, that is Italian on both the mother and father's side, who might not be in the phone book. Such as people with unlisted numbers, women who have married non-Italian men, or people without Italian sounding names. If you do, I would be interested in contacting them for my study.

    (   )   YES   (   )   NO   (   )   UNSURE

119. Could you give me their name, address, and phone number please?

    _____

    _____

Thank you very much for your time and cooperation

SHORT INTERVIEW FOR ITALIAN/MIXED ANCESTRY ONLY

SAMPLE NUMBER _____

   Before we begin, I would like to assure you that all information
   you give is complete confidential and that none of it will be
   released in any way that would permit identification of you or your
   family. Your participation is, of course, voluntary. You may
   decline to answer any question.

1. How long have you lived here in the Scottsdale area?

   _____ MONTHS (ONLY IF LESS THAN ONE YEAR)

   _____ YEARS

   (   ) LIVES IN SCOTTSDALE ONLY PART OF THE YEAR
         (For how many years?) _____

2. Where were you brought up? (What city and state?)
   (RECORD MULTIPLE RESPONSES)

   _____ (CITY OR TOWN AND STATE, IF U.S.)

   _____ (REGION (E.G., SICILY, LIGURIA) IF ITALY)

   _____ (COUNTRY IF NOT U.S. OR ITALY)

3. In what year were you born? _____

4. (INTERVIEWER: CHECK ONE)

   (   ) MALE   (   ) FEMALE

5. Are you single, married, divorced, widowed, separated, or what"

   (   ) SINGLE, NEVER MARRIED (GO ON)
   (   ) MARRIED
   (   ) DIVORCED
   (   ) WIDOWED
   (   ) SEPARATED
   (   ) OTHER _____

6. Have you ever had any children or adopted any children?

   (   ) YES (How many?) _____
   (   ) NO

7. Why did you move here? (INTERVIEWER READ OFF CHOICES). Because

( ) MY FAMILY DECIDED TO MOVE HERE
( ) I VACATIONED HERE
( ) JOB OR BUSINESS OPPORTUNITY
( ) RELATIVE MOVED HERE FIRST
( ) FRIEND MOVED HERE FIRST
( ) I WAS HERE (OR HUSBAND WAS) DURING THE SERVICE
( ) HEALTH REASONS
( ) COLLEGE
( ) CLIMATE
( ) OTHER _____

8. Where did you live right before you moved here? (What city and state?)

_____

9. How long did you live there? _____ YEARS

_____ MONTHS (ONLY IF LESS THAN ONE YEAR)

10. Could you tell me which side of your family is Italian? (Your father or mother's side?) And is that side all Italian or Italian and another nationality?

( ) FATHER'S SIDE ALL ITALIAN
( ) MOTHER'S SIDE ALL ITALIAN
( ) FATHER'S SIDE ITALIAN AND _____
( ) MOTHER'S SIDE ITALIAN AND _____

11. Could you tell me the nationality of the other side of your family. (INTERVIEW RECORD RESPONSE)

_____   _____

_____   _____

12. For the Italian side(s) of your family, could you tell me where in Italy your family originally came from? (INTERVIEWER RECORD CITY AND REGION SUCH AS SICILY, LIGURIA OR NORTH/SOUTH)

_____

_____

13. (ONLY IF MARRIED) What is the nationality (or ethnic background) of your husband/wife?

_____

14. Does your (husband/wife) have any relatives in the Scottsdale/Phoenix area or in nearby areas?

    (   ) YES   (   ) NO

15. Do you have any relatives in the Scottsdale/Phoenix area or in nearby areas?

    (   ) YES   (   ) NO   (GO ON)

16. Which side of the family (father's/mother's, or both) is here?

    (   ) MY PARENTS
    (   ) FATHER'S SIDE
    (   ) MOTHER'S SIDE
    (   ) BOTH SIDES

17. Could you tell me what your religious preference is: (READ CHOICES)

    (   ) CATHOLIC
    (   ) PROTESTANT (DENOMINATION) _____
    (   ) JEWISH
    (   ) MORMON
    (   ) NONE
    (   ) OTHER _____

18. (IF MARRIED) What is your (husband's/wife's) religious preference?

    (   ) CATHOLIC
    (   ) PROTESTANT (DENOMINATION) _____
    (   ) JEWISH
    (   ) MORMON
    (   ) NONE
    (   ) OTHER _____

19. How do you think of yourself? (READ CHOICES - INSERT NAME OF OTHER GROUP)

    (   ) ITALIAN
    (   ) ITALIAN AMERICAN
    (   ) AMERICAN ITALIAN
    (   ) ITALIAN AMERICAN AND _____
    (   ) I FIND MYSELF EMPHASIZING A DIFFERENT PART OF MY IDENTIFY DEPENDING ON WHICH GROUP I'M WITH
    (   ) OTHER _____

20. Do you feel any special sense of closeness to Italian Americans?

    (   ) YES   (   ) NO   (GO ON)

21. How close would you say you feel to Italian Americans?   (READ
    CHOICES)

    (   )   A SLIGHT SENSE OF CLOSENESS
    (   )   A MODERATE SENSE OF CLOSENESS
    (   )   A STRONG SENSE OF CLOSENESS
    (   )   A VERY STRONG SENSE OF CLOSENESS

22. What do you do for a living? _____

    _____

    (INTERVIEWER;   IF STUDENT OR HOUSEWIFE ASK FOR OCCUPATION OF HEAD
    OF HOUSEHOLD)

23. Has this always been your line of work?

    (   )   YES   (   )   NO   (GO ON)

24. What other kinds of work have you done?   (RECORD MULTIPLE RESPONSE)

    _____

    _____

25. Are you now a member of any political party, or do you favor any
    political party?

    (   )   YES   (   )   NO   (GO ON)

26. Which party would that be?   (DO NOT READ OFF CHOICES)

    (   )   DEMOCRAT
    (   )   REPUBLICAN
    (   )   INDEPENDENT
    (   )   OTHER _____

27. For your education from grammar school through (including) high
    school, did you go to public, parochial, or private schools?

    (   )   PUBLIC ELEMENTARY (K-8TH GRADE)
    (   )   PUBLIC HIGH SCHOOL
    (   )   PAROCHIAL ELEMENTARY
    (   )   PAROCHIAL HIGH SCHOOL
    (   )   PRIVATE ELEMENTARY
    (   )   PRIVATE HIGH SCHOOL

28. What is the highest grade or year you finished in school?

    _____   (GRADE OR YEAR FINISHED IN REGULAR SCHOOL)

    _____   (YEAR FINISHED IN COLLEGE)

29. Could you estimate the annual combined income of your household (that is income from wages and salaries, rental income, interest and any other money income received by all the people in the household who are related to you).

(What would be your best guess?)

( ) UNDER $10,000
( ) 10,000 to 15,000
( ) 15,000 to 20,000
( ) 20,000 to 30,000
( ) 30,000 to 40,000
( ) 40,000 to 50,000
( ) 50,000 to 60,000
( ) 60,000 AND OVER

30. Finally, do you know of anyone who is of Italian heritage, that is Italian on both the mother and father's side, who might not be in the phone book? Such as people with unlisted numbers, or people who have moved here within the last year? Or else someone who might not be easily identified as Italian such as a woman who married a non-Italian or someone without an Italian sounding name.

If you do know such a person, I'm interested in contacting them.

( ) YES
( ) NO
( ) UNSURE, WILL HAVE TO CHECK

31. Could you give me their name, phone number, and address please.

_____

_____

Thank you very much for your time and cooperation.

APPENDIX C

STATISTICAL ANALYSIS OF SCALES,

SCOTTSDALE SAMPLE

STATISTICAL ANALYSIS OF SCALES, SCOTTSDALE STUDY

The use of scales to measure ethnicity has grown in popularity as researchers seek ways to quantify complex and at times elusive social phenomena. Since several scales were used in this study, it is possible that other researchers will be interested in using all or parts of these scales in future research. The following analysis is presented in an effort to aid researchers by providing three types of statistical analyses of the scales. The analyses should give some insights which can aid in future modifications of scales used to measure ethnicity.

The three types of statistical analysis used are a Pearson correlation matrix of all the scales, a discriminant analysis, and a reliability analysis. The reasons for using each of these types of analysis are briefly explained. The findings are presented, and finally the implications for future research are discussed.

Pearson Correlation Matrix of All Scales

The Pearson product-moment correlation coefficient (r) is used to assess the "goodness of fit" between two variables in a linear regression relationship. Pearson's r not only indicates the goodness of fit of a linear relationship, but at the same time gives an indication of the strength of that relationship. Pearson's r ranges from -1.0 to +1.0, with an r of zero indicating little or no linear relationship between variables (Nie et al., 1975: 279).

A Pearson correlation matrix was computed for all the scales used in the Scottsdale study to assess to what extent the scales are related to each other. This information should prove useful if a researcher were interested in constructing a comprehensive scale that measured several aspects of ethnicity together.

As Table 37 shows in all but one instance the relationships between the scales are positive, with the one exception being the relationship between the National Ethnicity scale and the Food, Language, and Music scale. The relationship between these scales is a weak negative relationship.

The Italian American Family Attitude Scale (IAFA) has a fairly strong positive relationship between the Cultural Ethnicity scale (r=.48) and the National Ethnicity scale (r=.40). This seems to indicate that is would be feasible to construct a comprehensive scale for Italian Americans similar to Sandberg's ([1974] 1977) Group Cohesiveness Scale for Polish Americans. The IAFA would be substituted for the religious ethnicity component in Sandberg's scale. The IAFA also shows a fairly strong relationship with the Religious Ethnicity scale (r=.34), and with Identificational Ethnicity (r=.30). There is a weaker relationship between the IAFA scale and the Food, Language, and Music Scale (r=.27) and an even weaker relationship between it and the Structural Behavior Ethnicity Scale (SBES) (r=.21).

The Cultural Ethnicity scale shows its strongest relationship, as might be expected, with the National Ethnicity scale (r=.67). This is in fact the highest r found in this correlation matrix. There is also a strong correlation with the Identificational Ethnicity scale (r=.51). Fairly strong relationships are found between the Cultural Ethnicity scale and the SBES (r=.35). The weakest relationship, but still statis-

Table 37. Scottsdale Study, Pearson Correlation Matrix All Scales (r), with Probability (P)

Scales	Italian American Family	Cultural Ethnicity	National Ethnicity	Structural Behavior Ethnicity	Identificational Ethnicity	Religious Ethnicity	Food Language Music
Italian American Family	r=1.00 P=****	r=.48 P=.000c	r=.40 P=.000c	r=.21 P=.03a	r=.30 P=.002b	r=.34 P=.002b	r=.27 P=.005b
Cultural Ethnicity	———	r=1.00 P=****	r=.67 P=.000c	r=.39 P=.000c	r=.51 P=.000c	r=.35 P=.000c	r=.26 P=.007b
National Ethnicity		———	r=1.00 P=****	r=.26 P=.006b	r=.50 P=.000c	r=.24 P=.01a	r=-.05 P=.29
Structural Behavior Ethnicity			———	r=1.00 P=****	r=.37 P=.000c	r=.43 P=.000c	r=.37 P=.000c
Identificational Ethnicity				———	r=1.00 P=****	r=.39 P=.000c	r=.44 P=.000c
Religious Ethnicity					———	r=1.00 P=****	r=.38 P=.000c
Food, Language Music						———	r=1.00 P=****

a Significant at the .01 level or beyond.
b Significant at the .001 level or beyond.
c Significant beyond the .0001 level.

tically significant, is with the Food, Language, and Music scale (r=.26). The relation between the IAFA and the Cultural Ethnicity scale is fairly strong, as was mentioned (r=.48).

The National Ethnicity Scale has strong relationships with the IAFA (r=.40) and the Cultural Ethnicity scales (r=.67). There is a strong relationship with Identificational Ethnicity (r=.50). However, there is a drop in the strength of linear relationships when SBES (r=.25) and Religious Ethnicity (r=.24) are examined. Additionally, there is a weak, negative, and non-significant relationship with the Food, Language, and Music scale (r=-.05).

For SBES the strongest relationship is between SBES and Religious Ethnicity (r=.43). SBES also has a fairly strong relationships with the Food, Langauge, and Music Scale (r=.37) Identificational Ethnicity scale (r=.37), and the Cultural Ethnicity Scale (r=.39). There is a weak, although statistically significant, relationship between the SBES and the National Ethnicity scale (r=.26) and IAFA (r=.21) scale.

The Food, Language, and Music scale generally has weak to moderate relationships. Its relationship with Religious Ethnicity is moderate (r=.38), and a similar relationship is found with the SBES (r=.37) and Identificational Ethnicity scale (r=.39). A weaker, but significant, relationship is found with the IAFA (r=.27) and Cultural Ethnicity (r=.26) scales. A negative and non-significant relationship is found with the National Ethnicity scale (r=-.05). Identificational Ethnicity also has a fairly strong relationship with the Food, Language, and Music scale (r=.39) and Religious Ethnicity (r=.44), and SBES (r=.37). A weaker relationship is exhibited with the IAFA scale (r=.30).

Overall, there was found to be a general correlation among the scales, with the exception of the Food, Language, and Music scale and the National Ethnicity scale.

Discriminant Analysis

In addition to seeing how the scales relate to each other, it is useful to look at the individual scales to see which items give the most discriminating power between those who are high in ethnicity and those who are low in ethnicity, as determined by the frequency distribution of respondents' composite scores on all the ethnic scales for the Scottsdale study. All the analyses were done using stepwise regression. The purpose of using the discriminant analysis is as a guide to researchers who might want to "economize" on the items in a question-naire and cut down on the number of items included by eliminating those without much discriminating power. Generally, an item may not aid in discrimination for two reasons. There was either a general level of agreement with an item or a general level of disagreement with an item, no matter what group a respondent fell into. Caution should be used in any decision to eliminate an item, since a given item may relate to an attitude or behavior that is important to examine even if it did not aid in discriminating between groups in the Scottsdale sample. (See Appendix B for the complete wording of all the items on the seven scales discussed below.)

One fairly strong and statistically significant discriminant func-tion was derived for the Italian American Family Attitude scale. (See Table 38.) Two items contributed the most to the function. These were "Girls should be supervised more closely than boys, even when they are

Table 38. Scottsdale Study, Discriminant Function for Italian American
Family Attitude Scale

Eigen Value	Percent of Variance	Canonical Correlation	Wilks'* Lambda	Chi Square	Degrees of Freedom	Significance
1.5	91	.77	.35	88.3	16	0.0000[a]

Canonical Discriminant Function Coefficients

Item	Coefficient
Woman's Work Not Interfere with Family	.11
Wrong Reflects on the Family	.24
Family is All You Really Have	.28
Better to Put Trust in the Family	.32
Duty to Help Relatives	.34
Family Should Come Before Job	.36
Father Head of Family, Mother is Heart	.44
Girls Should be Supervised More	.49

[a]Significant beyond the .00001 level.
*Wilks' lambda is an inverse measure of residual discrimination. It
is converted into a chi-square test of significance. This is an
indirect test of the statistical significance of the function that (1)
indicates if there are statistically significant differences between the
groups used in discrimination, and (2) indicates if the first function
to be derived is statistically significant (Klecka, 1980: 38-42).

teenagers," (.49) and "The father is the head of the family, and the mother is the heart of the family" (.44).

Four variables were not included in the IAFA discriminant function because they were not useful in discriminating. These items were "A person should be willing to put the needs of their family ahead of their own needs," "One way a parent shows love for a child is be setting strict standards for the child," "Children show respect for their parents by being obedient and not talking back," and "A well kept home is the symbol of a sound family."

One discriminant function was derived for the Cultural Ethnicity scale (see Table 39) that was strong and statistically significant. Only one item was eliminated from the function. It was, "We need to know the history of the Italian people."

For the National Ethnicity scale one strong discriminant function was derived which was statistically significant. (See Table 40.) Two items were not included in this function. They were "we need stronger organizations to express the views of Italian Americans," and "If you're in trouble, you can count on Italian people to help you." The item "I feel more comfortable with Italian American people," contributed the most to the function (.57).

The Structural Behavior Ethnicity scale yielded one discriminant function that is moderately strong and statistically significant. (See Table 41.) Belonging to an Italian American organization (.73) clearly contributed the most to the SBES discriminant function.

There were several items not included in the derived discriminant function. Shopping in an Italian store did not contribute to the func-

Table 39. Scottsdale Study, Discriminant Function for Cultural
Ethnicity Scale

Eigen Value	Percent of Variance	Canonical Correlation	Wilks'* Lambda	Chi Square	Degrees of Freedom	Significance
1.7	97	.79	.32	89.9	10	0.0000[a]

Canonical Discriminant Function Coefficients

Item	Coefficient
Children Should Learn Italian Language	.20
Italian Tradition Not Carried on By Young	.30
Schools Should Teach More About Italians in America	.42
Willing to Give Money to Preserve Italian Tradition	.45
Children Should Learn Italian Dance and Music	.46

[a]Significant beyond the .00001 level.

Table 40. Scottsdale Study, Discriminant Function for National Ethnicity Scale

Eigen Value	Percent of Variance	Canonical Correlation	Wilks'* Lambda	Chi Square	Degrees of Freedom	Significance
1.1	97	.73	.46	67.4	8	0.0000[a]

Canonical Discriminant Function Coefficients

Item	Coefficient
Italian Families Are Warmer Than Other Families	.35
Italian Neighborhoods are Friendlier	.38
Can Be for Own People First, Still be Good American	.41
I Feel More Comfortable With Italian People	.57

[a]Significant beyond the .00001 level.

Table 41. Scottsdale Study, Discriminant Function for Structural
          Behavior Ethnicity Scale

Eigen Value	Percent of Variance	Canonical Correlation	Wilks'* Lambda	Chi Square	Degrees of Freedom	Significance
.73	88	.65	.52	54.5	12	0.0000[a]

Canonical Discriminant Function Coefficients

Item	Coefficient
Italian American Friends (Three Friends)	.13
Uses Services of Italian American (One)	.34
Italian American Friends (Four Friends)	.36
Uses Services of Italian American (Two)	.48
Frequency Shop at Italian Store	.53
Belongs to Italian Club	.73

[a]Significant beyond the .00001 level.

tion, nor did having one to two Italian American friends, or going to a social event sponsored by an Italian American organization, but not belonging to the organization.

The Identificational Ethnicity scale produced a significant function that is fairly strong. (See Table 42.) If a respondent was willing to vote for an Italian American, if other factors were equal, contributed the most to this function (.80). Items that were not included in the function were if a person felt close to fellow Italian Americans, how close the respondent felt to other Italian Americans, and if the respondent had a feeling of a common background with other Italian Americans.

The Food, Language and Music scale produced one discriminant function that was statistically significant, but somewhat weak. Two of the four items contributed to this function. The ability to read Italian and eating Italian food did not contribute to the function. A preference for Italian music (.88) clearly contributed the most to the function. (See Table 43.)

Finally, the Religious Ethnicity scale function was derived. (See Table 44.) Whether a person would like an Italian church locally or not was the most important item in this function (.55). The respondent being of Catholic faith was not included in the function, nor was church attendance included. The function was statistically significant and somewhat weak.

In general, the scales show a fairly good discriminant reliability, that is the ability to distinguish between two or more groups in a Sample. The next section is a discussion of a different type of reliability analysis.

Table 42. Scottsdale Study, Discriminant Function for Identificational
Ethnicity Scale

Eigen Value	Percent of Variance	Canonical Correlation	Wilks'* Lambda	Chi Square	Degrees of Freedom	Significance
.92	86	.69	.45	66.1	10	0.0000[a]

Canonical Discriminant Function Coefficients

Item	Coefficient
Feel Italians Still Face Prejudice	.13
Bothered by Negative News on Italians	.38
Would Change Name	.42
How Respondent Sees Self (e.g., Italian American)	.48
Vote, If Equal, for Italian American	.80

[a]Significant beyond the .00001 level.

Table 43. Scottsdale Study, Discriminant Function for Food, Language, Music Scale

Eigen Value	Percent of Variance	Canonical Correlation	Wilks'* Lambda	Chi Square	Degrees of Freedom	Significance
.30	84	.47	.73	26.7	4	0.0000[a]

Canonical Discriminant Function Coefficients

Item	Coefficient
Speak Italian	.34
Like Italian Music	.89

[a]Significant beyond the .00001 level.

Table 44. Scottsdale Study, Discriminant Function for Religious Ethnicity Scale

Eigen Value	Percent of Variance	Canonical Correlation	Wilks'* Lambda	Chi Square	Degrees of Freedom	Significance
.40	99	.53	.71	26.9	7	0.0001[a]

Canonical Discriminant Function Coefficients

Item	Coefficient
Devotion to a Saint	.42
Have a Catholic Spouse	.49
Like Italian Catholic Church	.55

[a]Significant beyond the .0001 level.

Reliability Analysis for All Scales

The subprogram RELIABILITY used to test the scales from the Scottsdale study gives the researcher a way to evaluate multiple-items scales by computing standard coefficients of reliability (Hull and Nie 1981). A variety of models are available for the RELIABILITY subprogram. The ALPHA model, based on Cronbach's alpha and standardized item alpha (Cronbach, 1951) that yields a conservative estimate of the internal consistency of a scale, was used for testing the Scottsdale scales.

The internal reliability of the scales ranged in general from good to fair with one exception, the Food, Language, and Music scale. The Italian American Family Attitude scale exhibited a good level of reliability (alpha=.74). Good reliability coefficients were also found for the Cultural Ethnicity scale (alpha=.76) and the National Ethnicity scale (alpha=.71). The similar level of reliability together with the fairly strong linear relations for these scales derived from the Pearson correlation matrix indicates that it would be reasonable to combine these three scales into a composite measure of Italian American ethnicity that would be similar to Sandberg's instrument for Polish Americans. Finally, the Structural Behavior Ethnicity scale showed a good level of reliability (alpha=.74).

Two other scales had coefficients that were in the fair range. They were the Identificational Ethnicity (alpha=.68) and Religious Ethnicity (alpha=.67). For future research it is useful to suggest some modifications that might improve the reliability of these two scales. The religious ethnicity component of the Scottsdale study was minimal, as noted in Chapter VI. This was because of the lack of an Italian American church locally. In an area with an Italian American Catholic church several questions could be asked to study the degree to which respondents were involved with traditional Italian religious practices or Italian American religious practices which emerged in America. These added questions could assess a range of religiosity that the Scottsdale scale did not provide due to its brevity.

The Identificational Ethnicity component of ethnicity, particularly in light of the discussion of symbolic ethnicity in Chapter VIII, is likely to be an increasingly important area to study study. A scale on Identificational Ethnicity could be enhanced in two ways. One way would be to divide the scale into three subscales. One subscale could examine the individual self-identity more closely. A second subscale could examine feelings toward fellow ethnics in detail. The third subscale could look at the individual's identification, or lack of identification, with the larger society in more detail. Or one expanded scale could be developed using questions similar to the Scottsdale scale, but adding some transitional questions as the emphasis is moved from the individual to fellow ethnics, and finally to the larger society.

The Food, Language, and Music scale did not show an acceptable reliability coefficient (alpha=.42). This is because the scale was not designed to measure the interrelations among the three areas of food, language, and musical preference. All that was being examined was the retention of three components of the Italian culture. By looking at the discriminant analysis and the reliability analysis for this scale, it seems doubtful that this is the best way to approach measures of acculturation. Rather, as was done in selecting the Italian family to study the Italian American attitudes, it would be best to focus on one aspect of culture to concentrate on in depth. However, if this is not possible, then a more extensive set of questions rather than a short scale might be more useful to study acculturative influences.

Conclusion

In reviewing the findings from the Scottsdale study it seems reasonable to conclude that while some progress has been made toward scales reflecting the ethnicity of Italian Americans, there is still a need for more work.

As has been noted at various points throughout this dissertation the study of ethnicity is compounded by the complexity of the area under study. The study of Italian Americans seems to be moving away from the participant approach observation characteristic of compact city-based neighborhoods towards the use of survey research in spatially more dispersed areas. While it is useful to be able to use statistical analysis to study this ethnic group the studies must be aided by reliable research instruments. The scales used for the Scottsdale study will need modifications for future studies, and it is hoped that researchers will take the time to do this.

It is possible to develop a reliable instrument to study a specific white ethnic group, however, it will take some time to develop a throughly satisfactory one. An instrument that can be used satisfactorily for all ethnic groups is even farther away.

APPENDIX D

FINDINGS ON MIXED ANCESTRY RESPONDENTS

FINDINGS ON MIXED ANCESTRY RESPONDENTS

The characteristics of the 23 mixed ancestry respondents are compared with those of the 91 full ancestry respondents in Tables 45 through Table 49. A few of the more salient aspects of the tables are discussed below. A discussion of the responses to the series of self identity questions follows.

Discussion of the General Characteristics (Table 45)

The mixed ancestry respondents are clearly concentrated in the middle birth cohort, in contrast to the full ancestry group which is more evenly distributed to the three birth cohorts. The median age for the mixed respondents is 41.8, and that of the full ancestry group 49 years old. The range of ages for both groups is similar. The mixed group ranged from 24 to 74 years old, and the full ancestry group ranged from 22 to 76 years of age.

The mixed group has a higher percentage of males. However, the percentage was close to that of the full ancestry group before exogamous females were added.

Although the full ancestry group, as discussed in Chapter IV, is higher in occupational status than recent studies indicate is the norm for the average urban Italian American, it is not as high as the mixed ancestry group. The mixed group is definitely concentrated in the professional and managerial group. Very few of the mixed group were found in the traditional blue-collar occupations.

A similar upward pattern is found in terms of educational mobility. Again, the higher than average level found for the full ancestry group is not as high as that of the mixed ancestry group. While 13 percent of

Table 45. General Characteristics of the Scottsdale Sample Mixed
Ancestry and Full Ancestry Italian American Respondents, by
Percentage*

Variables	Mixed Ancestry (N=23)	Full Ancestry (N=91)
BIRTH COHORT		
Pre 1914	4%	7%
1914-1929	9%	37%
1930-1945	61%	35%
1946-1960	26%	21%
SEX		
Male	74%	62%
Female	26%	38%
OCCUPATION		
Professional, Management	70%	55%
Sales, Clerical, Technical	17%	24%
Craftsmen, Operatives	13%	22%
EDUCATION		
High School	26%	41%
College	74%	59%
RELIGION		
Catholic	78%	76%
Protestant (Specific Denomination)	9%	4%
Christian (No Denomination)	13%	3%
None	0	11%
Other	0	5%

*Percentages may not add to 100 due to rounding.

the full ancestry group had not finished high school none of the mixed ancestry group failed to complete high school. Overall, 41 percent of the full ancestry group had a high school education or less, compared to 26 percent of the mixed ancestry. For the college group 22 percent of the mixed group had one year or more of college, without a four year degree, while 25 percent of the full ancestry group was in this category. Thirty five percent of the mixed ancestry group, compared to 25 percent of the full ancestry group, finished four years of college. The mixed ancestry group also had a higher percentage finishing graduate school, with 17 percent in this category compared to 9 percent of the full ancestry group.

One area in which the two groups were comparable was the percentage who were Catholics. Seventy-eight percent of the mixed group were Roman Catholics as was 76 percent of the full ancestry group.

Overall, in terms of these characteristics the mixed ancestry group is younger, found mainly in the 1930 to 1945 birth cohort, and more upwardly mobile than the full ancestry group. The groups were originally similar on their sex ratio, and still generally adhere to the Catholic faith.

Discussion of Migration Characteristics (Table 46)

Like the Italian American population in general, mixed ancestry respondents originally came from the East Coast. Forty-eight percent of the mixed group was from three states in that general region. However, New York was not as heavily represented as it was for the full ancestry

Table 46. Migration Characteristics of Scottsdale Sample Mixed Ancestry
and Full Ancestry Italian American Respondents, by Percentage

Variables	Mixed Ancestry (N=23)	Full Ancestry (N=91)
RAISED IN ITALIAN AMERICAN METROPOLIS		
Yes	57%	49%*
No	44%	51%
STATE RAISED IN**		
California	17%	3%*
Illinois	30%	20%
Massachusetts	13%	7%
Missouri	4%	1%
New York	22%	40%
Pennsylvania	13%	5%
MOVED PRIOR TO ARIZONA		
Yes	61%	51%
No	39%	49%
CITY SIZE PRIOR TO SCOTTSDALE		
Under 4,999	9%	11%
5,000 to 19,999	9%	13%
20,000 to 49,999	17%	14%
50,000 to 99,999	0	9%
100,000 to 499,999	13%	22%
500,000 to 1,000,000+	52%	31%
LENGTH OF TIME IN ARIZONA		
0 to 6 Years	61%	46%
7 or More Years	39%	54%
REASON FOR MOVE TO ARIZONA		
Job or Business Reasons	52%	20%
Family Moved Here	13%	8%
Climate/Life Style	13%	23%
Health	4%	22%
Relatives Already Here	4%	16%
Other	14%	11%

*Based on American born respondents, N=75.
**Comparison is only between states which contained both groups.

group. Illinois was the only state in the midwest from which the mixed ancestry group came. In contrast the full ancestry group came from several midwestern states.

Interestingly, a slightly higher percentage of mixed ancestry respondents were raised in Italian American metropolises than were those of the full ancestry group. Five respondents were from Chicago, three were from New York City, and one respondent each came from the following cities: Boston, Buffalo, Los Angeles, Saint Louis, and Pittsburgh.

In terms of prior geographic mobility, the mixed group was slightly more mobile than the full ancestry group. Also, the mixed group was more likely to have moved to Scottsdale from a large city with a population of 500,000 to a million or more inhabitants. Another contrast was shown in terms of the reason people moved to Arizona. The mixed ancestry group was most likely (52 %) to have moved for reasons related to their job or business. In contrast, the full ancestry group seemed to move equally for reasons of job (20%), health (22%), or climate (23%).

Discussion of Marital and Family Characteristics (Table 47)

In general the mixed ancestry group was close to the full ancestry group as far as marital status. The slightly higher percentage of single respondents may reflect the somewhat higher percentage of the mixed ancestry group in the youngest birth cohort. The mixed group is somewhat higher in terms of exogamy, and like the full ancestry group shows no clear pattern of out marriage preference for ethnicity. Non-Italian origin spouses were almost equally divided among Slavic, Irish, German, Anglo Saxon, and other European spouses.

Table 47. Scottsdale Sample Marital and Family Characteristics of Mixed
          Ancestry and Full Ancestry Italian Americans, by Percentage

Variables	Mixed Ancestry (N=23)	Full Ancestry (N=91)
MARITAL STATUS		
Married	65%	76%
Single	13%	8%
Divorced	13%	11%
Widowed	9%	5%
ENDOGAMOUS – ETHNICITY		
Yes	22%	36%
No	78%	64%
ENDOGAMOUS – RELIGION		
Yes	67%	65%
No	33%	35%
FAMILY LOCALLY		
Yes	26%	64%
No	74%	36%

In terms of the non-Italian parents of the mixed ancestry respondents, 22 percent had an Irish parent, 22 percent had an Anglo Saxon parent, 13 percent had a German parent, 4 percent had a Slavic parent, and the remaining 39 percent had a parent of mixed European origin.

The mixed group had a somewhat smaller family size than did the full ancestry group. The average number of children for the mixed group was 1.7 compared to 2.8 for the full ancestry group. Since the percentage of single respondents and those in the 1946 to 1960 birth cohort is somewhat higher for the mixed group, their average number of children may in time move somewhat closer to that of the full ancestry group. Or the mixed group may have different values regarding the desired number of children.

The mixed ancestry group was much less likely to have relatives locally than was the full ancestry group. Perhaps this is related to the tendency for the mixed ancestry group to move for job or business reasons, which would not include family considerations.

Discussion of Identification Ethnicity for Mixed Ancestry

One area which has been debated in recent articles is, as was discussed in Chapter IV, the question of ethnic identity for people of mixed ancestry. The respondents were given several choices to which to reply, allowing a range of identities to be expressed. (See Appendix B for the actual choices.) The respondents most typical choice was American Italian, with 35 percent choosing this identity. The next most typical response was a dual identity, with 26 percent of the respondents thinking of themselves as Italian American and another identity, such as

Irish American. Nine percent of the dual identity group noted that their identity depended on which ethnic group they were with, for example, the Italian or Irish side of their family. Thirteen percent of the respondents saw themselves as Italian American, while 17 percent saw themselves as Americans. No one chose the designation Italian. Nine percent of the mixed ancestry group identified with the other ethnic group in their heritage. (See Table 48.)

Overall, 48 percent of the mixed ancestry group had an ethnic identity solely related to their Italian American heritage. Twenty-six percent had an identity that was shared between Italian American and another ethnic group. Twenty-six percent of the respondents did not identify with the Italian American heritage at all.

In contrast, those of full Italian ancestry had a clearer identification with the Italian ethnic group. Fifty-two percent associated themselves with an Italian or Italian American identity. Another 29 pecent had an American Italian identity, so that 81 percent had some degree of identificational ethnicity. Only 18 percent of the group chose an American identification, while 2 percent had another type of identity.

To further assess a sense of identificational ethnicity, respondents were asked if they felt close to Italian Americans, and if they did feel close, how strong was that feeling of closeness. Twenty-two percent of the respondents did not feel a sense of closeness to those of Italian American ancestry. (See Table 49). The remaining 78 percent did feel a sense of closeness. However, the majority of the respondents (56%) who felt a sense of closeness indicated that it was a slight sense of

Table 48. Identificational Ethnicity for Scottsdale Sample Mixed
Ancestry and Full Ancestry Italian Americans by Percentage

Responses	Mixed Ancestry (N=23)	Full Ancestry (N=91)
ITALIAN	0	18%
ITALIAN AMERICAN	13%	34%
AMERICAN ITALIAN	35%	29%
AMERICAN	17%	18%
ITALIAN AMERICAN and OTHER	26%	0
OTHER ETHNIC	9%	0
OTHER	0	2%

Table 49. Feelings Toward Italian Americans, Scottsdale Study Mixed
Ancestry and Full Ancestry Italian Americans by Percentage

Responses	Mixed Ancestry (N=23)	Full Ancestry (N=91)
HAVE FEELING OF CLOSENESS		
Yes	78%	79%
No	22%	21%
STRENGTH OF FEELING OF CLOSENESS		
Very Strong	0	7%
Strong	11%	31%
Moderate	33%	41%
Slight	56%	21%

11 percent felt a strong sense of closeness.

A similar percentage of full ancestry respondents (79%) felt a sense of closeness to other Italian Americans, but the feeling was generally stronger. Overall, the mixed ancestry group exhibited an identificational ethnicity which was less pronounced than the sense of identity for those of full ancestry. There was, however, some evidence of identificational ethnicity.

These findings from the Scottsdale study indicate there is some sense of ethnicity that is salient for those of mixed ancestry. There is a need for research concentrated exclusively on groups of mixed ancestry to allow the ethnicity of this growing segment of white ethnics to be more fully understood.

APPENDIX E

ADDITIONAL DATA FOR VARIABLES

GENERATION AND BIRTH COHORT

Table 50. Italian American Family Attitude Scale, Additional t-test
Data for Selected Variables, Scottsdale Study

Variables		X	s	T Value	Degrees of Freedom
GENERATION					
First	(N=16)	54.0	8.0	-.48	46
Full Second	(N=32)	55.2	8.4		
First	(N=16)	54.0	8.0	1.16	31
Half Second	(N=17)	49.5	7.8		
First	(N=16)	54.0	8.0		
Third	(N=24)	48.5	8.2	2.07	38
Full Second	(N=32)	55.2	8.4		
Half Second	(N=17)	49.5	7.8	2.3	47
Full Second	(N=32)	55.2	8.4	3.0	54
Third	(N=24)	48.5	8.2		
Half Second	(N=17)	49.5	7.8		
Third	(N=24)	48.5	8.2	.39	39
BIRTH COHORT					
1914-1929	(N=34)	52.1	8.2	-.37	64
1930-1945	(N=32)	52.9	7.7		
1914-1929	(N=34)	52.1	8.2	1.84	51
1946-1960	(N=19)	47.3	10.7		
1930-1945	(N=32)	52.9	7.7	2.15	49
1946-1960	(N=19)	47.3	10.7		

Table 51. Cultural Ethnicity Scale, Additional t-test Data for Selected Variables, Scottsdale Study

Variables		X	s	T Value	Degrees of Freedom
GENERATION					
First	(N=16)	25.4	6.4	-.50	46
Full Second	(N=32)	26.2	4.7		
First	(N=16)	25.4	6.4	.98	31
Half Second	(N=17)	23.2	6.4		
First	(N=16)	25.4	6.4	.80	38
Third	(N=24)	23.9	5.1		
Full Second	(N=32)	26.2	4.7	1.87	47
Half Second	(N=17)	23.2	6.4		
Full Second	(N=32)	26.2	4.7	1.72	54
Third	(N=24)	23.9	5.1		
Half Second	(N=17)	23.2	6.4	-.40	39
Third	(N=24)	23.9	5.1		
BIRTH COHORT					
1914-1929	(N=34)	24.6	5.03	.03	64
1930-1945	(N=32)	24.6	5.08		
1914-1929	(N=34)	24.3	5.03	.19	51
1946-1960	(N=19)	24.3	7.5		
1930-1945	(N=32)	24.6	5.08	.21	49
1946-1960	(N=19)	24.3	7.5		

Table 52. National Ethnicity Scale, Additional t-test Data for Selected
Variables, Scottsdale Study

Variables		X	s	T Value	Degrees of Freedom
GENERATION					
First	(N=16)	20.3	8.6	-1.18	46
Full Second	(N=32)	22.8	6.0		
First	(N=16)	20.3	8.6	-.17	31
Half Second	(N=17)	20.7	6.3		
First	(N=16)	20.3	8.6	-.98	38
Third	(N=24)	22.4	4.9		
Full Second	(N=32)	22.8	6.0	1.12	47
Half Second	(N=17)	20.7	6.3		
Full Second	(N=32)	22.8	6.0	.28	54
Third	(N=24)	22.4	4.9		
Half Second	(N=17)	20.7	6.3	-.93	39
Third	(N=24)	22.4	4.9		
BIRTH COHORT					
1914-1929	(N=34)	20.8	7.3	-1.15	64
1930-1945	(N=32)	22.7	5.8		
1914-1929	(N=34)	20.8	7.3	-.26	51
1946-1960	(N=19)	21.3	5.1		
1930-1945	(N=32)	22.7	5.8	.87	49
1946-1960	(N=19)	21.3	5.1		

Table 53. Structural Behavior Ethnicity Scale, Additional t-test Data
         for Selected Variables, Scottsdale Study

Variables		X	s	T Value	Degrees of Freedom
GENERATION					
First	(N=16)	11.4	5.7	.89	46
Full Second	(N=32)	9.8	5.9		
First	(N=16)	11.4	5.7	2.81	31
Half Second	(N=17)	7.2	4.8		
First	(N=16)	11.4	5.7	2.00	38
Third	(N=24)	7.4	6.4		
Full Second	(N=32)	9.8	5.9		
Half Second	(N=17)	6.2	4.8	2.15	47
Full Second	(N=32)	9.8	5.9	1.44	54
Third	(N=24)	7.4	6.4		
Half Second	(N=17)	6.2	4.8		
Third	(N=24)	7.4	6.4	-.66	39
BIRTH COHORT					
1914-1929	(N=34)	8.7	5.6	.60	64
1930-1945	(N=32)	7.9	5.4		
1914-1929	(N=34)	8.7	5.6	-.11	51
1946-1960	(N=19)	9.0	7.4		
1930-1945	(N=32)	7.9	5.4	-.57	49
1946-1960	(N=19)	9.0	7.4		

Table 54. Food, Language, and Music Scale, Additional t-test Data for Selected Variables, Scottsdale Sample

Variables		X	s	T Value	Degrees of Freedom
GENERATION					
First	(N=16)	3.5	.63	1.98	46
Full Second	(N=32)	2.6	1.6		
First	(N=16)	3.5	.63	5.0	31
Half Second	(N=17)	1.8	1.1		
First	(N=16)	3.5	.63	8.3	38
Third	(N=24)	1.3	.87		
Full Second	(N=32)	2.6	1.6	1.85	47
Half Second	(N=17)	1.8	1.1		
Full Second	(N=32)	2.6	1.6	3.47	54
Third	(N=24)	1.3	.87		
Half Second	(N=17)	1.8	1.1	1.40	39
Third	(N=24)	1.3	.87		
BIRTH COHORT					
1914–1929	(N=34)	2.4	1.1	2.14	64
1930–1945	(N=32)	1.8	1.2		
1914–1929	(N=34)	2.4	1.1	1.29	51
1946–1960	(N=19)	2.0	1.3		
1930–1945	(N=32)	1.8	1.2	2.14	49
1946–1960	(N=19)	2.0	1.3		

Table 55. Identificational Ethnicity Scale, Additional t-test Data for
Selected Variables, Scottsdale Study

Variables		X	s	T Value	Degrees of Freedom
GENERATION					
First	(N=16)	7.9	1.9	.32	46
Full Second	(N=32)	7.7	2.3		
First	(N=16)	7.9	1.9	1.69	31
Half Second	(N=17)	6.2	3.4		
First	(N=16)	7.9	1.9	1.22	38
Third	(N=24)	7.1	1.9		
Full Second	(N=32)	7.7	2.3	1.71	47
Half Second	(N=17)	6.2	3.4		
Full Second	(N=32)	7.7	2.3	.92	54
Third	(N=24)	7.1	1.9		
Half Second	(N=17)	6.2	3.4	−1.04	39
Third	(N=24)	7.1	1.9		
BIRTH COHORT					
1914–1929	(N=34)	7.1	2.7	−.05	64
1930–1945	(N=32)	7.4	2.0		
1914–1929	(N=34)	7.1	2.7	.63	51
1946–1960	(N=19)	6.6	3.0		
1930–1945	(N=32)	7.4	2.0	1.15	49
1946–1960	(N=19)	6.6	3.0		

Table 56.   Religious Ethnicity Scale, Additional t-test Data for
            Selected Variables, Scottsdale Study

Variables		X	s	T Value	Degrees of Freedom
GENERATION					
First	(N=16)	2.7	1.5	-1.04	46
Full Second	(N=32)	3.2	1.4		
First	(N=16)	2.7	1.5	1.52	31
Half Second	(N=17)	1.8	1.6		
First	(N=16)	2.7	1.5	1.26	38
Third	(N=24)	2.0	1.8		
Full Second	(N=32)	3.2	1.4	2.84	47
Half Second	(N=17)	1.8	1.6		
Full Second	(N=32)	3.2	1.4	2.63	54
Third	(N=24)	2.0	1.8		
Half Second	(N=17)	1.8	1.6	-.28	39
Third	(N=24)	2.0	1.8		
BIRTH COHORT					
1914-1929	(N=34)	2.9	1.6	.81	64
1930-1945	(N=32)	2.5	1.8		
1914-1929	(N=34)	2.9	1.6	3.22	51
1946-1960	(N=19)	1.4	1.5		
1930-1945	(N=32)	2.5	1.8	2.29	49
1946-1960	(N=19)	1.4	1.5		

APPENDIX F

POINT BISERIAL CORRELATION

COEFFICIENTS

FINDINGS ON THE POINT BISERIAL CORRELATION COEFFICIENT

In the preceding analysis the t-test was used to indicate statistically significant differences between groups in the Scottsdale sample. The t-test shows that a significant difference exists, but it does not give information about the strength of a given relationship. So, it is also interesting to look at the proportion of variance in a continuous variable, in this case the different scales, that can be explained by being in one group or another. This can be done by computating the point biserial correlation cofficient, r_{pb} (Welkowitz, et. al., 1976). The squared r_{pb}^2 gives information analogus to r^2 which when expressed as a percentage shows what percent of the variance in scale scores can be explained by belonging to one group or another.

For example on Table 57, p. 355, for the IAFA scale the percent of the variance explained between any of the groups is rather small. Belonging to the first or third generation only accounts for about 10 percent of the differences among people on the IAFA; in contrast on the Food Language and Music scale it accounts for 64 percent of a person's score. This information lends support to the preceding discussion that considered 1) Italian family values still important to the Scottsdale respondents and 2) acculturation, as measured by the Food Language and Music scale, one of the first areas of assimilation. Overall, the largest proportions of variance are explained by the Food Language and Music, SBE, and Religious Ethnicity scales with the relationships on other scales being generally weak to moderate.

Table 57. Summary: r_{pb}^2 Expressed as a Percentage for Significant Differences Generation and Birth Cohort, All Scales In the Scottsdale Study

Variables	Italian American Family Attitude %	Cultural Ethnicity %	National Ethnicity %	Behavioral Ethnicity %	Identificational Ethnicity %	Religious Ethnicity %	Food Language Music %
GENERATION[1]							
1. First / Full Second							8
2. First / Half Second	4			20	8		45
3. First / Third	10			10			64
4. Full Second / Half Second	10	7		9	6	15	7
5. Full Second / Third	14	6				11	18
6. Half Second / Third						.2	
BIRTH COHORT[2]							
7. 1914–1929 / 1930–1945							7
8. 1914–1929 / 1946–1960	6					17	
9. 1930–1945 / 1946–1960	9					10	

[1]First Generation N=16, Full Second Generation N=32, Half Second Generation N=17, Third Generation N=24.
[2]1914 Birth Cohort N=32, 1930 Birth Cohort N=34, 1946 Birth Cohort N=19.

Table 58. Summary: r_{pb}^2 Expressed as a Percentage for Significant Differences Occupation, Education, and Gender, All Scales in the Scottsdale Study

Variables	Italian American Family Attitude %	Cultural Ethnicity %	National Ethnicity %	Behavioral Ethnicity %	Identificational Ethnicity %	Religious Ethnicity %	Food Language Music %
OCCUPATION[1]							
Blue-Collar	6						
White-Collar							
EDUCATION[2]							
High School or Less	7						
1 Year College or More							
MALES/FEMALES[3]							
Male							
Females			4	6			5

[1] Blue Collar, N=19; White Collar, N=60. [2] High School, N=34, College=48. [3] Males = 56; Females = 35.

Table 59. Summary: r_{pb}^2 Expressed as a Percentage for Significant Differences in Ties to the Italian American Community, All Scales in the Scottsdale Study

Variables	Italian American Family Attitude %	Cultural Ethnicity %	National Ethnicity %	Behavioral Ethnicity %	Identificational Ethnicity %	Religious Ethnicity %	Food Language Music %
TIES TO ITALIAN AMERICAN COMMUNITY							
Raised in an Italian American Metropolis[1]							
Yes	4		5				
No							
Endogamous[2]							
Yes		7		14		11	16
No							
Years in Arizona[3]							
0 to 6							
7 +							

[1]Raised in Italian American Metropolis, Yes N=37, No N=38. [2]Endogamous N=30; Exogamous, N=54. [3]Years in Arizona 0 to 6 N=42, 7 + N=45.

INDEX